TEACH YOURSELF BOOKS

FRENCH GRAMMAR

This book aims to present clearly and concisely the basic
rules of French grammar which must be mastered by all who
want to speak and translate French fluently. It is intended
for revision and quick reference, and assumes that the reader
already knows the elements of French grammar and the
irregular verbs.

This book is a real achievement. The material progresses logically from the simple sentence (Part I) to the complex sentence (Part II). The sections on the various translations of the English present participles, on *c'est* and *il est*, and on the use of the subjunctive are brilliantly clear. The book has everything to recommend it for 'O' level students or those starting 'A' level work.

The Times Educational Supplement

TEACH YOURSELF BOOKS

FRENCH GRAMMAR

E. S. Jenkins, B.A.

ST. PAUL'S HOUSE WARWICK LANE
LONDON EC4P 4AH

First printed 1961
Ninth impression 1974

This volume is published in the U.S.A. by David McKay Company Inc., 750 Third Avenue, New York, N.Y. 10017

ISBN 0 340 05785 8

Printed in Great Britain
for The English Universities Press, Ltd.,
by Richard Clay (The Chaucer Press), Ltd., Bungay, Suffolk

CONTENTS

CONTENTS

ACKNOWLEDGMENT

The author would like to express his gratitude to his colleagues V. A. Cullingworth, Esq., M.A., W. N. Jeeves, Esq., M.A., and Monsieur A. Theil, L. ès L. for their help and suggestions and also to the Editor-in-Chief, Leonard Cutts, Esq., for his kindness and encouragement.

PREFACE

This Grammar is not intended for absolute beginners who are learning a language for the first time. The reader should have worked conscientiously through a course such as *Teach Yourself French* or already made some progress in the language.

It has been written with certain purposes in mind. It is fairly exhaustive, but the author hopes that one will not find it exhausting. Much has been included that could have been left out: it is possible to make oneself understood with a bare minimum of grammatical knowledge. However, this is an inquiring age, and a student may well wish to find out the reason for certain turns of phrase in the works of some of the great authors. It therefore follows that the learner must not be disheartened if he cannot at once remember all the points in a book like this. If he did, he would know more about French grammar than the average Frenchman. In practice, he will discover that the grammatical puzzles which give him difficulty are the very ones that also trouble the native speaker.

It is hoped that the book will be used in two ways. First, that it will be read as a book from cover to cover or at least from beginning to end of a chapter: secondly, that it will serve as a reference. It will then explain a baffling sentence and help the student to speak and write French correctly. With these aims in view, we have set out at the beginning of the book a comprehensive list of contents. However, we must warn you that a grammar cannot include everything, and a good dictionary should never be far away.

French is a difficult language to write elegantly and correctly, and any attempt to gloss over this fact would be unfair to the student. However, even French people have sometimes to content themselves with something short of perfection, so we hope that this will help to console anyone worried about making a mistake. Your French *vis-à-vis* may be quite as uncertain about the correct preposition or tense as you are yourself!

To write a grammar book without using grammatical terms is an impossibility. Every branch of knowledge has its jargon, and the reader will learn more quickly if he knows the difference between a noun, a verb and an adjective. In fact, grammatical terms have been kept to a minimum, and if any explanation proves difficult there is always an example together with a translation to help.

The author has made an honest attempt to include the fruits of many years of teaching the French language. He hopes that this volume will prove of some benefit to all students.

INTRODUCTION

THE ORIGINS OF THE FRENCH LANGUAGE

Most French words are of Latin origin. During the first centuries of the Christian era, Roman soldiers, colonists and traders introduced into Gaul a popular kind of Latin which was very different from that used by Virgil, Cicero and Caesar. This gradually supplanted the native languages and slowly changed into a tongue called Gallo-Roman. Later, in the Middle Ages, many words were introduced by scholars who borrowed them from Classical Latin. In this way the same Latin word might be taken into French twice: for instance, auscultare became écouter in early popular speech and ausculter in later learned form. Naturally enough, the involved grammar of classical Latin was much simplified when it was brought into Gaul: Latin cases were dropped, declensions were reduced in number, tenses were more simply formed. This tendency increased with the passing of the years.

By the ninth century the various dialects spoken throughout the country had become two great groups: in the north that of the langue d'oïl, in the south the langue d'oc (so called because oïl and oc were their respective ways of saying 'yes'). Very gradually, between the twelfth and sixteenth centuries, the dialect spoken round Paris, in the region called the Ile de France, became the most important, mainly because it was there that the royal family lived.

As for the native language of Gaul, it had disappeared more or less completely by the end of the fourth century. Only a few traces remain in modern French—a handful of words and the method of counting in twenties.*

* This Celtic system of numbering has survived in France for the numbers 61 to 99. In the French-speaking parts of Switzerland septante (70), huitante (80) and nonante (90) are used: in Belgium septante (70) and nonante (90).

Like other European languages, French has also borrowed from Classical Greek, from the Frankish invaders in the fifth century and extensively in modern times from English and American. It is not surprising either, when we consider France's geographical position and political evolution, to find Scandinavian, Dutch, Italian, Spanish and Arabic words well represented in French.

Spelling

French is fairly logical in its spelling and not nearly so capricious as English. However, from the learner's point of view, it is quite bad enough. A word is not always pronounced as it is spelt, there are accents to deal with, and parasitical consonants like *h* which are never sounded. Two other examples of the latter tendency are the *p* in **sculpteur** (pronounced *sculteur*) and the *g* and *t* in **doigt** (pronounced *doi*).

Use of the Hyphen

The hyphen is used:

1. In certain compound words: **demi-heure**, half-hour; **avant-coureur**, forerunner.

2. Between the verb and the personal pronoun in the Interrogative and Imperative Affirmative: **parle-t-il?** is he speaking?; **dites-le-moi!** say it to me!

3. Between the emphatic pronoun and the adjective **même**: **lui-même**, himself.

4. In compound numbers from 17 to 99 inclusive: **quatre-vingts**, eighty; **vingt-six**, twenty-six.

5. With the particles **-ci**, **-là** in cases like **celui-ci**, this one; **cet homme-là**, that man.

6. With certain expressions: **pêle-mêle**, higgledy-piggledy; **au-delà**, beyond.

Use of Capital Letters

The capital letter is more rarely used in French than in English. It is found:

1. With the first word of a sentence or direct speech: Il a demandé: "Où avez-vous trouvé ce livre?" He asked: "Where did you find this book?"

2. With proper names: Jean Dupont, la France, la Seine.

3. With words like Dieu, God; Jésus, Jesus; le Seigneur, the Lord; la Vierge, the Blessed Virgin, etc.

4. With names of societies, organisations, etc.: L'Église, the Church; la Chambre des Députés, the House of Commons, le Ministère de la Justice, the Ministry of Justice.

5. With the names of feasts: Noël, Christmas; Pâques, Easter.

6. With titles of nobility or distinction: Sa Majesté, His Majesty; Monsieur le Président, Mr. President.

7. For titles of books, plays, pictures etc.: la Joconde, the Mona Lisa; Antigone, Antigone.

The capital letter is not used:

1. For adjectives of nationality: une ville française, a French town.

2. For names of languages: il apprend l'allemand, he is learning German.

3. For words like rue, street; place, square, etc.: il demeure rue Lepic, he lives in Lepic Street.

4. In monsieur, madame, mademoiselle, etc., with a name unless the words are abbreviated: avec un monsieur, but avec M. Boussion.

The Apostrophe

The vowels *a, e* are replaced by an apostrophe when le, la, je, me, te, se, ce que, de, ne come before a vowel or mute *h*: l'an, the year; j'ai, I have; je m'excuse, I excuse myself; il t'ennuie, he annoys you.

Similarly, **lorsque, puisque, quoique** lose their final *e* when followed by **il, ils, elle, elles, un, une, on: puisqu'il est là,** since he is there.

Jusque loses its *e* in **jusqu'à,** up to, until; **jusqu'alors,** up till then; **jusqu'ici,** up to now; **jusqu'où,** up to where; **jusqu'au bout,** to the end.

Quelque keeps its *e* except in the word **quelqu'un,** some-one.

Presque keeps its *e* except in **presqu'île,** peninsula.

Si, if, drops the *i* before il, ils: **s'il arrive,** if he arrives, but keeps it before **elle, elles, on: si elle chante,** if she sings.

In the Imperative Affirmative and the Interrogative, when **je, le, la, ce** come after the verb, there is no elision: **puis-je entrer?** may I come in?; **est-ce ici?** is it here?; **donnez-le à votre soeur!** give it to your sister!

Note the absence of the *e* in words like **grand'rue,** high-street; **grand'mère,** grandmother.

Diaeresis

This sign is used to show that contiguous vowels are to be pronounced separately and not to be combined into a diphthong. Thus **naïf,** (*na-if*), naive; **Moïse,** (*Mo-ïse*), Moses. In words like **aiguë** the sign shows that the word has two syllables **ai-guë** (pronounced *ay-gee*), acute.

Cedilla

The cedilla is used when it is necessary to give *c* the sound of *s* before the vowels *a, o, u*:

un **Français,** a Frenchman; nous **commençons,** we begin; **conçu,** conceived.

Punctuation

A comma is used in French for the English decimal point: 3,06 stands for our 3·06 (three point nought six). In figures the French put a full stop where we have a comma: 4.606 represents our 4,606 (four thousand six hundred and six).

Inverted commas to mark speech or to emphasise words are shown thus «   »:

«Donnez-le-moi!» dit-il. "Give it to me!", he said.

Accents

Accents are small signs written over vowels. They are used in two ways:

1. To indicate the pronunciation—

(*a*) An acute accent is put over the letter *e* to show it is pronounced something like the English *ay*; the phonetic symbol for this sound is e. Thus l'été, the summer; la gelée, frost.

(*b*) A grave accent placed over the letter *e* shows that è is to be pronounced like *e* in the English word "bet": the phonetic symbol is ɛ: la mère, the mother; il lève, he lifts.

(*c*) The circumflex accent generally lengthens the vowel: le mât, the mast; même, even, same.

2. Accents can also serve as a useful distinction between words otherwise indistinguishable in spelling and pronunciation: la, the; là, there; du, of the; dû, owed; ou, or; où, where.

h at the Beginning of a Word

The letter *h* should never be sounded in French. Most words beginning with *h* are treated as if the *h* did not exist at all and therefore elide the vowels *a* and *e* in the article: l'horizon, the horizon; l'humidité, wetness, etc. Some words begin with a so-called "aspirate" *h*, though in fact it is not sounded at all. All that happens is that the *h* is treated as if it were a proper consonant, with the result that there is no elision and no liaison before it. Thus la haie, the hedge; le haricot, the bean, with their plurals les haies, les haricots, where the *s* in les is not pronounced. In fact, a slight pause may be made between the preceding word and the word beginning with the aspirate *h*. This particular type of *h*, which occurs only at the beginning of a French word, is usually marked in a dictionary by a special sign, frequently an asterisk. To make a mistake over an aspirate *h* sounds just as bad to a Frenchman as a dropped aitch sounds to an Englishman.

The French Alphabet

French uses the same alphabet as we do, but the letter *w* is used only in words borrowed from other languages: **le wagon-lit**, sleeping-car; **le week-end**, the week-end; **le sandwich**, the sandwich; **le whist**, whist.

Division of a French Word into Syllables

The main distinction between English pronunciation and French is that we end a syllable with a consonant, whereas the French begin with a consonant. Thus, in very slow speech, we should say PAP-A, a Frenchman would say PA-PA. Compare **mo-dèle**, **pré-fé-rer**, **l'A-mé-rique** with the English mod-el, pref-er, Am-er-ic-a. When there are two consonants they are generally separated: **par-ler**, to speak; **quel-que**, some; **por-ta-tif**, portable, but if the second of the two consonants is *l* or *r* both consonants begin the syllable (except *rl*, *nr*, *nl*): **pro-gramme**, program; **tien-dra**, will hold.

Liaison

A feature of French pronunciation is the habit of running several words together. **Y en a-t-il?**, for instance, is sounded as if it were one single word. This joining of words is called in French **liaison**. It is useful to note that in liaison the letter *d* is pronounced as a *t*: **un grand homme**; *s* and *x* sound like *z*: **les hommes, deux enfants**.

When to make liaison

1. Between articles and nouns: **les enfants, les hommes, un exercice, des années**.

2. Between adjectives and following nouns: **un grand homme, mes enfants, le nouvel an.**

3. Between pronouns and verbs: **il y en a, cherchent-ils?, ils ont parlé.**

4. Between auxiliary and verb and after **avoir** and **être**: **vous avez été, ils sont arrivés, vous avez une plume, nous sommes innocents.**

5. After many prepositions, conjunctions and adverbs in a sense group of words: **en un instant, quand elle viendra, bien heureux, très aimable.**

6. Plural nouns generally pronounce the *s* or *x* before a following vowel: **des chevaux énormes.**

7. Between numerals and nouns: **trois années, vingt hommes.**

Do not try to make too many liaisons. It is better to make too few than too many.

When to avoid liaison

1. Do not make a liaison after a singular noun: do not, for instance, pronounce the *t* in a phrase like **un goût amer.**

2. The *t* in **et** is never sounded: **un homme et une femme.**

3. Do not make a liaison before **oui, onze, huit**: **mais oui, les onze joueurs, mes huit valises.**

CHAPTER I

THE NOUN

A noun is the name of a person, place or thing. The words Peter, England, book, silver, charity, pneumonia, rugby are all nouns.

Masculine and Feminine Gender

French nouns are divided into two genders—masculine and feminine. There is no neuter; to a Frenchman everything is a "he" or a "she". As a general rule, male animate beings are masculine, **le taureau,** the bull, while female animate beings are feminine, **la vache,** the cow. Very often, however, and especially in the case of smaller animals, no such distinction is made: i.e., **le ver,** the worm (masculine); **la panthère,** the panther (feminine). With inanimate things and abstractions there is no logical reason for the gender except form, analogy and etymology.

Before we go further let us remember that many other languages are similarly burdened with gender. For those who have learned Latin, it is useful to remember that masculine or feminine nouns usually kept their gender on becoming French. Neuter nouns generally became masculine. Mistakes in gender are serious, so you should endeavour to learn the gender of each noun as you come across it. Here are some rules which may prove helpful:

Gender Depending on the Meaning of the Word

(a) *Masculines*

1. Names of metals, trees, months, days of the week, seasons, languages: **le fer,** iron; **le chêne,** the oak; **le décembre,** December; **le dimanche,** Sunday; **le printemps,** Spring; **le français,** French.

2. Adjectives and Infinitives used as nouns: l'intérieur, the inside; le sourire, the smile.

3. Names of countries and towns not ending in *e*: le Portugal, Portugal; le Danemark, Denmark; le Japon, Japan.

(b) *Feminines*

1. Names of countries and towns ending in *e*: la France, France; l'Allemagne, Germany; la Suisse, Switzerland.

2. Flowers, fruits and vegetables ending in *e*: la rose, the rose; la pomme, the apple; la carotte, the carrot.

3. Names of festivals: la Pentecôte, Whitsun; la Toussaint, All Saints' Day. (La fête* is the French for festival.)

4. Names of sciences: la grammaire, grammar; la chimie, Chemistry; la physique, Physics.

Gender of the Letters of the Alphabet

The vowels are masculine, and the tendency is to make all the consonants masculine too, though some writers make them feminine if they sound as if they began with a vowel: thus un b, un c, un d, une f, un g, une h, etc.

Gender of Compound Nouns

In compound nouns such as le chef d'œuvre, masterpiece, the noun is masculine because the main part of it, le chef, is of that gender. Likewise la basse-cour, farmyard, is feminine because cour, yard, is feminine. Similar words are le bateau-mouche, m., passenger boat on the Seine; la chauve-souris, f., bat, whose gender depends on the fact that le bateau is masculine and la souris is feminine. On the other hand, such compounds as le tête-à-tête, confidential conversation (lit. "head to head"), and le passe-partout,

* This explains expressions like la mi-août, mid-August because one thinks of la fête de l'Assomption, Assumption Day, August 15. Following this pattern, we have la mi-février, mid-February; la mi-janvier and la mi-temps, half-time.

master-key (lit. "passes everywhere"), are so mixed up as to make any logical gender impossible. When the word is formed of a verb and a noun or a preposition and a noun it is usually masculine: le porte-plume, penholder (lit. "carries pen"); le sous-main, blotting pad (lit. "under the hand").

Gender Depending on the Ending of the Word

There are also characteristic masculine and feminine endings. Here are some masculine terminations: age, ail, eau, ège, eil, ice, ier, ment, oir, our: le ménage, household; le ruisseau, stream; l'artifice, artifice; le dentier, denture; le bâtiment, building; le trottoir, pavement; le tour, the trick. However, exceptions occur, the most common of which are la page, page (of a book); la cage, cage; la plage, beach; l'image, picture; l'eau, water; la peau, skin; la police, police; la jument, mare; la tour, tower; la cour, court or yard, all of which are feminine.

Similarly, the following are considered to be feminine endings: ade, aille, aison, ance, ée, eille, ence, esse, ette, ie, ière, ille, ion, ise, té, tié, tion, tude, ue, ure. Thus la bataille, battle; la saison, season; la chance, luck; la brassée, armful; la bouteille, bottle; l'insolence, insolence; la pie, magpie; la beauté, beauty; la gratitude, gratitude; la levure, yeast. Exceptions of course exist, among which we should note le lycée, grammar-school; le musée, museum; le silence, silence; le squelette, skeleton; le parapluie, umbrella; l'incendie, fire; le cimetière, cemetery, le murmure, murmur.

Nouns with Masculine and Feminine Forms

Often there is one word for the female of the species and another for the male. Here are a few well-known examples: le bouc, he-goat, la chèvre, nanny-goat; le cheval, horse, l'étalon, stallion, la jument, mare; le coq, cock, la poule, hen; le fils, son, la fille, daughter; le frère, brother, la sœur, sister; le gendre, son-in-law, la bru, daughter-in-law; le héros, hero, l'héroïne, heroine; le mari, husband, la femme, wife; le neveu, nephew, la nièce, niece; le parrain, godfather, la marraine, godmother; le taureau, bull, la vache, cow.

Nouns with One Form for Both Sexes

Others have only one form for both sexes: enfant, child; élève, pupil; artiste, artist; esclave, slave; hypocrite, hypocrite. We may therefore say un enfant (m.) or une enfant (f.); un élève or une élève, a male child, a female child, a boy pupil, a girl pupil, etc. With animals it is usual to add the words mâle or femelle, i.e., la souris mâle, male mouse, la souris femelle, female mouse. In the case of words which were once exclusively applied to men, the emancipation of women has led to difficulties. For some words like académicien, member of an academy; aviateur, airman; avocat, barrister; instituteur, teacher; there are feminine forms like académicienne, aviatrice, avocate, institutrice. For others, like auteur, author; écrivain, writer; professeur, professor or Grammar School master; imposteur, impostor; médecin, doctor of medicine; témoin, witness; sculpteur, sculptor; peintre, painter; there is no feminine. One is forced to say une femme auteur, a woman author; une femme écrivain, docteur, professeur if one wants to make oneself clear. In titles one writes Madame le docteur X or Madame X, docteur en médecine, etc. Otherwise one uses the masculine form: Cette femme est un imposteur mais c'est un grand écrivain. Elle a été mon professeur *: This woman is an impostor but she is a great writer. She was my Professor. However, in speaking of the wife of a prefect or general, one can say Madame la préfète or Madame la générale. Conversely, some words have no masculine forms, so that a man may be une personne, a person; une victime, a victim; une connaissance, an acquaintance; or une dupe, a dupe.

* It is interesting to note that in familiar speech, expressions like mon petit, mon chéri can be used when speaking to a woman.

Making a Masculine Word into Corresponding Feminine

Very often we can make a feminine word out of a masculine by adding an *e*. Thus le cousin, male cousin, la cousine, female cousin; le marquis, marquis, la marquise, marchioness; l'Espagnol, Spaniard, l'Espagnole, Spanish woman; l'ami, friend, l'amie, girl-friend; le marié, groom, la mariée, bride. Sometimes too, the final consonant is modified or doubled: le loup, wolf, la louve, she-wolf; le veuf, widower, la veuve, widow; le chat, cat, la chatte, she-cat; le chien, dog, la chienne, bitch; l'espion, spy, l'espionne, female spy; le Parisien, male inhabitant of Paris, la Parisienne, female inhabitant of Paris. This change of consonant does not always occur: l'avocat, barrister, becomes l'avocate; le chameau, camel turns into la chamelle.

Feminine of Words Ending in -EUR

Words ending in -EUR present a special difficulty. Some, comparative in meaning, add an *e* to the masculine; majeur(e), major; mineur(e), minor; meilleur(e), better; supérieur(e), superior. Others, which have the same stem as the present participle of the verb, change -EUR to -EUSE: voleur, thief, voleuse, woman thief; pêcheur, fisherman, pêcheuse, fisherwoman; vendeur, salesman, vendeuse, saleswoman. There are also a few which have a feminine form in -ERESSE: chasseur, hunter, chasseresse, huntress; pécheur, sinner, pécheresse, female sinner. Words ending in -TEUR, generally learned words, form their feminines in -TRICE: the most common are: acteur, actor, actrice, actress; empereur, emperor, impératrice, empress; lecteur, reader, lectrice, woman reader; protecteur, protector, protectrice, protectress. Enchanteur becomes enchanteresse, and here we might mention a few nouns in -e which have a feminine in -esse: nègre, negro, négresse, negress; comte, count, comtesse, countess; duc, duke, duchesse, duchess.

Nouns Masculine or Feminine According to Meaning

Certain words can be masculine or feminine. The doer of the action may be masculine, the action feminine: **un aide,** a helper, **une aide,** help; **un critique,** a critic, **une critique,** criticism. Sometimes, the difference in gender entails a difference in meaning. In such cases the similarity between the words may be purely accidental, the two words being derived from two different origins. Thus **le livre,** the book, **la livre,** the pound; **le manche,** the handle, **la manche,** the sleeve; **le mousse,** the cabin boy, **la mousse,** the moss; **le page,** the page-boy, **la page,** the page of a book; **le poêle,** the stove, **la poêle,** the frying pan; **le tour,** the trick, **la tour,** the tower; **le vase,** the vase, **la vase,** the mud. It is curious too that while **la chose,** thing, is feminine, **quelque chose,** something, is considered masculine: we say **quelque chose de nouveau,** something new.

Doubtful Gender

In the case of a few nouns, there is a certain amount of doubt concerning their gender. **L'après-midi,** afternoon, can be either masculine or feminine. **L'aigle** is masculine when referring to the bird, the eagle, but is feminine when it means a standard or military flag, i.e. "the eagles of Napoleon". **Couple** is masculine when it stands for a married or engaged couple, feminine when it means "two": **une couple d'œufs,** a couple of eggs.

Gender of GENS

The word **gens** needs special attention. Usually it is found in the masculine plural with the sense of "people". However, when an adjective comes immediately before it, this adjective becomes feminine, while any that come after remain masculine. Thus: **les vieilles gens,** old people, **les bonnes gens,** good people, and **les vieilles gens sont peureux,** old people are timid. If the preceding adjective is one that ends in a mute *e*, like **honnête** or **jeune**, for instance, the adjective and any other that precede stay masculine: **tous les honnêtes gens**, all honest people, **tous ces gens**, all these people.

The Gender of Towns and Ships

What is the gender of towns? When in doubt, we can always evade the issue by saying "**la ville de Paris**" or "**la ville de Metz**", in which case you automatically make them feminine for the purposes of agreement. Some, like **Le Mans, Le Caire** (Cairo), **Le Havre**, are obviously masculine. Others ending with a mute *e* are generally taken as feminine, thus **Rome, Séville, Genève**: those like **Paris, Dijon** are masculine. As for boats and ships, the French Academy has laid down that their names should be of the gender of the word used to distinguish the ship: thus **la Normandie**, named after the French Province, **la Normandie**. Despite this, many people use the masculine article, **le Normandie**, because, after all, it is a ship and both "**navire**", ship, and "**bateau**", boat, are masculine.

Plural of Nouns

Putting a noun into the plural presents fewer difficulties. Generally, the sign of the plural is the addition of the letter *s* to the noun: **garçon**, boy, **garçons**, boys; **livre**, book, **livres**, books. Nouns ending in *s*, *x* or *z* remain unchanged in the plural: **un nez**, a nose, **des nez**, noses; **un fils**, a son, **des fils**, sons; **la noix**, the nut, **les noix**, the nuts. Please remember that this plural *s* is not pronounced in French. Confusion between singular **garçon** and plural **garçons** is avoided by the use of an article or other accompanying word: **le garçon, les garçons**. While we are discussing pronunciation, it is worth while noting that with words like **œuf**, egg; **cerf**, stag; **bœuf**, ox, the *f* is pronounced in the singular but not in the plural. Similarly, the *s* in **os**, bone, is pronounced in the singular only.

Rules for Formation of the Plural

Not all French nouns take an *s* to form the plural.

1. Words ending in -AL change this termination to -AUX le cheval, the horse, les chevaux, the horses; le journal, the newspaper, les journaux, the newspapers. The most common exceptions here are bal, ball; carnaval, carnival; chacal, jackal; festival, festival; régal, feast; récital, recital, which add *s* to become bals, carnavals, chacals, etc.

2. Words ending in -EU, -AU, -EAU add the letter *x*: l'oiseau, the bird, les oiseaux; le feu, the fire, les feux. The principal exceptions are le pneu, tyre, les pneus; le bleu, bruise, les bleus.

3. The words bail, lease; corail, coral; émail, enamel; soupirail, air-hole; travail, work; vitrail, stained-glass window, become in the plural baux, coraux, émaux, soupiraux, travaux, vitraux.

4. Seven nouns ending in -OU: bijou, jewel; caillou, pebble; chou, cabbage; genou, knee; hibou, owl; joujou, plaything; pou, louse, add *x*: bijoux, cailloux, choux, etc.

Words with two plural forms

The word ciel, sky, can become in the plural cieux or ciels. Cieux means "the heavens" or "paradise", ciels is used only in phrases like ciels de tableaux, les ciels de Corot, les beaux ciels d'Italie, and refers to skies in works of art such as oil-paintings or climatic and picturesque ones. Œil, eye, becomes in the plural yeux, except in the word œils-de-bœuf, round windows. Aïeul, grandfather, can form as its plural aïeux, ancestors, or aïeuls (f. aïeules), grandfathers (f. grandmothers).

Plural of Compound Nouns

When a word is formed out of two or more elements like rouge-gorge, redbreast, the question of forming the plural is rather complicated. In some cases, like gendarme, police-nan; **vaurien,** good for nothing, we simply add an *s* and treat them like any other word: **gendarmes, vauriens.** To his class belong nouns like **grand'mère,** plural **grand'mères.** On the other hand, **gentilhomme, monsieur, madame, mademoiselle** become **gentilshommes, messieurs, mesdames, mesdemoiselles.**

When the two elements are separated the sense will help in many cases to decide the formation of the plural:

1. The noun consists of a noun and adjective* or of two nouns in apposition. Both elements become plural: **le chou-fleur,** cauliflower, **les choux-fleurs; le sourd-muet,** deaf-mute, **les sourds-muets; le cerf-volant,** kite (flying-stag), **les cerfs-volants.** However, learned compounds like **Anglo-Saxon, Indo-Chinois, Gallo-Romain** take the *s* only on the second element: **Anglo-Saxons, Indo-Chinois,** etc.

2. The compound consists of two nouns, one depending on the other with or without a preposition, of the following type: **le chef-d'œuvre,** masterpiece; **l'arc-en-ciel,** the rainbow. The first noun only takes the plural: **le chef-d'œuvre, les chefs-d'œuvre; l'arc-en-ciel, les arcs-en-ciel:** so also **le timbre-poste,** postage stamp, **les timbres-poste.**

In these examples, the use and position of the *s* are quite logical. **Chef-d'œuvre** (lit. chief of work), masterpiece, plural **chefs-d'œuvre:** the *s* is put where it would suit if the word were English, i.e., chiefs of work, masterpieces. Similarly, **arc-en-ciel** (arch in the sky), **arcs-en-ciel** (arches in the sky), rainbows; **timbre-poste,** stamp (of the) post, plural **timbres-poste,** stamps (of the) post.

3. The noun has in it a non-variable element or a verb. This part does not change, the other word takes the plural if the sense demands it. **L'avant-poste,** advanced position, **les avant-postes,** just as we should say in English forepost, foreposts: **le bouche-trou,** stop gap, **les bouche-trous,** stop gaps; **le gratte-ciel,** skyscraper, **les gratte-ciel** (no *s* here

---

* **demi** (half) in front of the noun is invariable: **une demi-heure,** half an hour, **des demi-heures.**

because **gratte-ciel** means literally "scrape sky", and a
plural "scrapes-sky" or "scrape-skies" would be ridiculous)

4. Words like le **tête-à-tête**, confidential conversation (lit.
head to head), les **tête-à-tête**; le **pick-up**, pick-up, les **pick
up**: le **passe-partout**, pass key (lit. passes everywhere), le
passe-partout remain invariable. In cases like this the diffi
culty of fixing the position of the *s* is so great that one jus
gives up and puts nothing at all!

Plural of Words Borrowed from Other Languages

Some, having become completely French, take the
normal plural: un **album**, des **albums**, un **bifteck**, steak, des
biftecks, un **meeting**, des **meetings**. Latin words like **maxi
mum** have plurals in -*a*, though **maximum** itself can take an
s. Italian words generally form their plurals in -*i*: **dillettante
dillettanti**; **libretto**, **libretti**. Nouns taken from English or
American have a tendency, especially as so many people
know English, to have their English plurals: un **barman**
des **barmen**; un **sportsman**, des **sportsmen**; un **baby**, des
babies; un **match**, des **matches** (or **matchs**!), un **sandwich**, des
sandwiches (or **sandwichs**).

Words Which Have no Plural Form

Family names do not change: Les **Dupont** sont ici, the
Duponts are here, unless the family is a particularly distin
guished one, les **Bourbons**, les **Tudors** or unless the name
stands for a type; les **Racines** sont rares, people like Racine
are rare. Some parts of speech, such as prepositions, ad
verbs, etc., when used as nouns do not vary: les **pour et les
contre**, the pros and the cons; les **non et les oui**, the ayes
and the nos.

Words Found in the Plural only

Some nouns have no singular form: les **archives**, archives
les **catacombes**, catacombs; les **échecs**, chess; les **vivres**,
victuals.

Words Found in the Singular only

Others have no plural: la botanique, botany; le midi, the south; l'or, gold; le bonheur, luck; le vrai, truth; le nord, the north. Lastly must be mentioned words which vary in meaning in singular and plural: la lunette, spyglass, les lunettes, spectacles.

The student may well find this chapter a very full one. Mistakes in plurals can be made even by those whose native language is French. When in doubt, it is of great value to consult a good dictionary. Make sure that it is a modern one, as practice may change with the passing of the years.

CHAPTER II

THE ARTICLES

THE DEFINITE ARTICLE

The Definite Article corresponds to the English word "the". Unlike the English word, it has many forms as the following table will show:

	Before a masculine word	Before a feminine word	Before a singular word beginning with a vowel or mute h	Before all plurals
THE	LE	LA	L'.	LES
OF *FROM* } *THE*	DU	DE LA	DE L'	DES
TO *AT* } *THE*	AU	À LA	À L'	AUX
Thus	le garçon *the boy*	la fillette *the girl*	l'homme *the man*	les ans *the years*
	du film *of the film*	de la femme *of the woman*	de l'eau *of the water*	des gens *of the people*
	au jardin *to the garden*	à la sœur *to the sister*	à l'enfant *to the child*	aux amis *to the friends*

Note the contracted forms **DU, DES, AU** and **AUX**. Formerly en les (in the) contracted to **ès**, which is still found in expressions like **docteur ès sciences**, doctor of science; **licencié ès lettres**, bachelor of arts.

You will notice that **LE** and **LA** change to **L'** before a word in the singular beginning with a vowel or a mute *h*: **l'or**, the gold; **l'heure**, the hour.

Initial H Aspirate

Some words, though beginning with the letter *h*, behave as though they began with consonants and have **LE** or **LA** efore them. They include the number **huit**, eight,* and ther words which, in order to distinguish them, are said to egin with an aspirate *h*. This *h* is, however, just as silent as he mute *h*, the letter never being pronounced in French. ome of the most common of these words are: **la hache**, axe; **a haie**, hedge; **la haine**, hatred; **la halte**, halt; **le hameau**, amlet; **le hamac**, hammock; **la hanche**, hip; **le hangar**, hed; **le harem**, harem; **le haricot**, bean; **la harpe**, harp; **le** asard, luck; **la hâte**, haste; **le havre**, haven; **le huit mars**, he eighth of March.

Use of the Definite Article

The Definite Article is more often used in French than its counterpart is in English. As in most cases the pronunciaion of the singular noun is the same as that of the plural, the se of the article is essential to clarify the expression. Maison, house, **maisons**, houses, would sound the same in French, so we must say **la maison**, **les maisons** to distinguish etween them. Just compare the following sentences with heir English equivalents:

> Horses are useful. **Les chevaux sont utiles.**
> Gold is a metal. **L'or est un métal.**
> Most people. **La plupart des gens.**

In English, when two or more nouns are used together, ven if the Article is put before the first, it is customary to eave out the Article before subsequent words. For instance, ve say "the father and mother of this child", "the horses, ows and sheep are in the field". This must not happen in French. The Article must be inserted before each noun: **le** ère **et la mère de cet enfant**; **les chevaux, les vaches et les** moutons **sont dans le champ**.

The Definite Article is used before the names of countries, ontinents, counties and many geographical names: **le**

* **onze**, eleven, is similarly used. We say "**le onze février**", the eleventh of February.

Portugal, la France, l'Europe, l'Asie, la Normandie, le Kent,
le Mont Blanc, le Havre, le Caire (Cairo). However, in the
case of feminine nouns of this type, the article is omitted
after EN, *to* or *in*, and DE, *from, of*: il va en France, il
revient d'Espagne, he is going to France, he comes back from
Spain. With masculine nouns of places, the article is re-
tained: Je vais au Havre, au Japon, au Portugal, au Canada,
aux Etats-Unis, je reviens du Pays de Galles: I am going to
le Havre, Japan, Portugal, Canada, the United States, I
come back from Wales.

We use the article:

(*a*) Before abstract nouns, l'argent ne fait pas le bonheur,
money does not make happiness.

(*b*) When we have a title and a name, la reine Élisabeth,
queen Elizabeth; le président de Gaulle, president de Gaulle,
and even when a name is preceded by an adjective: la
petite Marie, little Mary; la douce France, sweet land of
France.

(*c*) In familiar language the article can be used in front of
a name to express scorn: la Dubarry, that woman Dubarry;
la Louise, old Louise. On the other hand, used in front of
the names of famous woman artistes, it can express respect:
la Garbo, la Malibran, la Callas, la Lollobrigida, though this
usage seems to be dying out.

(*d*) Notice too the common use of expressions like
Monsieur le directeur, Headmaster; messieurs les voyageurs,
passengers; monsieur le curé, Vicar, used in addressing
people.

(*e*) Feast-days, with the exception of Pâques, Easter, and
Noël, Christmas, usually have la before them: Il reviendra à
la Trinité, à la Toussaint, à Pâques, à Noël, he will come back
on Trinity Sunday, All Saints' Day, Easter, Christmas.

(*f*) When price is mentioned, the French "the" takes the
place of the English "a": deux cents francs le kilo, two
hundred francs *a* kilo; cent francs la bouteille, a hundred

francs *a* bottle; **mille francs le mètre,** a thousand francs *a* yard; **quinze francs (la) pièce,** fifteen francs each (apiece).

(*g*) "Le" is used before days of the week when a customary action is referred to: **il vient ici le lundi,** he comes here of a Monday, on Mondays.

(*h*) The article is used with speeds: **L'auto faisait du cent à l'heure:** The car was doing a hundred (kilometres) *an* hour.

(*i*) The article is placed before the names of languages: **il connaît bien l'allemand,** he knows German well; **il apprend l'italien,** he is learning Italian. However, with the verb **parler,** it is usual to omit it: **ici on parle français,** here one speaks French; **parlez-vous français?,** do you speak French? If, however, you have any additional idea, the article returns: **il parle bien le français,** he speaks French *well.* **Presque tous les Gallois parlent l'anglais:** Nearly all Welsh people speak English (i.e., as well as or instead of their own language).

A very interesting use of the article is to use **au, à la, à l'** or **aux** in translating such expressions as "the man with the wooden leg", "the girl with the big mouth", "the woman with the fair hair". The usual word for "with", **avec,** is not employed because **avec** has the sense of "together with" or "accompanied by", and if put in the examples above would convey the idea of a man carrying a wooden leg, or of a woman with a supply of fair hair which she is about to make into a wig. So, to describe these persons with their characteristics, we say: **l'homme à la jambe de bois, la jeune fille à la grande bouche, la femme aux cheveux blonds.***

The Definite Article is also used in French where in English we should use the possessive adjective, especially with names of parts of the body. Study these examples:

He closes *his* eyes. **Il ferme les yeux.**

She opens *her* mouth. **Elle ouvre la bouche.**

* *a* man with *a* wooden leg = **un homme à jambe de bois.** Similarly *a* woman with fair hair = **une femme à cheveux blonds.**

I rub *my* foot. Je me frotte le pied.
I seized *her* arm. Je lui ai saisi le bras.
They brush *their* hair. Elles se brossent les cheveux.

You will notice that if only one part of the body is involved, if one just moves a limb in a simple, singular movement, we have this type of sentence:

Il ferme les yeux. He closes his eyes.
Elle ouvre la bouche. She opens her mouth.
Il tourne la tête. He turns his head.
Levez la main! Raise your hand!

When an action is done to one part of the body using another, "I scratch my nose (i.e., with my finger)", or if an action is performed on another person, "*I* seized *her* arm", a pronoun must be introduced to show to whom the action is being done.

Il se gratte le nez. He scratches his nose (lit. he scratches to himself the nose).
Je lui ai saisi le bras. I seized her arm (lit. I seized the arm to her).

Unless lui was inserted, we should not know whose arm was seized.

A similar type of sentence is used to describe a person's physical characteristics:

Il a les yeux bleus. He has blue eyes.
Mon frère a le nez long. My brother has a long nose.

Why, then, in view of the above rules, do we sometimes find sentences like the following?

J'admirais ses beaux cheveux. I admired her lovely hair.
Ses mains sont propres. His hands are clean.

The possessive adjectives "her" and "his" must be used here, because otherwise the sentences would mean something quite different. **J'admirais les beaux cheveux** would mean "I admired lovely hair (i.e., anybody's as long as it was lovely)"; **les mains sont propres** would give no indication whose hands were clean!

Under this heading, we have one last point to note. When we speak of words like **la bouche** mouth; **la vie**, life; **le nez**, nose, etc., things of which a person has one only, we use the singular of the word in French:

> **Je leur ai sauvé la vie.** I saved their lives (lit. the life to them).
>
> **Ils gardaient le chapeau à la main.** They kept their hats in their hands.

Omission of the Article

It is so usual to put in the article, that perhaps it would have been easier to learn when to leave it out. It is often omitted:

In proverbs—

> **Pauvreté n'est pas vice.** Poverty is no vice.

Before names of streets—

> **Il demeure rue Lepic.** He lives in Lepic Street.

In rapid enumerations—

> **Hommes, femmes, enfants, tous se sauvèrent.** Men women, children, all ran away.

There is no article when nouns are used in apposition, i.e., when two nouns referring to the same object are placed next to each other as **Londres** and **capitale** are in the next sentence:

> **J'arrivai à Londres, capitale de la Grande-Bretagne.** I arrived at London, the capital of Great Britain.

"The" is not translated before a comparative:

> **Moins il travaille, plus il gagne.** The less he works, the more he earns.

With titles too we leave out an article: la **Banque de France**, the Bank of France; le **roi d'Espagne**, the King of Spain. In expressions like les **vins de France**, wines from France, French wines; des **tapis de Perse**, carpets from Persia, Persian carpets, where **de France** and **de Perse** have an adjectival meaning, no article is used. However, we include the article when we refer to a geographical entity: les **richesses de l'Angleterre**, the riches of England (of the whole of England).

With north, south, east and west, usage varies with the points of the compass: talking of winds, we say le **vent du nord**, le **vent du sud**, le **vent d'est** and le **vent d'ouest**.

Articles are left out when addressing people: **Bonjour, Docteur**, good morning, doctor, and are generally omitted after the prepositions **par, en, avec, sans** and **de: par avion**, by plane; en **auto**, by car; avec **soin**, with care; sans **exception**, without exception; un **verre de vin**, a glass of wine. No article is needed with expressions like **avoir raison**, to be right; **avoir tort**, to be wrong; **avoir sommeil**, to be sleepy; **faire fortune**, to make a fortune; vous **avez tort comme toujours**, you are wrong as usual; j'ai **sommeil après mon bain**, I'm sleepy after my bathe. With months, days and times too the article is left out: en **avril**, in April; **dimanche prochain**, next Sunday; à **midi**, à **deux heures**, at noon, at two o'clock.

THE INDEFINITE ARTICLE

	Masc.	Fem.	Meaning
Singular	UN	UNE	A or An
Plural	DES		SOME or ANY

Un journal, a newspaper; une **chose**, a thing; des **chiens**, some dogs.

The Indefinite Article is derived from the Latin numeral

unus, so that it is wise to remember that **un** or **une** can also mean "one": **une seule chose,** one single thing.

Uses of the Indefinite Article

The uses of the Indefinite Article in French and English are very similar. However, it is left out in French in the following cases:

1. When we are describing a person's profession, nationality, rank, religion, etc., together with the verbs **être, devenir, élire.**

> **Elle est Anglaise.** She is an Englishwoman.
> **Il est docteur.** He is a doctor.
> **Il a été élu président.** He has been elected president.

2. Before the words **cent** and **mille.**

> **cent hommes,** a hundred men.
> **mille fois,** a thousand times.

3. After **quel, sans, ni.**

> **Quel garçon!** what a boy!
> **sans argent* ni espoir,** without money or hope

4. After **par** in such phrases as:

> **trois fois par jour,** three times a day.
> **mille francs par semaine,** a thousand francs a week.

5. When **jamais** begins a sentence:

> **Jamais écolier ne fut plus heureux que lui.** Never was a schoolboy happier than he.

Sometimes, the article is included where in English we should leave it out. We say, just as we do in English: **avec courage, avec soin, avec patience,** with courage, with care,

---

* In the sentence **Il est rentré sans l'argent que vous lui avez donné**: He came home without the money that you gave him, the article is included because the noun is particularised. We are not saying that "he returned without money" but that "he returned without the particular money he had been given".

with patience. If we add an adjective the article is used, thus: **avec patience**, with patience, but **avec une grande patience**, with great patience; **avec soin**, with care, but **avec une soin minutieux**, with minute care. Similarly, **un homme de talent**, a man of talent, becomes, if supplied with an adjective, **un homme d'un talent rare**, a man of rare talent.

THE PARTITIVE ARTICLE

Masculine Singular	Feminine Singular	Singular word beginning with a vowel or mute *h*	Plural	Meaning
DU	DE LA	DE L'	DES	*SOME, ANY*

Du pain, some bread; **avez-vous de la viande?** have you any meat?; **il a trouvé de l'or**, he found some gold; **il y avait des pommiers dans le jardin**, there were some apple-trees in the garden.

Use of the Partitive Article

Very similar to English usage, but it should be remembered that the Partitive Article must not be omitted in French, even though it often is in English.

> He has money. **Il a de l'argent.**
> There are flowers in the vase. **Il y a des fleurs dans le vase.**

DE (*or* **D'** *before a vowel or mute* h) *is used instead of* **DU, DE LA, DE L'** *or* **DES** *in the following cases:*

1. After a negative—*

> **Je n'ai pas de pain.** I have not any bread.

* It is possible to use **du, de la, de l', des** after a negative in a sentence like this: **Ce n'est pas du thé, c'est du café.** It isn't tea, it's coffee. There is a negative, but it is a negative with a difference. You are not saying that you *haven't anything*. You have *something* but it isn't tea!

Il n'a plus d'argent. He no longer has any money.
Ne buvez pas de vin. Do not drink any wine.
Elle n'a pas de plume.* She hasn't a pen.
Sans casser d'œufs. Without breaking any eggs.
Rien de nouveau. Nothing new.

2. When an adjective comes before a PLURAL NOUN—

de belles choses, some lovely things
d'autres choses, some other things
de bons élèves, some good pupils

This rule does not apply to a singular noun: du bon tabac, some good tobacco; de la bonne viande, some good meat, or when the adjective comes *after* the noun: des animaux dangereux, some dangerous animals.]

The French do not use this rule when the noun and adjective are used so often together that they have come to be regarded as a single entity: des jeunes filles, some girls; des jeunes gens, youths; des petits pois, peas; des faux pas, mistakes.

* "Not a" may also be translated by pas un or pas une (f.), but here the meaning is "not a single one". Thus: "Je n'ai pas un sou." I have not a (single) penny!

CHAPTER III
ADJECTIVES

An adjective is a word used with a noun to give some additional meaning or description. Thus we may say: a good boy, a tall boy, a lazy boy, a fat boy. *Good, tall, lazy, fat* are adjectives describing *boy*.

AGREEMENT OF ADJECTIVES

In French the adjective has several forms: the word "grand" (big) may be spelt, in different circumstances, grand, grande, grands or **grandes**. The adjective is said to "agree" with its noun, thus if a noun is feminine singular, its adjective must also become feminine singular and add an -e. Similarly, with a masculine plural noun it will generally add an -s, with a feminine plural -es. Perhaps the following examples will make this clearer.

Le garçon est grand.	Masculine Singular
Les garçons sont grands.	Masculine Plural (-s)
La dame est grande.	Feminine Singular (-e)
Les dames sont grandes.	Feminine Plural (-es)

le petit village, the little village; les petits villages, the little villages: la petite ferme, the little farm; les petites fermes, the little farms.

Formation of the Feminine Singular

1. In the majority of cases we add the letter -e to the adjective: grand, grande; petit, petite; ouvert, ouverte.

Le magasin est ouvert. The shop is open.
La fenêtre est ouverte. The window is open.

2. Adjectives which end with an -e in the masculine remain unchanged in the feminine singular. **Jeune** (young);

. jeune; brave, f. brave; agréable (pleasant), f. agréable: un jeune homme, a young man: une jeune femme, a young woman. [Maître (master) and traître (treacherous) become maîtresse and traîtresse: la carte maîtresse, the master card; la montagne est traîtresse, the mountain is treacherous.]

3. In the case of adjectives ending in -el and -eil [as well as gentil (nice) and nul (no)], the l is doubled before the feminine e. Cruel, f. cruelle; vermeil (vermilion), f. vermeille; gentil, f. gentille; nul, f. nulle. Des lèvres (lips) vermeilles. Une mère cruelle.

(a) Jumeau (twin) becomes jumelle. Des frères jumeaux, twin brothers; des sœurs jumelles, twin sisters.

(b) Beau, beautiful, handsome; nouveau, new; vieux, old; mou, soft; fou, mad, become in the feminine singular belle, nouvelle, vieille, molle, folle.

[Before a masculine singular noun which begins with a vowel or a mute h we use the forms bel, nouvel, vieil, mol, fol.* Un beau garçon, a handsome lad; un bel homme, a handsome man. Une belle femme, a beautiful woman. In the plural the usual masculine plural is used: de beaux garçons, de beaux hommes.

Similarly, le Nouveau Testament, the New Testament; le nouvel an, the new year: un vieil homme, an old man.]

4. Adjectives ending in -en and -on double the n before a feminine e. Bon (good), f. bonne; ancien (old, former), f. ancienne; parisien (Parisian), f. parisienne. Une famille ancienne, an old family.

[Paysan (peasant) becomes paysanne but note bénin (benign), f. bénigne; malin (evil), f. maligne. La maligne influence, the evil influence.]

5. Most adjectives ending in -et double the t [note too sot (foolish), f. sotte]. Muet (dumb), f. muette; net (clean), f. nette.

* When these adjectives come before et (and), one may use either form for the masculine singular: un beau et charmant enfant or un bel et charmant enfant.

Les grandes douleurs sont muettes. Great griefs are the ones not spoken of.

[Complet, complete; concret, concrete; inquiet, anxious; replet, stout; secret, secret; désuet, obsolete become complète, concrète, inquiète, replète, secrète, désuète.]

Idiot becomes idiote. Une réflexion idiote.

6. Bas, low; gras, fat; las, tired; épais, thick; gros, big become basse, grasse, lasse, épaisse, grosse. Une porte basse, a low door. [Other adjectives in -s simply add an e: gris (grey), f. grise, etc.]

7. Faux, false; roux, russet red; exprès, express become fausse, rousse, expresse. Fausses dents, false teeth.

8. Frais, fresh becomes fraîche; favori, favourite becomes favorite. Des fleurs fraîches, fresh flowers; ma couleur favorite, my favourite colour.

9. Adjectives ending in -er change this termination to -ère. Amer, bitter; premier, first become amère, première. L'onde amère, the bitter sea.

10. Adjectives ending in -x change this letter to -se. Joyeux (joyous), f. joyeuse; jaloux (jealous), f. jalouse. [Doux, sweet, gentle becomes douce.]

11. Adjectives change final -f to -ve in the feminine. Neuf (new), f. neuve; naïf (artless, naive), naïve [bref, brief becomes brève]. Une idée neuve, a new idea.

12. Final -c changes to -que. Public (public), f. publique; turc (Turkish), f. turque. [Note that grec (Greek) becomes grecque.] La langue turque, the Turkish tongue.

13. Blanc, white; franc, frank; sec, dry become blanche, franche, sèche. La race blanche, the white race.

14. Final -g changes to -gue. Long (long), f. longue; oblong (oblong), f. oblongue. Une longue rue: a long street.

15. Final -gu changes to -guë. (The mark is placed over the e to show that the u is to be pronounced. See Diaeresis on page xviii.) Aigu (sharp, acute), f. aiguë; exigu (exiguous), f. exiguë. Une chambre exiguë, a tiny bedroom.

Feminine of Adjectives ending in -EUR

1. Adjectives ending in -eur which are derived from verbs whose stem is also the stem of the present participle, i.e., **pêcher**, to fish, **pêchant**, fishing, **pêcheur**; **mentir**, to lie, **mentant, menteur** form their feminine in -euse. **Une réponse flatteuse**, a flattering reply. [Exceptions are **enchanteur**, enchanting; **pécheur**, sinning; **vengeur**, avenging which become **enchanteresse, pécheresse, vengeresse: la femme pécheresse**, the woman who was a sinner.]

2. Some adjectives in -teur, not formed from the present participle, change to -trice. **Protecteur** (protecting), f. **protectrice**; **consolateur** (consoling), f. **consolatrice**. **Une épaule protectrice**, a protecting shoulder.

3. Ten adjectives, comparative in form and originally at any rate comparative in meaning, simply add an -e. **Antérieur**, anterior, **extérieur**, exterior, **inférieur**, inferior, **intérieur**, interior, **majeur**, major, **meilleur**, better, **mineur**, minor, **postérieur**, posterior, **supérieur**, superior, **ultérieur**, ulterior. **Une meilleure méthode**, a better method; **la mâchoire inférieure**, the lower jaw.

Special Cases

1. **Grand** does not change in a few hallowed expressions though allied to a feminine; **grand'chose**, much, a lot; **grand'mère**, grandmother; **grand'messe**, high mass; **grand' route**, highroad; **grand'rue**, main street, though the apostrophe marks the place where the feminine -e should be found.*

2. Some adjectives have no special feminine form: **chic**, smart, **rococo**, rococo, **snob**, snobbish. **Une femme chic**, a smart woman; **une pendule rococo**, a clock in the rococo

---

* These words may also be spelt without the apostrophe: **grand chose, grand mère, grand messe, grand route, grand rue** [plurals des **grand(s) mères**, des **grand(s) messes**, des **grand(s) routes**, des **grand(s) rues**]. To this class belong also **grand faim, grand honte, grand soif** and **grand tante**.

style; **maman est un peu snob,** mummy is a little snobbish. Similarly, some adjectives are found only in the feminine: **enceinte,** pregnant.

PLURAL OF ADJECTIVES

The same rules apply to the plural of adjectives as apply to the plural of nouns. All feminine adjectives add -s in the plural: it's only the masculines which give trouble! **Un bon garçon, de bons garçons; un journal loyal, des journaux loyaux; le nouveau bateau, les nouveaux bateaux; un gros tas, de gros tas.**

A few adjectives ending in -al have their masculine plurals in -als: naval, navals; fatal, fatals; natal, natals; final, finals; banal, banals (or banaux). **Des compliments banals,** banal compliments; **des conseils fatals,** fatal advice.

Adjectives with no Plural Form

Some too have no plural form: **rococo, chic, kaki, sterling.**

> **Elles ne sont pas chic.** They are not smart.
> **Des uniformes kaki,** khaki uniforms.
> **Cent livres sterling,** a hundred pounds sterling.

Tout

Tout, all, every, demands attention. In the masculine plural it loses a *t* and becomes **tous: tous les hommes,** all (the) men. The feminine plural is regular: **toutes les dames.**

Adjective Describing Two or More Nouns

When an adjective refers to several nouns it is put into the plural.

> **le père et son fils sont charmants.** The father and son are charming.

If the nouns are of different genders the adjective is used in the masculine plural form.

> **Madame Dubras et son fils sont charmants.** Mrs. Dubras and her son are charming.

When the adjective has a characteristic feminine form, and the nouns are of different genders, the masculine noun should be placed nearer the adjective.

> **Avec une intonation et un accent parfaits.** With perfect intonation and accent.

Agreement with a Complex Noun

In the case of two nouns joined by **DE**, common sense has to be used to decide with which noun the adjective must agree.

> **Le verre d'eau traditionnel.** The traditional glass of water. (The glass is traditional, not the water.)
>
> **Un régiment d'infanterie complet.** A complete infantry regiment. (The regiment is complete, not the infantry.)
>
> **Un bol de porcelaine blanc (or blanche).** A white porcelain bowl. (The bowl is white and so is the porcelain.)

Avoir l'air

In expressions using "**avoir l'air**", i.e., to translate sentences like "she looks happy", "she looks sad", etc., one may make the adjective agree either with the subject of the sentence or with the masculine word "**l'air**".

> She looks cross. **Elle a l'air fâchée (or fâché).**

However, there is a little difference in meaning between the two renderings. **Elle a l'air fâché** means "she *looks* angry", she has an angry look on her face, whereas **elle a l'air fâchée** means "she *seems* angry".

When we are speaking of a thing and not a person the adjective generally agrees with the subject, because a thing cannot change its appearance at will:

> **Cette maladie a l'air très sérieuse.** This illness seems looks serious.

If you find this difficult, you can always play safe by inserting **d'être** and making the adjective agree with the subject.

> **Cette chaise a l'air d'être neuve.** This chair seems new.

Vous

The polite plural "**Vous**" referring to one person is, of course, counted as a singular.

> **Vous êtes poli, monsieur.** You are polite, sir.

But titles like **Majesté, Excellence,** even when referring to men, are of feminine gender, and therefore require a feminine adjective.

> **Votre Majesté a été très bonne.** Your Majesty has been most kind.

But add a masculine word and then the adjective will remain masculine.

> **Sa majesté le roi est content de vous voir.** His Majesty the King is pleased to see you.

Adjectives of Colour

Simple adjectives of colour agree with their noun.

> **Il a les cheveux noirs.** He has black hair.
> **La fleur est blanche.** The flower is white.

Compound adjectives of colour are invariable: **des yeux bleu clair,** light blue eyes; **une robe vert pomme,** an apple-green dress. A noun used to indicate a colour likewise remains unchanged.

> **Des rubans orange.** Orange (coloured) ribbons.

Compound Adjectives

(*a*) A compound adjective may consist of two adjectives, both of which qualify the noun. In this case, both parts agree: **des enfants sourds-muets**, deaf and dumb children.*

(*b*) If the compound adjective is made up of an invariable word or of one adjective used as an adverb, only the second part changes.

> **Des rayons ultra-violets.** Ultra-violet rays.
> **Des personnes haut placées.** Highly placed people.

Other examples are **tard-venus**, late comers; **nouveau-nés**, newly born.

[This rule is by no means universal. **Frais, large, grand, bon** agree even when used adverbially: **une rose fraîche cueillie**, a freshly picked rose; **les deux pages grandes ouvertes**, both pages wide open; similarly, **raide-mort**, stone-dead; **ivre-mort**, dead-drunk, become **raides-morts, ivres-morts** in the masculine plural.]

Demi (half)

When **demi** is used before a noun to which it is attached by a hyphen it is invariable: **une demi-heure**, half an hour; **elle est demi-morte**, she is half dead. Placed after a noun, **demi** agrees: **trois heures et demie**, half-past three. **Mi** (half) is always invariable and does not exist except when joined to a word by a hyphen: **la mi-janvier**, mid January; **la mi-été**, midsummer; **la mi-temps**, half-time (in these cases the compound is feminine); **les yeux mi-clos**, eyes half-closed.

Excepté

Excepté, except; **ci-joint**, enclosed; **y compris**, including; **franc de port**, post-free, remain invariable when placed

---

* However, one says, **une fille mort-née**, a still-born daughter, without making **mort** feminine, though the child is both born and dead.

before a noun or pronoun: **excepté elle**, except for her; **ci-joint sa lettre**, her letter is enclosed; **y compris la France**, including France. Like **demi**, when placed after a noun they agree.

Feu * (late, deceased)

Feu, used in the singular only, agrees if it is preceded by an article or possessive adjective. Thus **feu la reine** or **la feue reine**, the late queen; **feu mes oncles**, my deceased uncles; **ma feue sœur**, my late sister.

Haut (high), bas (low)

Haut and **bas** are used adverbially in expressions like **haut les mains!** up with your hands! **bas les pattes!** down with your paws! and so do not agree.

Nu (bare, naked)

Nu used before a noun is invariable and is joined to it by a hyphen: **nu-jambes**, bare-legged; **nu-pieds**, bare-footed; **nu-bras**, bare-armed. After the noun, it agrees: **la tête nue**, bare-headed; **marcher pieds nus**, to walk bare-footed.

Possible

Possible does not change in expressions using **le plus, le moins**.

> **Courez le moins de risques possible.** Run the fewest risks possible.

Adjectives Used as Adverbs

In expressions like **voler bas**, to fly low; **sentir bon**, to smell good; **marcher droit**, to walk straight; **couper court**,

---

* Feu is used only in the literary language. Otherwise one says **mon défunt père**, my late father, **ma défunte mère**, my deceased mother.

to cut short; **chanter faux,** to sing out of tune; **parler haut,** to speak up, the adjectives **bas, bon, droit,** etc., are used as adverbs, and therefore do not agree.

> les cheveux coupés **court,** hair cut short
> **Cette viande sent bon.** That meat smells good.

POSITION OF THE ADJECTIVE

The general rule is that the adjective follows its noun: la langue française, the French language; la maison blanche, the white house; la table ronde, the round table.

However, the adjective may come in front of the noun when both are considered as a single idea, a single unit of thought: la jeune fille, the girl; le petit pois, the pea; un jeune homme, a youth; un petit chien, a pup.

These rules have numerous exceptions, especially in the literary language, where for purposes of style all kinds of variations of usage are possible.

Put the Adjective before the Noun

1. When the adjective is a short and common one, and especially when the noun has several syllables: **un petit appartement,** a small flat; **un long voyage,** a long journey. Other adjectives which generally precede are **grand,** big, tall; **gros,** big; **haut,** high; **beau,** beautiful; **joli,** pretty; **vilain,** ugly; **jeune,** young; **vieux,** old; **court,** short; **bon,** good, kind; **mauvais,** bad.

2. When the adjective is considered as the usual and fitting one: le **brave soldat,** the brave soldier; la **verte Irlande,** green Ireland; la **douce mère,** the sweet mother; la **terrible catastrophe,** the terrible catastrophe; **votre charmante sœur,** your charming sister.

Put the Adjective after the Noun

1. When the adjective is a long one, especially if the noun is monosyllabic: **un chant harmonieux**, a sweet song.

2. When it is an adjective of colour or shape: **un champ oblong**, an oblong field; **une robe noire**, a black dress.

3. If it is an adjective of nationality: **un livre français**, a French book.

4. If the adjective is followed by a phrase: **une chambre grande comme la main**, a bedroom as big as your hand.

5. When you are in doubt. (Most adjectives follow the noun!)

Adjectives Which Vary in Meaning According to their Position

Some adjectives vary in meaning when they are put before or after a noun. Here are some examples:

Before	*After*
un ancien élève, a former pupil	**une maison ancienne**, an old house
un brave homme, a worthy man	**un homme brave**, a brave man
ma chère femme, my beloved wife	**une robe chère**, an expensive dress
le dernier jour de la semaine, the last day of the week (last of a series)	**mercredi dernier**, last Wednesday (the one that's just gone)
un grand homme, a great man	**un homme grand**, a tall man
une pauvre femme, an unfortunate woman	**une femme pauvre**, a poor (without money) woman
ma propre main, my own hand	**les mains propres**, clean hands
la seule chose, the only thing	**une femme seule**, a woman on her own
une triste affaire, a wretched business	**une journée triste**, a sorrowful day

Nouveau and Neuf

Both mean "new", but **neuf** is used with the sense of "brand-new", "fresh from the shop", "just made".

Ma nouvelle voiture n'est pas neuve. My new car is not a brand-new one.

Two or More Adjectives with the Same Noun

This requires care. If one adjective normally comes before, the other after, there is no problem: **une petite table ronde**, a little round table. When the adjective and noun are linked closely—**une petite fille**, a little girl—you may add another in its normal position: **une jolie petite fille**, a pretty little girl; **une petite fille intelligente**, a clever little girl. In most cases you join the two adjectives together by **et** and for preference put them after the noun: **une table longue et basse**, a long, low table.

Position of Adjective with a Complex Noun

When we have a complex noun like **hôtel de ville**, town hall; **cahier d'écolier**, (schoolboys') exercise book, the adjective is put in its usual place: **un bel hôtel de ville**, a fine town hall; **un cahier d'écolier vert**, a green exercise book. When, however, there would be ambiguity, the adjective is not placed after the second noun: **un sale cahier d'écolier**, a dirty exercise book (it's the book, and not the schoolboy, which is dirty!).

POSSESSIVE ADJECTIVES

Possessive adjectives, as their name implies, are attached to a word to show ownership: *my* book, *thy* book, *his* book, *her* book, *our* book, *your* book, *their* book.

Meaning	Before Masculine Singular Nouns	Before Feminine Singular Nouns	Before Plural Nouns
my	mon	ma	mes
thy	ton	ta	tes
his, her, its, one's	son	sa	ses
our	notre	notre	nos
your	votre	votre	vos
their	leur	leur	leurs

Examples: ma pomme, my apple; son livre, his or her book; sa mère, his or her mother; nos plumes, our pens; leurs chapeaux, their hats; le ciel et sa beauté, the sky and its beauty; on aime sa patrie, one loves one's country.

Use of the Possessive Adjectives

1. *His* or *her*; translated by the same word in French. Son or sa depend on the gender of the *noun*, not of the *possessor*: son livre, his or her book; sa mère, his or her mother. If you are really afraid of not making yourself perfectly clear, say sa mère à lui, *his* mother; sa mère à elle, *her* mother.

2. Mon, ton, son are used instead of ma, ta, sa if a feminine singular word begins with a vowel or mute h: mon encre (f.), my ink; ton auto (f.), thy car; son âme (f.), his or her soul; son inoubliable histoire (f.), his, her or its unforgettable story.

3. In English the possessive adjective may be understood and therefore omitted: in French it must be repeated: his pen and book, sa plume et son livre; my brother and sister, mon frère et ma sœur.

4. A soldier * speaking to an upper rank always says **mon lieutenant, mon capitaine, mon général** when spoken to by an officer.

5. When an owner possesses only one of the objects, the singular of the adjective and noun is generally used.

> **Les oiseaux font leur nid au printemps.** Birds make their nests in spring.
>
> **Ils ôtèrent leur chapeau.** They removed their hats.

If, however, there is an insistence on the number or variety, then the plural is used:

> **Les marchands ouvrent leurs boutiques aujourd'hui.** Shopkeepers open their shops today.

Sometimes too it is essential to use the plural to avoid producing a ludicrous effect:

> **L'après-midi les messieurs se promenaient avec leurs femmes.** In the afternoon the gentlemen used to walk with their wives.

(The singular "femme" might imply a society in which the gentlemen shared a wife!)

6. As already pointed out in Chapter II, the possessive adjective is replaced by the Definite Article when there is no doubt about the identity of the possessor, especially where parts of the body are concerned.

> **Il leva la tête.** He raised his head.
>
> **On lui attacha les pieds.** One tied his feet (lit. the feet to him).

Of course, the possessive adjective is allowed when some additional emphasis is required:

> **Il a toujours sa grippe.** He still has his influenza (that influenza of his).
>
> **Tes beaux yeux!** Your lovely eyes!

* A civilian would say simply **monsieur** or **lieutenant**, etc.

DEMONSTRATIVE ADJECTIVES

Demonstrative Adjectives are used to point out the nouns with which they are associated.

	Masculine	Feminine	Meaning
Singular	ce or cet	cette	this *or* that
Plural	ces		these *or* those

Examples: **ce crayon**, this pencil, that pencil; **cet homme**, this man, that man; **cette maison**, this house, that house; **ces amis**, these friends, those friends.

In the masculine *singular*, **cet** is used before a vowel or mute h: **cet ami**, this friend; **cet autre livre**, this other book; **cet homme**, this man.

This adjective may be reinforced by placing the particles -ci or -là after the noun:

-ci (here) gives the idea of nearness: **ce livre-ci**, *this* book.
-là (there) gives the impression of distance: **ce livre-là**, *that* book.

     Voulez-vous cette chambre-ci ou cette chambre-là? Do you want *this* bedroom or *that* bedroom?

INTERROGATIVE ADJECTIVES

1. **Quel?** (which?, what?). The interrogative adjective **quel** (which? *or* what?) has four forms in French: **quel**, masculine singular, **quelle**, feminine singular, **quels**, masculine plural, **quelles**, feminine plural.

     Quel livre désirez-vous? Which book do you want?
     Quelle femme est là? Which woman is there?
     Quelle est cette odeur agréable? What is that pleasant smell?

De quelle couleur est cette robe? What colour is this
dress?

Quelle heure est-il? What time is it?

2. Quel! (what a!, what!). This adjective may also be used
to indicate astonishment.

Quel chien! What a dog!
Quelle ville! What a town!
Quels élèves! What pupils!

Notice the absence of the article "a" in the above
examples.

3. Quel may also be used with the subjunctive in clauses
like these:

Quel que soit votre avis . . . Whatever may be your
opinion . . .

Quelle que soit la maladie . . . Whatever the illness may
be . . .

Quelles que soient vos raisons . . . Whatever your
reasons may be . . .

4. Quel is also used in conjunction with n'importe and
je ne sais:

Achetez n'importe quel journal! Buy any paper you
please! (No matter which.)

Il est sorti pour je ne sais quelle raison. He went out for
some reason or other. (I don't know what.)

INDEFINITE ADJECTIVES

Here is a list of some indefinite adjectives with examples
of their uses:

aucun, nul, no, not any

Il n'a donné $\begin{Bmatrix} \text{aucune} \\ \text{nulle} \end{Bmatrix}$ raison. He gave no reason.

sans aucune protection, without any protection

autre, other

> **un autre jour,** another day
>
> **d'autres livres,** other books
>
> **les autres tables,** the other tables
>
> **Il n'est pas comme les autres.** He isn't like the others (the rest).
>
> **nous autres Anglais,** we English people
>
> **Il y a autre chose.** There's something else.
>
> **Avez-vous autre chose à me montrer?** Have you anything else to show me?

certain, certain

> **un certain homme,** a certain man
>
> **une chose certaine,** a sure thing
>
> **la mort certaine,** certain, sure death
>
> **Certains l'ont déjà dit.** Certain people have already said so.

chaque, each, every

> **Chaque jour il fait la même chose.** Every day he does the same thing.
>
> **Chaque fois qu'il y entre . . .** Every time he goes in . . .

même, same, very, self

> **la même chose,** the same thing
>
> **le même prix,** the same price
>
> **Les officiers mêmes refusèrent d'obéir.** The very officers refused to obey.
>
> **Ma sœur est la bonté même.** My sister is kindness itself.
>
> **Je le ferai, moi-même.** I shall do it myself.

When **même** is used in front of the article and a noun, it is invariable.

> **Même les chiens refusent de manger cela.** Even the dogs refuse to eat that.

It does not change if used similarly before an adjective or a verb.

Ils sont bons et même indulgents. They are kind and
  even indulgent.
Ils veulent même venir avec nous. They even want to
  come with us.

plusieurs, several

plusieurs enfants, several children
plusieurs femmes, several women

quelque(s), some, a few

quelque chose de nouveau, something new
quelque part, somewhere
quelques fleurs, a few flowers

quelconque, some or other

une idée quelconque, some idea or other
un livre quelconque (familiar style), a very ordinary
  kind of book

tel, such

un tel garçon, such a boy
une telle chose, such a thing
de tels livres, such books
Telle fut sa patience que . . . Such was her patience
  that . . .
Telle qu'elle est, je l'aime. I love her just as she is.
Monsieur un Tel, Mr. So-and-so

tout, toute, every, all (sing.)

tous, toutes, all (plur.)

tout ceci, all this
tout le jour, all day, the whole day
toute ma famille, all my family, the whole of my family
tous les jours, every day
tous les deux jours, every other day
tous (les) deux, both
tous trois, all three

Tout homme bien élevé aurait fait la même chose.

Any ⎫
Every ⎭ well-brought-up man would have done the
same thing.

COMPARISON OF ADJECTIVES

Adjectives are said to have degrees of comparison: positive, comparative and superlative. If we take a common adjective like "high", then we can say "high" (positive), "higher" (comparative), "highest" (superlative). With longer adjectives we do not use this method: instead we employ "more" and "most": thus, "beautiful" (positive), "more beautiful" (comparative), "most beautiful" (superlative). This latter method is the French way of doing it,

Positive	*Comparative*	*Superlative*
haut (high)	plus haut (higher)	le plus haut (highest)
confortable (comfortable)	plus confortable (more comfortable)	le plus confortable (most comfortable)
long (long)	plus long (longer)	le plus long (longest)

and is used for most French adjectives.

Exceptions

In English we have a few exceptions like "good, better, best", "bad, worse, worst". Here are the exceptions in French:

bon (good)	meilleur (better)	le meilleur (best)
mauvais (bad)	pire (worse)	le pire (worst)
petit (little)	moindre (less, lesser)	le moindre (least)

Mauvais and petit can also be compared with plus, thus:

mauvais	plus mauvais	le plus mauvais
petit (small)	plus petit (smaller)	le plus petit (smallest)

There is a slight difference in meaning between the two forms. For instance, le plus petit stands for the smallest in size.

De tous les enfants, c'est Jean qui est le plus petit. Jean is the smallest of the children.

Le moindre has the sense of "the slightest", and is used with abstract nouns.

Il l'a fait sans la moindre difficulté. He did it without the slightest difficulty.

Similarly, le plus mauvais means "worst" in a concrete sense: les plus mauvais souliers, les plus mauvais habits, the worst shoes, the worst clothes, whereas le pire means "worst" referring to moral matters: la pire corruption, the worst corruption.

Examples of Comparison

Now let us have a few examples of comparison:

Jean est grand. Jean is tall.

Jean est plus grand que son frère. Jean is taller than his brother.

Jean est le plus grand garçon de la classe. Jean is the tallest boy in the class.

Note that "than" is expressed by que and that whereas in English we say "in" after a superlative, "the tallest boy *in* the class, the prettiest house *in* the street, the best restaurant *in* Paris", the French always use de, "of the class, of the street, of Paris".

Suzanne est aussi grande que Pierre. Suzanne is as tall as Pierre.

Suzanne n'est pas $\left.\begin{array}{c}\text{si}\\\text{aussi}\end{array}\right\}$ grande que Pierre. Suzanne is not $\left.\begin{array}{c}\text{so}\\\text{as}\end{array}\right\}$ tall as Pierre.

Suzanne est moins grande que Pierre. Suzanne is $\left.\begin{array}{l}\text{less tall than}\\\text{not so tall as}\end{array}\right\}$ Pierre.

Note the use of **que** in all the above examples.

> **Suzanne est le moins beau de mes enfants.** Suzanne is the least beautiful of my children.

Thus, using **moins** (less), and **le moins** (least), we can make unflattering comparisons: **confortable** (comfortable), **moins confortable** (less comfortable), **le moins confortable** (least comfortable).

The position of the adjective need not worry you: it goes into its normal place, either before or after the noun: **Le plus beau tableau du musée**, the most beautiful picture in the museum; **le garçon le plus intelligent**, the most intelligent boy; **les exercices les plus difficiles**, the most difficult exercises.

When a possessive adjective is used with a superlative and the adjective is one which precedes the noun the article is omitted: **ma plus belle photo**, my finest photo, *but* **mes livres les plus intéressants**, my most interesting books.

Most

There is also a use of "most" which is not really a direct comparison. We say "he is a most charming gentleman", meaning "he is exceedingly charming" and without consciously comparing him with anyone else. In this case we should translate by **un monsieur des plus charmants** or **un monsieur très charmant**: similarly, **un livre des plus intéressants**, a most interesting book. We could also say: **un livre fort intéressant** or **un livre bien intéressant**, a very interesting book, which amounts more or less to the same thing.

Other phrases worth learning are **de plus en plus**, more and more; **de moins en moins**, less and less: **de plus en plus sérieux**, more and more serious; **de plus en plus grand**, bigger and bigger; **de moins en moins important**, less and less important.

Comme

There remains yet another way of comparing, using **comme: fort comme un âne**, as strong as an ass (strong like an ass); **doux comme un agneau**, as gentle as a lamb.

You will have noticed already that when a definite article is used there is no difference in form between a comparative and a superlative adjective, thus: **fort**, strong; **plus fort**, stronger; **le plus fort**, the stronger. **Le plus fort** may, as we have already seen, also mean "the strongest". Now look at these two sentences:

> Jacques is the stronger (of my two sons).
> Jacques is the strongest (of my three sons).

In both cases, the sentences would begin in French:

> **Jacques est le plus fort . . .**

Expletive NE in Comparison

One last point. In sentences like "He is stronger than you think" and "He talks more than he works", the comparative is followed in the **que** clause by an untranslated or expletive **ne**.

> Il est plus fort que vous ne pensez.
> Il parle plus qu'il ne travaille.

CARDINAL NUMBERS

0 zéro	9 neuf
1 un (m.), une (f.)	10 dix
2 deux	11 onze
3 trois	12 douze
4 quatre	13 treize
5 cinq	14 quatorze
6 six	15 quinze
7 sept	16 seize
8 huit	17 dix-sept

18	dix-huit	60	soixante
19	dix-neuf	61	soixante et un
20	vingt	66	soixante-six
21	vingt et un	70	soixante-dix
22	vingt-deux	71	soixante et onze
23	vingt-trois	72	soixante-douze
24	vingt-quatre	73	soixante-treize
25	vingt-cinq	74	soixante-quatorze
26	vingt-six	75	soixante-quinze
27	vingt-sept	76	soixante-seize
28	vingt-huit	77	soixante-dix-sept
29	vingt-neuf	78	soixante-dix-huit
30	trente	79	soixante-dix-neuf
31	trente et un	80	quatre-vingts
32	trente-deux	81	quatre-vingt-un
40	quarante	82	quatre-vingt-deux
41	quarante et un	83	quatre-vingt-trois
43	quarante-trois	84	quatre-vingt-quatre
50	cinquante	90	quatre-vingt-dix
51	cinquante et un	91	quatre-vingt-onze
55	cinquante-cinq	92	quatre-vingt-douze

100	cent
101	cent un
102	cent deux
200	deux cents
201	deux cent un
1000	mille
1001	mille un
2000	deux mille
1,000,000	un million
2,000,000	deux millions
1,000,000,000	un milliard

Uses of Cardinal Numbers

Cardinal numbers may be simple, **un, deux, trois** or compound, **dix-sept, vingt et un, quatre-vingt-treize.** French compound numbers from 17 to 99 inclusive have hyphens between their component parts except when et is used as a joining word: 21, 31, 41, 51, 61, 71; vingt et un, trente et un, quarante et un, etc. After 71 no et is used: quatre-vingt-un (81), quatre-vingt-onze (91), cent un (101). Vingt and cent take an -s when multiplied by another number:* quatre-vingts (80), quatre cents (400), but not if another number follows: quatre-vingt-trois (83), quatre cent dix (410). The only number which has a feminine form is UN, so that we say une maison, one house; vingt et une maisons, twenty-one houses. Mille, a thousand, has no plural form: trois mille hommes, three thousand men. Million and milliard are nouns, and therefore we must say trois millions de francs (3,000,000 francs) and un milliard de livres (£1,000,000,000). Cardinal numbers are used (with the exception of premier, first) with names of kings and in dates: Louis premier, Louis I, but Louis deux, Louis II, Louis trois, Louis III, etc., le premier décembre, December 1st, but le deux décembre, le trois décembre, etc.

Cardinal numbers are generally placed before the noun, trois sacs, three bags: they come afterwards to indicate the order of kings, popes, etc., Louis quatorze, Louis XIV, and to give a reference, chapitre cinq, chapter five.

ORDINAL NUMBERS

1st premier (m.), première (f.)	6th sixième
2nd deuxième, second(e)	7th septième
3rd troisième	8th huitième
4th quatrième	9th neuvième
5th cinquième	10th dixième

21st vingt et unième
33rd trente-troisième

---

* In expressions like page deux cent, page quatre-vingt, where the number follows the noun, no -s is required.

Use, Formation and Position of Ordinals

They indicate order: **le premier homme**, the first man; **le cinquième jour**, the fifth day; **il est arrivé le septième**, he came in seventh. They are formed, with the exception of premier, from the cardinal numbers by the addition of -ième. Of course, with numbers ending in -e, like **quatre, quatorze, quarante,** the **e** is dropped before the ending: **quatrième, quatorzième, quarantième.** Note too that **cinq** adds a u to become **cinquième** and that the f of neuf becomes a **v** in neuvième.

There are two words for second: **deuxième** and **second** (pronounced *zegond*). In compound numbers we always use deuxième; **vingt-deuxième,** twenty-second. In other cases either deuxième or second may be used: **le deuxième livre, le second livre.*** Deuxième seems to be more common than second.

Ordinal adjectives come before the noun and, of course, agree like normal adjectives: **ma première auto,** my first car.

---

* It used to be stated that, when speaking of two things only, **second** should be used, of more than two, **deuxième** was better.

CHAPTER IV

THE VERB

TENSES AND PERSONS

The verb is the most important word in the sentence: it expresses the action that takes place. Unfortunately it is also the most difficult word to use correctly. A verb is generally found in tenses, which give evidence of the occasion when the action takes place, whether in the past, the present or the future. Each tense has six forms, 1st, 2nd and 3rd Persons Singular and 1st, 2nd and 3rd Persons Plural. Thus the Present Tense of the verb "to like" can be written down thus in English:

	Singular	*Plural*
1st Person	I like	we like
2nd Person	thou likest	you like
3rd Person	he, she, it likes	they like

This in French would be written like this:

1st Person	j'aime	nous aimons
2nd Person	tu aimes	vous aimez
3rd Person	il, elle aime	ils, elles aiment

TU

The 2nd Person Singular form **Tu** (thou), which has almost died out in English, is very common in French, being used when members of a family are speaking to each other, in conversation between close friends and when calling animals. In prayer, Catholics use **Vous** (You) in addressing God, Protestants **Tu** (Thou).

MOODS

The Verb has also Moods: the Indicative Mood, the Conditional Mood, the Imperative, the Subjunctive and the Infinitive Moods.

Tenses of the Indicative Mood

Here are the four simple tenses of the Indicative of the verb **donner** (to give) with their equivalents in English:

Present Tense: **je donne**, I give, I am giving, I do give
Imperfect Tense: **je donnais**, I was giving, I used to give
Past Historic Tense: **je donnai**, I gave, I did give
Future Tense: **je donnerai**, I shall give

Compound Tenses

In addition to these four simple tenses, there are four compound tenses (i.e., where the verb is made up of two parts).

Perfect Tense: **j'ai donné**, I have given, I gave
Pluperfect Tense: **j'avais donné**, I had given
Past Anterior Tense: **j'eus donné**, I had given
Future Perfect Tense: **j'aurai donné**, I shall have given

Conditional Mood

The Conditional Mood has two tenses only:

Conditional Tense: **je donnerais**, I should give
Conditional Perfect Tense: **j'aurais donné**, I should have given

Imperative Mood

The Imperative Mood is used to give commands.

2nd Person Singular: **donne!** give!
1st Person Plural: **donnons!** let us give!
2nd Person Plural: **donnez!** give!

The Subjunctive Mood

The Subjunctive has four tenses whose meanings are generally the same as the corresponding tenses of the Indicative.

Present Tense: **je donne**
Imperfect Tense: **je donnasse**
Perfect Tense: **j'aie donné**
Pluperfect Tense: **j'eusse donné**

The Infinitive

The Infinitive has two forms:

Present Infinitive: **donner,** to give
Perfect Infinitive: **avoir donné,** to have given

Participles

Present Participle: **donnant,** giving
Past Participle: **donné,** gíven

Active and Passive Voice

Every tense can be in the active voice or in the passive voice. Here are two examples:

Present Tense (Active Voice): **je punis,** I punish
Present Tense (Passive Voice): **je suis puni,** I am punished
Future Tense (Active Voice): **je punirai,** I shall punish
Future Tense (Passive Voice): **je serai puni,** I shall be punished

After the above preliminaries, let us go into more detail. There are thousands of French verbs, and learning them thoroughly is a task which every student must tackle boldly. To make things easier, it is usual to divide verbs into families or conjugations. Here is the usual classification:

CONJUGATIONS

1. The first conjugation: Verbs ending in -ER, like donner, to give.

2. The second conjugation: Verbs ending in -IR, like finir, to finish.

3. The third conjugation: Verbs ending in -RE, like vendre, to sell.

There remain the Irregular Verbs which, as their name implies, do not always behave like the verbs of the three conjugations. A list of these verbs is given later in this chapter.

THE FIRST CONJUGATION

Verbs whose Infinitive ends in -ER.

This conjugation is by far the most important, containing over four thousand verbs. Moreover, any new verb brought into the language—kidnapper, to kidnap; interviewer, to interview—goes into this category.

Donner, to give

Indicative Mood

Present Tense.

je donne, I give, am giving, do give
tu donnes, thou givest, etc.
il (elle) donne, he (she) gives, etc.
nous donnons, we give, etc.

vous donnez, you give, etc.
ils (elles) donnent, they give, etc.

Imperfect Tense.

je donnais, I was giving, used to give
tu donnais, thou wast giving, etc.
il donnait, he was giving, etc.
nous donnions, we were giving, etc.
vous donniez, you were giving, etc.
ils donnaient, they were giving, etc.

Past Historic.

je donnai, I gave, I did give
tu donnas, thou gavest, etc.
il donna, he gave, etc.
nous donnâmes, we gave, etc.
vous donnâtes, you gave, etc.
ils donnèrent, they gave, etc.

Future.

je donnerai, I shall give
tu donneras, thou wilt give
il donnera, he will give
nous donnerons, we shall give
vous donnerez, you will give
ils donneront, they will give

Compound Tenses

Perfect.	Pluperfect.
j'ai donné, I have given, I gave	j'avais donné, I had given
tu as donné, thou hast given, etc.	tu avais donné, thou hadst given
il a donné, he has given, etc.	il avait donné, he had given
nous avons donné, we have given, etc.	nous avions donné, we had given
vous avez donné, you have given, etc.	vous aviez donné, you had given
ils ont donné, they have given, etc.	ils avaient donné, they had given

Past Anterior.	Future Perfect.
j'eus donné, I had given	j'aurai donné, I shall have given
tu eus donné, thou hadst given	tu auras donné, thou wilt have given
il eut donné, he had given	il aura donné, he will have given
nous eûmes donné, we had given	nous aurons donné, we shall have given
vous eûtes donné, you had given	vous aurez donné, you will have given
ils eurent donné, they had given	ils auront donné, they will have given

Conditional Mood

Conditional.	Conditional Perfect.
je donnerais, I should give	j'aurais donné, I should have given
tu donnerais, thou wouldst give	tu aurais donné, thou wouldst have given
il donnerait, he would give	il aurait donné, he would have given
nous donnerions, we should give	nous aurions donné, we should have given
vous donneriez, you would give	vous auriez donné, you would have given
ils donneraient, they would give	ils auraient donné, they would have given

Subjunctive Mood

Present.	Imperfect.
je donne	je donnasse
tu donnes	tu donnasses
il donne	il donnât
nous donnions	nous donnassions
vous donniez	vous donnassiez
ils donnent	ils donnassent

Perfect.	Pluperfect.
j'aie donné	j'eusse donné
tu aies donné	tu eusses donné
il ait donné	il eût donné
nous ayons donné	nous eussions donné
vous ayez donné	vous eussiez donné
ils aient donné	ils eussent donné

Imperative Mood

Affirmative.	Negative.
donne! give (thou)!	ne donne pas! do not give!
donnons! let us give!	ne donnons pas! let us not give!
donnez! give (you)!	ne donnez pas! do not give!

Infinitive Mood

Present.	Past.
donner, to give	avoir donné, to have given

Participles

Present.	Past.
donnant, giving	donné, given
	ayant donné, having given

All verbs ending in **-ER**, with the exceptions of **aller** and **envoyer**, are like **donner**.

Minor Peculiarities of the First Conjugation

A few verbs ending in **-ER**, while not irregular, have a few minor peculiarities. We shall deal with these now.

Verbs Ending in -CER

Examples: commencer, to commence; lancer, to throw.
Verbs ending in **-CER** have a cedilla under the **c** before **a** and **o** in order to keep the same soft **c** sound.

commencer   nous commençons   je commençais

Verbs Ending in -GER

These add a mute or silent e before endings that begin with a and o in order to keep the soft g sound.

| manger | nous mangeons | ils mangeaient |
| plonger | nous plongeons | il plongeait |

Verbs Ending in -YER

These change the y to i before a mute or silent e.*

essayer	il essaie	nous essaierons
broyer	je broie	tu broieras
essuyer	ils essuient	ils essuieront

Verbs Like RÉGNER, CÉDER, PROTÉGER

These change the é to è before a mute e in the endings of the Present Tense.

céder: je cède but vous cédez
pénétrer: ils pénètrent but nous pénétrons

In the Future and Conditional Tenses the accents are not changed: je céderai, il protégerait, ils céderaient.

Verbs Like SEMER, LEVER, PROMENER, ACHETER, GELER

These verbs take a grave accent over the e when there is a mute e following: semer, je sème; lever, ils lèvent; promener, je promènerai; acheter, elle achètera; geler, il gèle.

Other Verbs Ending in -ELER and -ETER

These double the l or t in similar circumstances: jeter, ils jettent; appeler, j'appellerai but vous appelez.

* Verbs ending in ayer, i.e., payer, may either keep the y or change it to i: payer, je paye or je paie.

SECOND AND THIRD CONJUGATIONS
(Verbs ending in -IR and -RE)

There are far fewer verbs ending in **-IR** and only a small number ending in **-RE**.

Second Conjugation	Third Conjugation
FINIR, to finish	**VENDRE**, to sell

Indicative Mood

Present.	Imperfect.	Present.	Imperfect.
I finish	{ *I was finishing* { *I used to finish*	*I sell*	{ *I was selling* { *I used to sell*
je finis	je finissais	je vends	je vendais
tu finis	tu finissais	tu vends	tu vendais
il finit	il finissait	il vend	il vendait
nous finissons	nous finissions	nous vendons	nous vendions
vous finissez	vous finissiez	vous vendez	vous vendiez
ils finissent	ils finissaient	ils vendent	ils vendaient

Past Historic.	Future.	Past Historic.	Future.
I finished	*I shall finish*	*I sold*	*I shall sell*
je finis	je finirai	je vendis	je vendrai
tu finis	tu finiras	tu vendis	tu vendras
il finit	il finira	il vendit	il vendra
nous finîmes	nous finirons	nous vendîmes	nous vendrons
vous finîtes	vous finirez	vous vendîtes	vous vendrez
ils finirent	ils finiront	ils vendirent	ils vendront

Compound Tenses

Perfect.	Pluperfect.	Perfect.	Pluperfect.
I have finished	*I had finished*	*I have sold*	*I had sold*
j'ai fini	j'avais fini	j'ai vendu	j'avais vendu
tu as fini	tu avais fini	tu as vendu	tu avais vendu
il a fini	il avait fini	il a vendu	il avait vendu
nous avons fini	nous avions fini	nous avons vendu	nous avions vendu
vous avez fini	vous aviez fini	vous avez vendu	vous aviez vendu
ils ont fini	ils avaient fini	ils ont vendu	ils avaient vendu

Conditional Mood

Conditional.	Conditional Perfect.	Conditional.	Conditional Perfect.
I should finish	*I should have finished*	*I should sell*	*I should have sold*
je finirais	j'aurais fini	je vendrais	j'aurais vendu
tu finirais	tu aurais fini	tu vendrais	tu aurais vendu
il finirait	il aurait fini	il vendrait	il aurait vendu
nous finirions	nous aurions fini	nous vendrions	nous aurions vendu
vous finiriez	vous auriez fini	vous vendriez	vous auriez vendu
ils finiraient	ils auraient fini	ils vendraient	ils auraient vendu

Subjunctive Mood

Present.	Imperfect.	Present.	Imperfect.
je finisse	je finisse	je vende	je vendisse
tu finisses	tu finisses	tu vendes	tu vendisses
il finisse	il finît	il vende	il vendît
nous finissions	nous finissions	nous vendions	nous vendissions
vous finissiez	vous finissiez	vous vendiez	vous vendissiez
ils finissent	ils finissent	ils vendent	ils vendissent

Perfect.	Pluperfect.	Perfect.	Pluperfect.
j'aie fini	j'eusse fini	j'aie vendu	j'eusse vendu
tu aies fini	tu eusses fini	tu aies vendu	tu eusses vendu
il ait fini	il eût fini	il ait vendu	il eût vendu
nous ayons fini	nous eussions fini	nous ayons vendu	nous eussions vendu
vous ayez fini	vous eussiez fini	vous ayez vendu	vous eussiez vendu
ils aient fini	ils eussent fini	ils aient vendu	ils eussent vendu

Imperative Mood

finis! finish (thou)!		vends! sell (thou)!	
finissons! let us finish!		vendons! let us sell!	
finissez! finish!		vendez! sell!	

Infinitive

Present: **finir**, to finish   **vendre**, to sell
Perfect: **avoir fini**, to have finished   avoir vendu, to have sold

Participles

Present: **finissant**, finishing   **vendant**, selling
Past: **fini**, finished   **vendu**, sold
ayant fini, having finished   **ayant vendu**, having sold

AVOIR and ÊTRE

You will have noticed that in the Compound Tenses another verb, **avoir**, is brought in to help. There are two such auxiliary verbs: **avoir**, to have, and **être**, to be. We must look at them at once.

Avoir, to have   **Être**, to be

Indicative Mood

Present.	Imperfect.	Present.	Imperfect.
I have	*I had* *I was having* *I used to have*	*I am*	*I was* *I used to be*
j'ai	j'avais	je suis	j'étais
tu as	tu avais	tu es	tu étais
il a	il avait	il est	il était
nous avons	nous avions	nous sommes	nous étions
vous avez	vous aviez	vous êtes	vous étiez
ils ont	ils avaient	ils sont	ils étaient

Past Historic.	Future.	Past Historic.	Future.
I had	*I shall have*	*I was*	*I shall be*
j'eus	j'aurai	je fus	je serai
tu eus	tu auras	tu fus	tu seras
il eut	il aura	il fut	il sera
nous eûmes	nous aurons	nous fûmes	nous serons
vous eûtes	vous aurez	vous fûtes	vous serez
ils eurent	ils auront	ils furent	ils seront

Compound Tenses

Perfect.	Pluperfect.	Perfect.	Pluperfect.
I have had	*I had had*	*I have been*	*I had been*
j'ai eu	j'avais eu	j'ai été	j'avais été
tu as eu	tu avais eu	tu as été	tu avais été
il a eu	il avait eu	il a été	il avait été
nous avons eu	nous avions eu	nous avons été	nous avions été
vous avez eu	vous aviez eu	vous avez été	vous aviez été
ils ont eu	ils avaient eu	ils ont été	ils avaient été

Past Anterior.	Future Perfect.	Past Anterior.	Future Perfect.
I had had	*I shall have had*	*I had been*	*I shall have been*
j'eus eu	j'aurai eu	j'eus été	j'aurai été
tu eus eu	tu auras eu	tu eus été	tu auras été
il eut eu	il aura eu	il eut été	il aura été
nous eûmes eu	nous aurons eu	nous eûmes été	nous aurons été
vous eûtes eu	vous aurez eu	vous eûtes été	vous aurez été
ils eurent eu	ils auront eu	ils eurent été	ils auront été

Conditional Mood

Conditional.	Conditional Perfect.	Conditional.	Conditional Perfect.
I should have	*I should have had*	*I should be*	*I should have been*
j'aurais	j'aurais eu	je serais	j'aurais été
tu aurais	tu aurais eu	tu serais	tu aurais été
il aurait	il aurait eu	il serait	il aurait été
nous aurions	nous aurions eu	nous serions	nous aurions été
vous auriez	vous auriez eu	vous seriez	vous auriez été
ils auraient	ils auraient eu	ils seraient	ils auraient été

Subjunctive Mood

Present.	Imperfect.	Present.	Imperfect.
j'aie	j'eusse	je sois	je fusse
tu aies	tu eusses	tu sois	tu fusses
il ait	il eût	il soit	il fût
nous ayons	nous eussions	nous soyons	nous fussions
vous ayez	vous eussiez	vous soyez	vous fussiez
ils aient	ils eussent	ils soient	ils fussent

Perfect.	Pluperfect.	Perfect.	Pluperfect.
j'aie eu	j'eusse eu	j'aie été	j'eusse été
tu aies eu	tu eusses eu	tu aies été	tu eusses été
il ait eu	il eût eu	il ait été	il eût été
nous ayons eu	nous eussions eu	nous ayons été	nous eussions été
vous ayez eu	vous eussiez eu	vous ayez été	vous eussiez été
ils aient eu	ils eussent eu	ils aient été	ils eussent été

Imperative

aie! have! (thou)	sois! be! (thou)
ayons! let us have!	soyons! let us be!
ayez! have! (you)	soyez! be! (you)

Infinitive

Present: **avoir**, to have	**être**, to be
Perfect: **avoir eu**, to have had	**avoir été**, to have been.

Participles

Present: **ayant**, having	**étant**, being
Past: **eu**, had	**été**, been
ayant eu, having had	**ayant été**, having been

Verbs Conjugated with ÊTRE

Some verbs form their compound tenses, not with **avoir**, but with the help of the verb **être**. Here is a list of these verbs:

aller, to go	**venir**, to come; **devenir**, to become; **revenir**, to come back
arriver, to arrive	**partir**, to set out; **repartir**, to set out again
entrer, to enter	**sortir**, to go out; **ressortir**, to go out again
rentrer, to come home	**retourner**, to go back
naître, to be born	**mourir**, to die
monter, to go up	**descendre**, to go down
remonter, to go up again	**redescendre**, to go down again
tomber, to fall	**rester**, to remain
retomber, to fall again	

You will notice that most of these verbs concern motion, but do not be led into thinking that **être** is used with all verbs of motion. That is not true: **courir**, to run; **sauter**, to jump; **danser**, to dance; **marcher**, to walk, are all used with **avoir**: j'ai couru, il avait sauté, nous avons dansé, ils auront marché.

Compound Tenses of a Verb Conjugated with ÊTRE

Arriver, to arrive

Perfect.	Pluperfect.
I have arrived	*I had arrived*
je suis arrivé(e)	j'étais arrivé(e)
tu es arrivé(e)	tu étais arrivé(e)
il est arrivé	il était arrivé
elle est arrivée	elle était arrivée
nous sommes arrivé(e)s	nous étions arrivé(e)s
vous êtes arrivé(e)(s)	vous étiez arrivé(e)(s)
ils sont arrivés	ils étaient arrivés
elles sont arrivées	elles étaient arrivées

Past Anterior.	Future Perfect.
I had arrived	*I shall have arrived*
je fus arrivé(e)	je serai arrivé(e)
tu fus arrivé(e)	tu seras arrivé(e)
il fut arrivé	il sera arrivé
nous fûmes arrivé(e)s	nous serons arrivé(e)s
vous fûtes arrivé(e)(s)	vous serez arrivé(e)(s)
ils furent arrivés	ils seront arrivés

Conditional Perfect.

I should have arrived

je serais arrivé(e)	nous serions arrivé(e)s
tu serais arrivé(e)	vous seriez arrivé(e)(s
il serait arrivé	ils seraient arrivés

Subjunctive.

Perfect.	Pluperfect.
je sois arrivé(e)	je fusse arrivé(e)
tu sois arrivé(e)	tu fusses arrivé(e)
il soit arrivé	il fût arrivé
nous soyons arrivé(e)s	nous fussions arrivé(e)s
vous soyez arrivé(e)(s)	vous fussiez arrivé(e)(s)
ils soient arrivés	ils fussent arrivés

Infinitive.

Present: **arriver,** to arrive
Perfect: **être arrivé(e)(s),** to have arrived

Participles.

arrivé(e)(s), arrived
étant arrivé(e)(s), having arrived

Note that with this type of verb, the Past Participle agrees with the subject of the verb, the doer of the action:

> *Nous* sommes *montés* dans le train. We got into the train.
>
> *Il* était *tombé* dans l'escalier. He had fallen on the stairs.
>
> *Elle* est *née* en France et est *morte* en Italie. She was born in France and died in Italy.
>
> Mes deux *sœurs* sont *parties* pour l'Amérique. Both my sisters have left for America.

Some of the above verbs may also be conjugated with **avoir**, but they then have different meanings and can take an object.

Compare the following sentences in which **descendre**, **monter** and **rentrer** are used with **être** and **avoir**.

With être.	With avoir.
Elle est descendue du train.	Elle a descendu les bagages.
She got down from the train.	She brought the luggage downstairs.
Elle était montée à sa chambre.	Elle avait monté ma valise.
She had gone up to her room.	She had taken my case upstairs.
Elle est rentrée à six heures.	Elle a rentré mon vélo.
She came home at six.	She has brought my bicycle indoors.

THE PASSIVE VOICE

The passive voice is formed by adding the Past Participle of the verb to the correct tense of **être**. This is exactly the same as the English usage. Thus the Present Tense of the Passive of **punir**, to punish, goes like this:

e suis puni(e), I am punished	nous sommes puni(e)s, we are punished
u es puni(e), thou art punished	vous êtes puni(e)(s), you are punished
est puni, he is punished	ils sont punis, they are punished
lle est punie, she is punished	elles sont punies, they are punished

Similarly other tenses can be formed:

Past Historic: je fus puni(e), I was punished
Future: je serai puni(e), I shall be punished
Perfect: j'ai été puni(e), I have been punished
Pluperfect: j'avais été puni(e), I had been punished
Past Anterior: j'eus été puni(e), I had been punished
Future Perfect: j'aurai été puni(e), I shall have been punished
Conditional: je serais puni(e), I should be punished
Conditional Perfect: j'aurais été puni(e), I should have been punished
Present Subjunctive: je sois puni(e)
Imperfect Subjunctive: je fusse puni(e)
Perfect Subjunctive: j'aie été puni(e)
Pluperfect Subjunctive: j'eusse été puni(e)
Imperative: sois puni(e), soyons puni(e)s, soyez puni(e)(s)
Infinitive: Present: être puni(e)(s), to be punished
           Past: avoir été puni(e)(s), to have been punished
Participle: étant puni(e)(s), being punished

Note that in the Passive Voice the Past Participle agrees with the Subject of the sentence:

La jeune *fille* a été *punie*. The girl has been punished.
Les *vaches* avaient été *vendues* au marché. The cows had been sold at the market.

Avoiding the Passive

The French often avoid using the Passive Voice. Instead of a rather cumbrous sentence like

La fenêtre a été réparée. The window has been repaired.

they often prefer to say:

On a réparé la fenêtre. One has repaired the window.

Here are some other examples of how to evade the complicated Passive Voice:

It is said that . . . **On dit que** (one says that) . . .

He will be respected. **On le respectera** (one will respec him).

He was seen entering the house. **On l'a vu entrer dan la maison.**

The Passive Must not Be Used with Verbs that Take the Dative

The construction with **on** *must* be used if the French verb takes a dative (or indirect object). For instance, in French one says **répondre à une question**, to answer *to* a question **demander à un homme**, to ask (*to*) a man; **dire à quelqu'un** to tell *to* someone. In cases like this, the passive may not be used: one must not say in French: "his question is answered", "the man was asked", "the woman will be told" The sentences must be recast, using one (**on**).

One answers (to) his question. **On répond à sa question.** One asked (to) the man. **On demanda à l'homme.** One will tell (to) the woman. **On dira à la femme.**

REFLEXIVE VERBS

Reflexive Verbs are easily recognised in a dictionary: they have the word **SE** in front of them: **se laver,** to wash oneself; **se raser,** to shave oneself; **s'habiller,** to dress oneself. With this kind of verb, the action, instead of passing on to another person, reflects back on the doer. The subject and object are the same person; one is doing something to oneself.

Below is a simple example of a reflexive verb. Notice that in the Compound Tenses **ÊTRE** is used. The endings are the normal ones.

SE LAVER, to wash oneself

Indicative Mood

Present.	Imperfect.
je me lave, I wash myself	*I was washing myself*
tu te laves, thou washest thyself	*I used to wash myself*
il se lave, he washes himself	je me lavais
elle se lave, she washes herself	tu te lavais
nous nous lavons, we wash ourselves	il se lavait
vous vous lavez, you wash { yourself / yourselves	nous nous lavions
	vous vous laviez
ils se lavent } they wash themselves / elles se lavent }	ils se lavaient

Past Historic.	Future.
I washed myself	*I shall wash myself*
je me lavai	je me laverai
tu te lavas	tu te laveras
il se lava	il se lavera
nous nous lavâmes	nous nous laverons
vous vous lavâtes	vous vous laverez
ils se lavèrent	ils se laveront

Compound Tenses

Perfect.	Pluperfect.
I have washed myself	*I had washed myself*
je me suis lavé(e)	je m'étais lavé(e)
tu t'es lavé(e)	tu t'étais lavé(e)
il s'est lavé	il s'était lavé
elle s'est lavée	nous nous étions lavé(e)s
nous nous sommes lavé(e)s	vous vous étiez lavé(e)(s)
vous vous êtes lavé(e)(s)	ils s'étaient lavés
ils se sont lavés	
elles se sont lavées	

Past Anterior.	Future Perfect.
I had washed myself	*I shall have washed myself*
je me fus lavé(e)	je me serai lavé(e)
tu te fus lavé(e)	tu te seras lavé(e)
il se fut lavé	il se sera lavé
nous nous fûmes lavé(e)s	nous nous serons lavé(e)s
vous vous fûtes lavé(e)(s)	vous vous serez lavé(e)(s)
ils se furent lavés	ils se seront lavés

Conditional Mood

Conditional.	Conditional Perfect.
I should wash myself	*I should have washed myself*
je me laverais	je me serais lavé(e)s
tu te laverais	tu te serais lavé(e)
il se laverait	il se serait lavé
nous nous laverions	nous nous serions lavé(e)s
vous vous laveriez	vous vous seriez lavé(e)(s)
ils se laveraient	ils se seraient lavés

Subjunctive Mood

Present.	Imperfect.	Perfect.	Pluperfect.
je me lave	je me lavasse	je me sois lavé(e)	je me fusse lavé(e)
tu te laves	tu te lavasses	tu te sois lavé(e)	tu te fusses lavé(e)
il se lave	il se lavât	il se soit lavé	il se fût lavé
nous nous lavions	nous nous lavassions	nous nous soyons lavé(e)s	nous nous fussions lavé(e)s
vous vous laviez	vous vous lavassiez	vous vous soyez lavé(e)(s)	vous vous fussiez lavé(e)(s)
ils se lavent	ils se lavassent	ils se soient lavés	ils se fussent lavés

Imperative

lave-toi! wash thyself!
ne te lave pas! do not wash thyself
lavons-nous! let us wash ourselves!
ne nous lavons pas! let us not wash ourselves!
lavez-vous! wash { yourself! / yourselves! }

ne vous lavez pas! do not wash { yourself! / yourselves! }

Infinitive

se laver, to wash oneself   s'être lavé, to have washed oneself

Participles

se lavant, washing oneself   s'étant lavé, having washed oneself

Notice that the Reflexive Verb has the normal endings, but the Past Participle in the Compound Tenses agrees with the preceding direct object, in this case the reflexive pronouns **me, te, se, nous, vous, se.** This is the usual state of affairs, the reflexive pronoun being also the direct object:

Elle *s'*est *lavée.* She has washed herself.
Nous *nous* sommes *coupés.* We have cut ourselves.

However, occasionally the reflexive pronoun may be an indirect object, and then there is no agreement:

Ils se sont dit. They said to themselves.
Nous nous sommes demandé. We asked (to) ourselves.

AUXILIARY VERBS: AVOIR OR ÊTRE?

Whether to use **avoir** or **être** with a verb is a problem which worries every student of the French language: it even worries some Frenchmen! Let us sum up briefly.

1. *All* transitive verbs (i.e., verbs that take a direct object) and most instransitive verbs use **avoir** in compound tenses.

Il avait fait la connaissance de cette femme. He had made the acquaintance of this woman.
J'ai décidé de ne pas le faire. I decided not to do it.

2. A verb in the passive voice takes **être**.

J'avais vingt ans. J'aimais; j'étais aimé. I was twenty. I was in love, I was loved.
Dans ce combat Orso fut vaincu. In this fight Orso was beaten.

3. *All* reflexive verbs take **être**.

Elle s'est couchée tout de suite. She went to bed at once.
Je m'étais levé de bonne heure. I had got up early.

4. The following intransitive verbs: **aller, arriver, entrer, rentrer, naître, monter, remonter, tomber, retomber, venir,**

devenir, revenir, partir, sortir, mourir, descendre, redescendre, rester take être.

Il est né en France. He was born in France.
Nous y serions restés longtemps. We should have stayed there a long time.

IRREGULAR VERBS

If a verb does not behave as an **-ER**, **-IR** or **-RE** verb generally does, it is called an irregular verb. It simply does not obey the usual rules. Learning these verbs is one of the curses of studying a language. However, the important ones are soon learned, because, oddly enough, they include some of the most common verbs. You meet them so often that you acquire them almost unconsciously. Later on in this chapter we shall give a fairly complete list. We do not give all the tenses, because some you can easily form for yourself.

Rules for the Formation of the Tenses

1. If you know the Past Participle you can form the Compound Tenses with the help of the auxiliary **avoir** or **être**.

2. The Imperfect and Conditional of *all* verbs have the same endings: **-AIS, -AIS, -AIT, -IONS, -IEZ, -AIENT.**

3. The *stem* of the Future and Conditional is *always* the same: the future of **être** is je **serai**, the conditional is je **serais**; the future of **aller** is j'**irai**, the conditional is j'**irais**.

4. The Future is nearly always formed by adding endings to the Infinitive. The endings of the Future are the same for *all* verbs: **-AI, -AS, -A, -ONS, -EZ, -ONT**: The Future of the irregular verb **FUIR** is je **fuirai**.

5. To form the Imperfect Indicative, remove the **-ONS** from the 1st Person Plural of the Present Indicative of **a**

verb and add the endings -AIS, -AIS, -AIT, -IONS, -IEZ, -AIENT. Thus savoir, Present Indicative nous savons, remove the -ONS, sav-, Imperfect je savais, etc.

(The only exception to this rule is être, which has j'étais as its Imperfect.)

6. The Imperative (with the exceptions of avoir, être, savoir and vouloir) is formed from the Present Indicative by removing the pronouns from the 2nd Person Singular, 1st Person Plural and 2nd Person Plural. Thus finis, finissons, finissez. -ER verbs lose the s in the 2nd Person Singular, thus donner: donne, donnons, donnez.

7. In the Past Historic:

(a) -ER verbs have the endings -AI, -AS, -A, ÂMES, -ÂTES, -ÈRENT.

(b) Most -IR and -RE verbs end in -IS, -IS, -IT, -ÎMES, -ÎTES, -IRENT.

(c) Most verbs in -OIR and -OIRE end in -US, -US, -UT, -ÛMES, -ÛTES, -URENT.

(d) TENIR and VENIR are quite distinctive: tenir becomes tins, tins, tint, tînmes, tîntes, tinrent; venir becomes vins, vins, vint, vînmes, etc.

8. The endings of the Present Subjunctive (with the exceptions of avoir and être) are -E, -ES, -E, -IONS, -IEZ, -ENT. The stem can generally be found by removing the -ENT of the 3rd Person Plural of the Present Indicative. Thus boire, ils boivent, boiv-, je boive, etc.

If the stem of the Present Indicative changes during the tense, the stem of the Present Subjunctive generally follows suit. Thus boire, Present Indicative: bois, bois, boit, *buvons, buvez*, boivent; Present Subjunctive: boive, boives, boive, *buvions, buviez*, boivent.

9. The Imperfect Subjunctive is *always* formed by adding -SE to the 2nd Person Singular of the Past Historic. Thus venir, tu vins, je vinsse, etc.

Principal

Infinitive.	Participles.	Present Indicative.	Imperfect Past Historic.
acquérir, *to acquire*	acquérant	acquiers, -iers, -iert	acquérais
	acquis	acquérons, -érez, acquièrent	acquis
*aller, *to go*	allant	vais, vas, va	allais
	allé	allons, allez, vont	allai
asseoir, *to seat*	asseyant	assieds, assieds, assied,	asseyais
	assis	asseyons, -ez, -ent	assis
avoir, *to have*	ayant	ai, as, a,	avais
	eu	avons, avez, ont	eus
battre, *to beat*	battant	bats, bats, bat,	battais
	battu	battons, -ez, -ent	battis
boire, *to drink*	buvant	bois, bois, boit,	buvais
	bu	buvons, buvez, boivent	bus
bouillir, *to boil*	bouillant	bous, -s, -t,	bouillais
	bouilli	bouillons, -ez, -ent	bouillis
conclure, *to conclude*	concluant	conclus, -s, -t,	concluais
	conclu	concluons, -ez, -ent	conclus
connaître, *to know*	connaissant	connais, -s, connaît,	connaissais
	connu	connaissons, -ez, -ent	connus
coudre, *to sew*	cousant	couds, couds, coud,	cousais
	cousu	cousons, -ez, -ent	cousis
courir, *to run*	courant	cours, -s, -t,	courais
	couru	courons, -ez, -ent	courus
couvrir, *to cover*	couvrant	couvre, -es, -e,	couvrais
	couvert	couvrons, -ez, -ent	couvris
craindre, *to fear*	craignant	crains, -s, -t,	craignais
	craint	craignons, -ez, -ent	craignis
croire, *to believe*	croyant	crois, -s, -t,	croyais
	cru	croyons, -ez, croient	crus
croître, *to grow*	croissant	crois, croîs, croît,	croissais
	crû, crue	croissons, -ez, -ent	crûs
cueillir, *to gather*	cueillant	cueille, -es, -e,	cueillais
	cueilli	-ons, -ez, -ent	cueillis
cuire, *to cook*	cuisant	cuis, cuis, cuit,	cuisais
	cuit	cuisons, -ez, -ent	cuisis
devoir, *to owe*	devant	dois, dois, doit,	devais
to have to	dû, due	devons, devez, doivent	dus
dire, *to say*	disant	dis, -s, -t,	disais
	dit	disons, dites, disent	dis
dormir, *to sleep*	dormant	dors, dors, dort,	dormais
	dormi	dormons, -ez, -ent	dormis
écrire, *to write*	écrivant	écris, -s, -t,	écrivais
	écrit	écrivons, -ez, -ent	écrivis
envoyer, *to send*	envoyant	envoie, -es, -e,	envoyais
	envoyé	envoyons, -ez, envoient	envoyai
être, *to be*	étant	suis, es, est,	étais
	été	sommes, êtes, sont	fus
faillir, *to fail*	—	faut (rare)	—
	failli		faillis
faire, *to make, do*	faisant	fais, fais, fait,	faisais
	fait	faisons, faites, font	fis
falloir, *to be necessary*	—	il faut	il fallait
	fallu		il fallut
fuir, *to flee from*	fuyant	fuis, fuis, fuit,	fuyais
	fui	fuyons, -ez, fuient	fuis
haïr, *to hate*	haïssant	hais, hais, hait,	haïssais
	haï	haïssons, -ez, -ent	
joindre, *to join*	joignant	joins, -s, -t,	joignais
	joint	joignons, -ez, -ent	joignis

* Conjugated with the verb être.

Irregular Verbs

Present Subjunctive.	Future Conditional.	Imperative.	Remarks. So conjugate.
acquière, -es, -e,	acquerrai	acquiers,	conquérir
acquérions, -iez, acquièrent	acquerrais	acquérons, acquérez	
aille, ailles, aille,	irai	va,	
allions, alliez, aillent	irais	allons, allez	
asseye, -es, -e	assiérai	assieds, asseyons,	*s'asseoir
asseyions, -iez, -ent	assiérais	asseyez	
aie, aies, ait,	aurai	aie,	
ayons, ayez, aient	aurais	ayons, ayez	
batte, -es, -e,	battrai	bats, battons,	combattre
-ions, -iez, -ent	battrais	battez	abattre
boive, -es, -e,	boirai	bois, buvons,	
buvions, -iez, boivent	boirais	buvez	
bouille, -es, -e,	bouillirai	bous, bouillons,	intransitive verb, l'eau bout, *the water boils,* but je fais bouillir l'eau, *I boil the water*
-ions, -iez, -ent	bouillirais	bouillez	
conclue, -es, -e,	conclurai	conclus, concluons,	
-ions, -iez, -ent	conclurais	concluez	
connaisse, -es, -e,	connaîtrai	connais, connaissons,	paraître
-ions, -iez, -ent	connaîtrais	connaissez	
couse, -es, -e,	coudrai	couds, cousons,	
-ions, -iez, -ent	coudrais	cousez	
coure, -es, -e,	courrai	cours, courons,	
-ions, -iez, -ent	courrais	courez	
couvre, -es, -e,	couvrirai	couvre, couvrons,	ouvrir, offrir
-ions, -iez, -ent	couvrirais	couvrez	souffrir
craigne, -es, -e,	craindrai	crains, craignons,	plaindre, joindre,
-ions, -iez, -ent	craindrais	craignez	teindre, peindre
croie, -es, -e,	croirai	crois, croyons,	
croyions, -iez, croient	croirais	croyez	
croisse, -es, -e,	croîtrai	croîs, croissons,	Notice the circumflex accent to distinguish it from croire
-ions, -iez, -ent	croîtrais	croissez	
cueille, -es, -e,	cueillerai	cueille, cueillons,	accueillir
-ions, -iez, -ent	cueillerais	cueillez	
cuise, -es, -e,	cuirai	cuis, cuisons,	
-ions, -iez, -ent	cuirais	cuisez	
doive, -es, -e,	devrai	dois, devons,	Je dois cent francs, *I owe 100 francs* Je dois partir, *I must go*
devions, -iez, doivent	devrais	devez	
dise, -es, -e,	dirai	dis, disons	
-ions, -iez, -ent	dirais	dites	
dorme, -es, -e,	dormirai	dors, dormons,	mentir, *partir, servir,
-ions, -iez, -ent	dormirais	dormez	sentir, *sortir
écrive, -es, -e,	écrirai	écris, écrivons,	décrire
-ions, -iez, -ent	écrirais	écrivez	
envoie, -es, -e,	enverrai	envoie, envoyons,	
envoyions, -iez, envoient	enverrais	envoyez	
sois, sois, soit,	serai	sois, soyons,	
soyons, -ez, soient	serais	soyez	
—	faudrai	—	j'ai failli attendre, *I nearly waited*
	faudrais		
fasse, -es, -e,	ferai	fais, faisons,	
fassions, -iez, -ent	ferais	faites	
il faille	il faudra	—	
	il faudrait		
fuie, -es, -e,	fuirai	fuis, fuyons,	
fuyions, -iez, fuient	fuirais	fuyez	
haïsse, -es, -e,	haïrai	hais, haïssons,	
-ions, -iez, -ent	haïrais	haïssez	
joigne, -es, -e,	joindrai	joins, joignons,	plaindre, craindre,
-ions, -iez, -ent	joindrais	joignez	teindre

Principal

Infinitive.	Participles.	Present Indicative.	Imperfect Past Historic.
lire, *to read*	lisant lu	lis, lis, lit, lisons, -ez, -ent	lisais lus
luire, *to shine*	luisant lui	luis, luis, luit, luisons, -ez, -ent	luisais luisis
mentir, *to lie*	mentant menti	mens, -s, -t, mentons, -ez, -ent	mentais mentis
mettre, *to put*	mettant mis	mets, mets, met, mettons, -ez, -ent	mettais mis
moudre, *to grind*	moulant moulu	mouds, mouds, moud, moulons, -ez, -ent	moulais moulus
*mourir, *to die*	mourant mort	meurs, -s, -t, mourons, -ez, meurent	mourais mourus
mouvoir, *to move*	mouvant mû	meus, -s, -t, mouvons, -ez, meuvent	mouvais mus
*naître, *to be born*	naissant né	nais, nais, naît, naissons, -ez, -ent	naissais naquis
plaire, *to please*	plaisant plu	plais, -s, plaît, plaisons, -ez, -ent	plaisais plus
pleuvoir, *to rain*	pleuvant plu	il pleut	il pleuvait il plut
pouvoir, *to be able*	pouvant pu	puis } peux ʃ, peux, peut, pouvons, -ez, peuvent	pouvais pus
prendre, *to take*	prenant pris	prends, prends, prend, prenons, -ez, prennent	prenais pris
recevoir, *to receive*	recevant reçu	reçois, -s, -t, recevons, -ez, reçoivent	recevais reçus
rire, *to laugh*	riant ri	ris, ris, rit, rions, riez, rient	riais ris
rompre, *to break*	rompant rompu	romps, romps, rompt, rompons, -ez, -ent	rompais rompis
savoir, *to know*	sachant su	sais, sais, sait, savons, -ez, -ent	savais sus
suffire, *to suffice*	suffisant suffi	suffis, -is, -it, suffisons, -ez, -ent	suffisais suffis
suivre, *to follow*	suivant suivi	suis, suis, suit, suivons, -ez, -ent	suivais suivis
taire, *to silence*	taisant tu	tais, tais, tait, taisons, taisez, taisent	taisais tus
tenir, *to hold*	tenant tenu	tiens, tiens, tient, tenons, tenez, tiennent	tenais tins
tressaillir, *to quiver*	tressaillant tressailli	tressaille, -es, -e, -ons, -ez, -ent	tressaillais tressaillis
vaincre, *to conquer*	vainquant vaincu	vaincs, vaincs, vainc, vainquons, vainquez, vainquent	vainquais vainquis
valoir, *to be worth*	valant valu	vaux, vaux, vaut, valons, valez, valent	valais valus
*venir, *to come*	venant venu	viens, viens, vient, venons, venez, viennent	venais vins
vêtir, *to dress*	vêtant vêtu	vêts, vêts, vêt, vêtons, vêtez, vêtent	vêtais vêtis
vivre, *to live*	vivant vécu	vis, vis, vit, vivons, -ez, -ent	vivais vécus
voir, *to see*	voyant vu	vois, -s, -t, voyons, -ez, voient	voyais vis
vouloir, *to wish*	voulant voulu	veux, veux, veut, voulons, voulez, veulent	voulais voulus

* Conjugated with the verb être.

Irregular Verbs

Present Subjunctive.	Future Conditional.	Imperative.	Remarks. So conjugate.
lise, -es, -e,	lirai	lis, lisons,	élire
-ions, -iez, -ent	lirais	lisez	
luise, -es, -e,	luirai	luis, luisons,	
-ions, -iez, -ent	luirais	luisez	
mente, -es, -e,	mentirai	mens, mentons,	*sortir, *partir
-ions, -iez, -ent	mentirais	mentez	
mette, -es, -e,	mettrai	mets, mettons,	
-ions, -iez, -ent	mettrais	mettez	
moule, -es, -e,	moudrai	mouds, moulons,	
-ions, -iez, -ent	moudrais	moulez	
meure, -es, -e,	mourrai	meurs, mourons,	
mourions, -iez, meurent	mourrais	mourez	
meuve, -es, -e,	mouvrai	meus, mouvons,	
mouvions, -iez, meuvent	mouvrais	mouvez	
naisse, -es, -e,	naîtrai	nais, naissons,	
-ions, -iez, -ent	naîtrais	naissez	
plaise, -es, -e,	plairai	plais, plaisons,	déplaire
-ions, -iez, ent	plairais	plaisez	
il pleuve	il pleuvra	qu'il pleuve	
	il pleuvrait		
puisse, -es, -e,	pourrai	—	
-ions, -iez, -ent	pourrais		
prenne, -es, -e,	prendrai	prends, prenons,	comprendre
prenions, -iez, prennent	prendrais	prenez	
reçoive, -es, -e,	recevrai	reçois, recevons,	
recevions, -iez, reçoivent	recevrais	recevez	
rie, ries, rie,	rirai	ris, rions,	sourire
riions, -iez, -ent	rirais	riez	
rompe, -es, -e,	romprai	romps, rompons,	corrompre,
-ions, -iez, -ent	romprais	rompez	interrompre
sache, -es, -e,	saurai	sache, sachons,	
-ions, -iez, -ent	saurais	sachez	
suffise, -es, -e,	suffirai	suffis, suffisons,	
-ions, -iez, -ent	suffirais	suffisez	
suive, -es, -e,	suivrai	suis, suivons,	poursuivre
-ions, -iez, -ent	suivrais	suivez	
taise, -es, -e,	tairai	tais, taisons,	
-ions, -iez, -ent	tairais	taisez	
tienne, -es, -e,	tiendrai	tiens, tenons,	
tenions, -iez, tiennent	tiendrais	tenez	
tressaille, -es, -e,	tressaillirai	tressaille, tressaillons,	
-ions, -iez, -ent	tressaillirais	tressaillez	
vainque, -es, -e,	vaincrai	vaincs, vainquons,	
-ions, iez, -ent	vaincrais	vainquez	
vaille, -es, -e,	vaudrai	—	
valions, -iez, vaillent	vaudrais		
vienne, -es, -e,	viendrai	viens, venons,	*devenir
venions, -iez, viennent	viendrais	venez	*revenir
vête, -es, -e,	vêtirai	vêts, vêtons,	
-ions, -iez, -ent	vêtirais	vêtez	
vive, -es, -e,	vivrai	vis, vivons,	
-ions, -iez, -ent	vivrais	vivez	
voie, -es, -e,	verrai	vois, voyons,	entrevoir
voyions, voyiez, voient	verrais	voyez	prévoir (fut. prévoirai)
veuille, -es, -e,	voudrai	veuille, veuillons,	
voulions, vouliez, veuillent	voudrais	veuillez	

You will notice that not even irregular verbs are different all the time. They are irregular only in certain tenses.

IMPERSONAL VERBS

Impersonal Verbs are verbs used in the 3rd Person Singular only. Examples are **neiger,** to snow: **il neige,** it snows; **il neigeait,** it was snowing; **pleuvoir,** to rain: **il pleut,** it is raining; **il a plu,** it has been raining; **il pleuvra,** it will rain. Two very important ones which require more explanation are **FALLOIR** (to be necessary) and **IL Y A *** (there is, there are). Here are their tenses and meanings:

Y AVOIR	FALLOIR
Present: **il y a,** there is, there are	**il faut,** it is necessary
Imperfect:	**il fallait,** it was (used to be) necessary
il y avait, { there was, were / there used to be	
Past Historic: **il y eut,** there was, were	**il fallut,** it was necessary
Future: **il y aura,** there will be	**il faudra,** it will be necessary
Perfect: **il y a eu,** there has (have) been	**il a fallu,** it has been necessary
Pluperfect: **il y avait eu,** there had been	**il avait fallu,** it had been necessary
Past Anterior: **il y eut eu,** there had been	**il eut fallu,** it had been necessary
Future Perfect: **il y aura eu,** there will have been	**il aura fallu,** it will have been necessary
Conditional: **il y aurait,** there would be	**il faudrait,** it would be necessary
Conditional Perfect: **il y aurait eu,** there would have been	**il aurait fallu,** it would have been necessary
Present Subjunctive: **il y ait**	**il faille**
Imperfect Subjunctive: **il y eût**	**il fallût**
Perfect Subjunctive: **il y ait eu**	**il ait fallu**
Pluperfect Subjunctive: **il y eût eu**	**il eût fallu**

* Do not confuse **il y a** with **voilà** (also meaning "there is" or "there are"), which may be used in conversation only when you are actually pointing to someone or something.

Examples

1. Y AVOIR.

Il y a beaucoup de monde dans les rues. There are a lot of people in the streets.

Il y aura deux cents personnes au bal. There will be two hundred people at the dance.

Il y a is also used with the sense of "ago".

il y a une semaine, a week ago

il y a dix jours, ten days ago

2. FALLOIR.

Il faut aller à l'hôpital.
{ It is necessary to go to the hospital.
You must go to the hospital.
One must go to the hospital. }

Il me faudra lire le livre.
{ It will be necessary for me to read the book.
I shall have to read the book. }

Il faut de la patience.
{ It is necessary (to have) patience.
Patience is needed. }

HOW TO MAKE A VERB NEGATIVE

The French equivalent for "not" with a verb is made up of two words, **ne** and **pas**. Ne (**n'** before a vowel or mute **h**) is placed before the verb, **pas** almost always comes after.

J'aime, I like   **Je n'aime pas,** I do not like

il parlait, he was speaking   **il ne parlait pas,** he was not speaking

In compound tenses, **ne** or **n'** comes before the auxiliary verb **avoir** or **être**, **pas** is placed before the Past Participle.

il était entré, he had entered   **il n'était pas entré,** he had not entered

nous aurions cru, we should have thought   **nous n'aurions pas cru,** we should not have thought

In the case of the Infinitive, both **ne** and **pas** are put before the verb:

> Je préfère ne pas y aller ce soir. I prefer not to go there tonight.

THE INTERROGATIVE

To turn a verb into its question form, the pronoun is placed after the verb or, in the compound tenses, after its auxiliary. Thus:

> Vous venez. You come.
> Venez-vous? Are you coming?
> Ils ne voient pas. They do not see.
> Ne voient-ils pas? Do they not see?
> J'ai fini. I have finished.
> Ai-je fini? Have I finished?
> Vous n'êtes pas sorti. You did not go out.
> N'êtes-vous pas sorti? Did you not go out?

In the 3rd Person Singular of the Present Tense of the -ER conjugation, in the 3rd Person Singular of the Future Tense of all verbs, in the 3rd Person Singular of the Past Historic of -ER verbs and of the Present Tense of **avoir**, the letter **t** is inserted before the **il** or the **elle** in order to prevent a clash of vowels:

il donne, he gives	donne-t-il? does he give?
elle fera, she will make	fera-t-elle? will she make?
il envoya, he sent	envoya-t-il? did he send?
elle a, she has	a-t-elle? has she?

When the subject of the verb is a noun the noun is placed first, followed by the verb and the corresponding pronoun:

> Mes parents sont ici. My parents are here.
> Mes parents sont-ils ici? Are my parents here?
> L'autobus n'est pas parti. The bus has not left.
> L'autobus n'est-il pas parti? Has not the bus left?

An alternative method of making a verb interrogative is to put **Est-ce que** (is it that?) before the verb without altering the word order. As this way avoids the use of inversion, it is very frequently used in conversation.

> **Il va.** He goes.
> **Est-ce qu'il va?** Is he going?
> **Vous parlez.** You speak.
> **Est-ce que vous parlez?** Are you speaking?
> **Les parents sont déjà partis.** The parents have already left.
> **Est-ce que les parents sont déjà partis?** Have the parents already left?
> **Où est-ce que vous avez vu mon père?** Where did you see my father?

This **Est-ce que** method is also the usual one for the 1st Person Singular of the Present Tense of **-ER** verbs. One always says and writes **Est-ce que je donne?** Am I giving? and one uses **est-ce que** with most monosyllabic forms: **est-ce que je crains?** do I fear? where the alternatives would give a harsh sound. On the other hand, the forms **ai-je?** have I?; **dois-je?** must I?; **puis-je?** may I?; **sais-je?** do I know?; **vais-je?** am I going?; **suis-je?** am I? are very common.

A further method of forming the Interrogative is to make a statement and follow it by **n'est-ce pas?** (is it not?).

> **Il est intelligent, n'est-ce pas?** He is intelligent, isn't he?
> **Nous allons à Paris, n'est-ce pas?** We are going to Paris, aren't we?
> **Elles sont déjà arrivées, n'est-ce pas?** They have already arrived, haven't they?

Note that whatever person or tense is used, **n'est-ce pas** remains unchanged.

USING THE TENSES AND MOODS

In this section we shall mention only those tenses which are likely to prove difficult to the student.

The Infinitive

The infinitive may be used as subject, complement or object of a verb and also after a preposition.

> **Voir c'est croire,** to see is to believe
> **je veux chanter,** I want to sing
> **il aime à rire,** he loves to laugh
> **sans mentir,** without telling lies
> **pour réussir,** in order to succeed
> **afin de s'amuser,** in order to enjoy oneself

It is also occasionally used on public notices as an imperative:

> **Ne pas se pencher au dehors!** Do not lean out!

in a few expressions like:

> **Que faire?** What's to be done?

and as an exclamation:

> **Mentir tout le temps! Quelle horreur!** Tell lies all the time! Ugh!

The Present Indicative

Do not forget that the Present Tense **je donne** may have three possible translations into English: I give, I am giving, I do give. The "am" and the "do" are generally used to translate the negative or interrogative forms:

> **Je ne crois pas.** I don't think.
> **Y allez-vous?** Are you going there?

As in English, the Present is also used to express an immediate future:

> **Cet après-midi je pars pour Avignon.** This afternoon I am leaving for Avignon.

There is also a dramatic use of the Present, the so-called Historic Present, where an author uses the tense to make an account of past events more vivid and exciting:

> **À ce moment, quelque chose pousse la porte, l'ouvre doucement et entre dans ma chambre.** At that moment, something pushes the door, opens it gently and comes into my bedroom.

The Present is also employed, generally in conjunction with the preposition **depuis**, to describe an action already begun but still unfinished.

> **Je suis ici depuis trois heures.** I have been here for three hours (and I'm still here!)
>
> **Il attend depuis longtemps.** He has been waiting a long time (and he's still waiting!)
>
> **J'étudie le français depuis cinq ans!** } I have been
> **Il y a cinq ans que j'étudie le français!** } studying French for five years (and I'm still at it!)

The Imperfect Indicative

The usual translations of the Imperfect are "was (were)" and "used to".

1. It is used to describe an action that was going on when another took place:

> **Il descendait la rue quand il remarqua quelque chose de curieux.** He was going down the street when he noticed something strange.

2. Or an habitual action in the past:

> **Il quittait son bureau tous les jours à la même heure.** He { used to / would } leave his office every day at the same time.

3. It is also the tense of description:

Monsieur Dubois avait les yeux bleus. Mr. Dubois had blue eyes.

Le soleil brillait dans le ciel bleu, les oiseaux chantaient dans les haies. The sun shone (was shining) in the blue sky, the birds were singing (sang) in the hedges.

4. The Imperfect is used in conjunction with the preposition **depuis** to describe an action, already begun, which was still going on at the time of the narrative.

Il pleuvait depuis trois jours. It had been raining for days (and was still raining at the time!).

Il attendait l'autobus depuis vingt minutes quand j'arrivai en voiture. He had been waiting twenty minutes for the bus when I arrived in my car (when I arrived, he was still waiting).

The Past Historic

The Past Historic (also called the Preterite, the Past Definite or the Simple Past in some grammar-books) is the tense used in a narrative to bring the story one step forward. It describes what happened next.

Il se leva de sa chaise, courut vers la porte, l'ouvrit et descendit vite l'escalier. He got up from his chair, ran to the door, opened it and quickly went downstairs.

It is also the tense used to describe actions in the past which are considered as finished for good and all, having no connection with the present.

Louis XIV mourut en 1715: il régna soixante-douze ans. Louis XIV died in 1715: he reigned for seventy-two years.

Apart from a few parts of verbs used in Southern France, the Past Historic is never used in *spoken* French (unless, of course, the speaker is quoting from a book or newspaper).

It is the past tense used for events described in books, news-papers, etc. In conversation we should say, instead of the sentence above:

> Louis XIV est mort en 1715: il a régné soixante-douze ans.

The Perfect Indicative

The Perfect has the same meaning as the Past Historic, which it replaces in conversation and letter-writing. Remember that **J'ai écrit** may mean "I have written" or "I wrote" (or indeed "I did write" in negative or interrogative sentences).

> Elle répondit «Je ne l'ai pas fait. Je suis allée en ville ce matin et je ne suis rentrée qu'à midi et demi.» She replied: "I did not do it. I went to town this morning and didn't get back until half past twelve."

The Pluperfect Indicative and the Past Anterior

The Pluperfect Indicative and the Past Anterior have the same meaning. **J'avais donné, j'eus donné,** both mean "I had given". However, in a compound sentence introduced by a conjunction of time, such as **après que,** after; **quand** or **lorsque** (when); **aussitôt que** or **dès que** (as soon as), these conjunctions are followed by the Past Anterior if the verb in the Main Clause is in the Past Historic.*

$\left.\begin{array}{l}\text{Après que}\\\text{Quand}\\\text{Lorsque}\\\text{Aussitôt que}\\\text{Dès que}\end{array}\right\}$ Jean eut fini de lire son livre, il se coucha.

$\left.\begin{array}{l}\text{After}\\\text{When}\\\text{As soon as}\end{array}\right\}$ Jean had finished reading his book, he went to bed.

---

* Often in conversation, where the Past Historic is, of course, never used, a kind of compound tense replaces the Past Anterior: Quand Jean a eu fini de lire son livre, il s'est couché.

There is a similar construction, but with inversion after—

> à peine . . . que, hardly (scarcely) . . . than
>
> À peine le voleur fut-il entré dans la maison que l'agent sauta sur lui. Scarcely had the robber entered the house than the policeman jumped on him.

If there is no conjunction of time, the Pluperfect is used.

> À vingt ans, j'avais fini mes études. At the age of twenty I had finished my studies.
>
> Il en avait déjà parlé à son père. He had already spoken of it to his father.

The Future

The Future describes an action that is to come:

> Il pleuvra demain. It will rain tomorrow.
>
> Je partirai sans toi si tu n'es pas sage. I shall leave without you if you are not well-behaved.
>
> Un seul Dieu tu adoreras. One God only shalt thou worship.

In addition to translating "shall" and "will", the Future is sometimes used in French where we should use a Present in English, especially after conjunctions of time like quand, lorsque, when; aussitôt que, dès que, as soon as.

> Quand vous irez en vacances, n'oubliez pas de m'envoyer une carte. When you (will) go on holiday, don't forget to send me a card.

A similar use of the Future Perfect for the English Perfect is made:

> Aussitôt que vous aurez écrit la lettre, vous viendrez me la montrer. As soon as you (will) have written the letter, you will come and show it to me.

Do not be tempted into using the Future after the conjunction "if". "If" is never followed by the Future or Conditional.

> **S'il pleut demain, je resterai à la maison.** If it rains tomorrow, I shall stay at home.

"Shall" and "will" are not always a sign of the Future Tense. When "shall" indicates duty or obligation the verb **devoir,** to have to, should be used.

> **Vous devez obéir.** You shall obey. (= You have to $\left.\begin{array}{l} \text{You have to} \\ \text{must} \end{array}\right\}$ obey.)

Willingness or determination are expressed by **vouloir,** to wish:

> **Voulez-vous entrer?** Will you come in?
> **Je ne veux pas le faire.** I will not do it.

The Conditional ("should" or "would")

The Conditional has two main uses. It is used in conjunction with the Imperfect in sentences like this:

> **S'il pleuvait, j'irais au cinéma.** If it were to rain, I should go to the cinema.

Similarly, the Conditional Perfect is used with the Pluperfect:

> **S'il avait plu, je serais allé au cinéma.** If it had rained, I should have gone to the cinema.

It is also a common tense in reported speech:

> **Il dit qu'il le ferait tout de suite.** He said that he would do it at once.

After conjunctions of time, the Conditional is used where in English we should put the Imperfect:

> **Je leur dis de partir quand ils seraient prêts.** I told them to leave when they were (would be) ready.

Similarly, the Conditional Perfect replaces the English Pluperfect:

> **Il promit de venir quand il aurait fini son travail.** He promised to come when he had (would have) finished his work.

The Conditional Mood is also used to make a statement when the writer is not quite ready to vouch for its authenticity.

> **D'après le journal, il serait arrivé à Paris hier soir.** According to the paper, he arrived in Paris last night.

Another curious use of the Conditional is to put it after Quand or Quand même to translate "though" or "even if":

> **Quand même il me le dirait, je ne le croirais pas.** Even if he told me so, I should not believe it.

Lastly, do not forget that "should" may, in certain circumstances, mean "ought to", in which case the verb **devoir** is used.

> You should (ought to) drink less wine. **Vous devriez boire moins de vin.**

The Imperative Mood

The Imperative has three forms only: **viens!** come (thou)!; **venons!** let us come!; **venez!** come (you)! If a third person is required, it is borrowed from the Present Subjunctive: **qu'il entre!** let him come in! **qu'ils meurent!** let them die!

AGREEMENT OF VERB AND SUBJECT

As a general rule, the verb agrees in number with the subject. If the subject is singular, so is the verb; a plural subject has a plural verb.

> **L'homme disparut.** The man disappeared.
> **Les hommes disparurent.** The men disappeared.

It is when we have a collective noun as subject that trouble appears. Even in English most of us do not know whether to say "The Government has decided" or "The Government have decided". In French we use a singular verb if the collective noun is in the singular:

> Après la révolution, le clergé avait perdu toute sa richesse. After the revolution the clergy had lost all its wealth.
>
> L' ennemi va nous attaquer demain. The enemy is going to attack us tomorrow.

If, however, the collective noun is followed by a plural complement, the verb may be put into the singular or plural: it depends whether the writer is thinking of an undivided whole or a number of individuals:

> Une partie des soldats se sauva (or se sauvèrent). A section of the soldiers ran away.

Beaucoup, many; peu, few; combien, how many; trop, too many; la plupart, most, the majority, all take a plural verb:

> La plupart des habitants ont quitté la ville. Most of the inhabitants have left the town.
>
> Peu de gens croient cela. Few people believe that.

What happens when a verb has more than one subject? With ni . . . ni . . . ne, neither . . . nor, the verb is generally in the plural:

> Ni son père ni sa mère ne sont ici. Neither his father nor his mother is here.

In the case of l'un et l'autre (both) and l'un ou l'autre (either), you are free to use a singular or plural verb:

> L'un et l'autre arrivèrent (or arriva). Both arrived.
>
> L'un ou l'autre arriva (or arrivèrent). Either arrived.

When the subjects are of different persons, great care must be exercised. Suppose the subject is **Mon frère et moi,** my brother and I, then obviously the verb must go into the 1st Person Plural: "my brother and I" can be replaced by "we":

Mon frère et moi sommes bien contents de vous revoir.
My brother and I are very pleased to see you again.

Similarly, any other combination can be solved in the same way. **Vous et votre père,** you and your father, will have a verb in the 2nd Person Plural—**vous,** you.

Vous et votre père partirez aujourd'hui. You and your father will leave today.

SOME AUXILIARY VERBS

There are a number of very important verbs which are often used before the Infinitive of other verbs: here is a list with some examples:

(*a*) **aller,** to go

> **Je vais l'accompagner.** I am going to accompany him.

(*b*) **devoir,** to have to

> Present: **Je dois parler.** I have to, I must speak.
> Imperfect: **Je devais parler.** I used to have to speak, I had to speak.
> Past Historic: **Je dus obéir.** I had to obey.
> Future: **Je devrai me laver.** I shall have to wash myself.
> Perfect: **J'ai dû le faire.** I had to do it, I must have done it.
> Conditional: **Je devrais écrire.** I ought to (I should) write.
> Conditional Perfect: **J'aurais dû le faire.** I ought to have done it, I should have done it.

(*c*) **pouvoir,** to be able

> Present: **Je peux le porter.** I can carry it.
> **Puis-je entrer?** May I come in?

Imperfect: **Je pouvais faire cela quand j'étais jeune.**
I was able to (I could) do that when I was young.

Conditional: **Je pourrais y aller si je voulais.** I should
be able to (could) go there if I wanted to.

Conditional Perfect: **J'aurais pu le faire si j'avais été
là.** I should have been able to do it (I could have
done it, might have done it) if I had been there.

Note that the Imperfect and the Conditional both can
mean "could".

(*d*) **savoir,** to know * (how to)

Present: **Je sais jouer du piano.** I can (know how to)
play the piano.

Imperfect: **Je savais bien parler le français.** I could
(used to know how to) speak French well.

You will have noticed that both **pouvoir** and **savoir** may
mean "can" or "could". **Pouvoir** is used when we refer to a
physical ability or permission, **savoir** when we mention an
ability one has learnt by a mental process. Thus:

I can speak French. **Je sais parler français.**
He cannot walk (because he has broken his leg). **Il ne
peut pas marcher.**

(*e*) **venir,** to come

Venez me voir demain. Come and see me tomorrow.

venir à, to happen to

Un homme vint à passer. A man happened to pass by.

venir de, to have just (found in two tenses only, the
Present and Imperfect).

Present: **il vient d'arriver,** he has just arrived
Imperfect: **il venait d'arriver,** he had just arrived.

---

* **Connaître** also means "to know", but in the sense of "to be
acquainted with".
Je connais son frère. I know his brother.
Connaissez-vous bien Paris? Do you know Paris well?

CONSTRUCTIONS AFTER THE VERB FAIRE, TO MAKE, TO CAUSE TO

As is the case with all French verbs, a verb dependent on another is put into the Infinitive:

Je vous fais travailler. I make you work.
Il a fait pleurer Marie. He made Mary cry.
Il fera lire l'élève. He will make the pupil read.
Il la fera lire. He will make her read.

Faire, when used in this way, can also mean "to cause":

Il fait bâtir une maison. { He is causing a house to be built.
He is having a house built.

If the dependent infinitive has an object of its own the object of faire becomes indirect:

Il fera lire la fillette. He will make the girl read.
Il la fera lire. He will make her read.
but Il fera lire le livre à la fillette. He will make the girl read the book.
Il lui fera lire le livre. He will make her read the book.
Il le lui fera lire. He will make her read it.

As the above sentence Il fera lire le livre à la fillette may be ambiguous, meaning either "He will make the girl read the book" or "He will cause the book to be read to the girl", it is better in cases like this to change to:

Il fera lire le livre par la fillette. He will have the book read by the girl.

When a reflexive verb is used, the reflexive pronoun is often omitted:

Je les fais asseoir. I make them sit down (s'asseoir).
Nous la faisons taire. We make her keep silence (se taire).

Similar constructions are used with the verbs voir, to see; entendre, to hear; laisser, to let, allow.

Il vous a vu venir. He saw you coming.

Je l'ai entendu parler de cela. I heard him talking about that.

Ils ne vont pas nous laisser sortir. They are not going to let us get out.

THE DEPENDENT INFINITIVE

As we mentioned above, when two verbs are used together in French, the second one is put into the Infinitive:

(a) Je l'entends jouer. I hear him playing.

(b) Il aime à chanter. He likes singing.

(c) Elle résolut de partir. She decided to set out.

(d) Vous finirez par accepter. You will end up by accepting.

The infinitive may, as you can see from the above examples, follow immediately the previous verb (a) or be separated from it by à (b), de (c) or par (d). To know whether to put in a preposition and which one to use is one of the most difficult features of French grammar. Here is a list of common French verbs together with the preposition which follows them and separates them from the next verb:

aider à	décider de	faire
aimer mieux	se dépêcher de	falloir
aller	désirer	finir de
s'amuser à	devoir	s'habituer à
apprendre à	empêcher de	se hâter de
avoir à	entendre	hésiter à
avoir peur de	entrer	inviter à
cesser de	envoyer	laisser
commencer à	espérer	se mettre à
consentir à	dire de	monter
continuer à	essayer de	ordonner de
craindre de	éviter de	oser
croire	s'excuser de	oublier de

passer son temps à	prier de	réussir à
perdre son temps à	promettre de	savoir
permettre de	proposer de	sembler
pouvoir	refuser de	se souvenir d
préférer	regretter de	tâcher de
paraître	remercier de	voir
parler de	retourner	vouloir
se préparer à		

Thus, using the above information, one says:

Il se met à courir. He starts running.
Nous hésitons à le dire. We hesitate to say so.
Il m'a empêché de parler. He prevented me from
   speaking.
Vous n'osez pas entrer. You dare not go in.

THE PRESENT PARTICIPLE

1. The Present Participle can be used as an adjective and then follows the usual rules of agreement: **votre charmante sœur,** your *charming* sister; **des soucoupes volantes,** *flying* saucers.

2. It can also assume the functions of a finite verb, having objects or being qualified by adverbs. It is then invariable.

Cherchant un appartement, nous avons consulté tous les habitants du quartier. Looking for a flat, we consulted everybody in the district.

3. **En** with the Present Participle: **en chantant,** singing, while singing, by singing; as I, you, he, she, we, etc., sing, sang, etc.

En faisant ceci, vous vous ferez détester. By doing this you will cause yourself to be hated.
Il traversa la rue en courant. He ran across the street (he crossed while running).

4. **Tout en** with the *Present Participle* is used when the two actions are occurring at the same time.

Tout en descendant la rue, il lisait son journal. While going down the street, he read his paper.

English Present Participle Translated by the French Infinitive

When using the Present Participle in this way with the function of a verb, remember that the Present Participle refers to the subject of the sentence. We should not use it in a sentence like this:

I saw him coming downstairs.

"I" is the subject of the sentence, while the person coming downstairs is "he". In cases like this, to avoid ambiguity we must use a dependent infinitive:

Je l'ai vu descendre l'escalier.

English Present Participle Translated by a French Past Participle

Be careful when translating "sitting, kneeling, lying, hanging", etc. The French consider these to be past participles, **assis, agenouillé, couché, pendu,** because any action involved has already been accomplished.

Elle était assise* au coin du feu. She was sitting (seated) at the fireside.

Il est agenouillé devant l'autel. He is kneeling before the altar.

Le chien est couché au soleil. The dog is lying in the sun.

Appuyé, leaning; **étendu,** lying; **accroupi,** squatting; **penché,** leaning, stooping; **accroché,** hanging from a hook, are similarly used.

---

* Be careful not to confuse **être assis,** to be sitting or seated, with **s'asseoir,** to seat oneself, to take a seat, to sit down.

Elle est assise. She is sitting.
Elle s'assied. She sits down.

English Continuous Tenses

Do not use a participle when translating English continuous tenses into French:

I am speaking. **Je parle.** (I speak.)
He was speaking. **Il parlait.**
She had been writing. **Elle avait écrit.** (She had written.)

English -ING after a Preposition

All prepositions, with the exception of **EN** are followed by an infinitive.

without speaking, **sans parler**
before going, **avant d'aller**

THE AGREEMENT OF THE PAST PARTICIPLE

1. The Past Participle too may be used alone as an adjective agreeing with the noun it qualifies:

une table **couverte** d'une nappe blanche, a table *covered* with a white cloth
des soldats **blessés**, *wounded* soldiers
une bouteille **cassée**, a *broken* bottle

2. When, however, the Past Participle is used as part of a compound tense it agrees like an adjective with its direct object, provided that this object precedes the verb. When the object follows the verb, there is no agreement:

Il *nous* a *vus.* He has seen us.
Il a *vu les hommes.* He has seen the men.
Elle *s'est lavée.* She washed herself.
Elle a *lavé la table.* She washed the table.
Voici les *lettres* que nous avons *écrites.* Here are the letters that we wrote.
Nous avons *écrit les lettres.* We wrote the letters.
Elle *s'est coupée* au doigt. She cut herself on the finger.
Elle s'est *coupé le doigt.* She cut her finger.

3. You will notice from the last two examples above that it is necessary to use special care with reflexive verbs. Where the reflexive pronoun is the direct object of the verb the past participle agrees with it:

Elle *s'est blessée.* She has hurt *herself.*
Ils *se* sont *lavés.* They have washed *themselves.*

However, the reflexive pronoun may be an indirect object: study the following examples:

Elle s'est dit. She said to herself.
Ils se sont menti. They lied to themselves.

Here there is no agreement.

A frequent case of this usage is found in the type of sentence in which the reflexive pronoun is used with a part of the body:

Elle s'est *coupé* la *main.* She has cut her hand (the hand to herself).

There is no agreement because the direct object, la main, comes after the verb.

A few reflexive verbs like se **souvenir**, to remember; s'apercevoir, to realise; se **moquer,** to mock, make fun of; se taire, to be silent, cannot take an object either direct or indirect, and their Past Participles always agree with the reflexive pronoun.

Ils se sont moqués de moi. They made fun of me.
Elle s'est souvenue de son nom. She remembered his name.
Les oiseaux se sont tus. The birds kept silent.

4. Now let us return to those verbs mentioned on page 58, which form their compound tenses with être: aller, venir, arriver, partir, entrer, sortir, naître, mourir, monter, descendre, tomber, rester, retourner. These are intransitive verbs and cannot agree with an object: they agree with the subject.

Ma *mère* est *née* à Paris. My mother was born in Paris.

Ses *sœurs* étaient *restées* à la maison. His sisters had stayed at home.

Le *père* et la *mère* n'y sont pas *retournés*. The father and mother did not go back there.

5. In the Passive Voice the Past Participle is really an adjective describing the subject and agrees with it.

Madeleine a été invitée au bal. Madeleine has been invited to the dance.

La table sera couverte d'une belle nappe. The table will be covered with a beautiful cloth.

Some Exceptions

The Past Participle does not agree with a preceding direct object which refers to price, weight or distance:

Les quelques *francs* que ce crayon m'a *coûté* . . . The few francs that this pencil cost me . . .

Les six *kilomètres* que nous avons *marché* . . . The six kilometres that we walked . . .

There is also no agreement with the pronoun EN.

Des serpents! J'*en* ai *vu* au bord de la route. Snakes! I saw some on the roadside.

THE SUBJUNCTIVE MOOD

Everyone, even French people,* finds it difficult to use the Subjunctive correctly. My advice is to find sentences which do not require this mood!

Use of the Subjunctive

(1) *Principal Clauses*

We rarely find the Subjunctive in principal clauses except in time-honoured expressions like **Vive le roi!** Long live the

* For instance, the Imperfect Subjunctive is practically never used in conversation. It would sound too unpleasant to a Frenchman.

King!; **Plût à Dieu que** ... Would to God that ... ; **Advienne que pourra!** Come what may! The Present Subjunctive is sometimes used to form a 3rd Person Singular for the Imperative: **Qu'il meure!** May he die!; **qu'ils entrent!** let them come in!

(2) *The Subjunctive in Subordinate Clauses*

It is in subordinate clauses that the subjunctive is most frequently used. We find it:

(*a*) After certain conjunctions. Here are the most common—

quoique **bien que** } although		**sans que,** without
pour que **afin que** } in order that		**jusqu'à ce que,** until
avant que, before		**pourvu que,** provided that
à moins que . . . ne, unless		
de peur que . . . ne **de crainte que . . . ne** } for fear that		

Quoiqu'il n'ait que vingt-trois ans, il est déjà docteur. Although he is only twenty-three, he is already a doctor.

Pourvu qu'il fasse beau! Provided (if only) the weather is fine!

Nous attendrons jusqu'à ce qu'il arrive. We shall wait until he arrives.

You will have noticed that three of these conjunctions, **à moins que, de peur que, de crainte que,** have an expletive or untranslated **ne** before the following verb:

à moins que vous n'y alliez tout de suite . . . unless you go there at once . . .

de peur qu'il ne vienne . . . for fear that he may come . . .

(*b*) After verbs and expressions of emotion: to be glad, to be sorry, to fear, etc.:

Je suis content que vous soyez ici. I am pleased that you are here.

Il regrette que je sois malade. He is sorry that I am ill.

Je ne crains pas qu'il vienne. I am not afraid* of him coming.

(c) After verbs of wishing, desiring or doubting:

Je veux que vous y alliez ce soir. I want you to go there tonight.

Maman préfère que je rentre avant dix heures. Mother prefers me to be home before ten o'clock.

(d) After verbs of thinking, believing or saying used negatively or interrogatively:

Croyez-vous qu'il soit mort? Do you think that he is dead?

Je ne dis pas que vous ayez tort. I am not saying that you are wrong.

(e) After verbs of commanding, permitting and forbidding:

Nous exigeons qu'on nous réponde. We demand that we be answered.

Je défends que vous vous absentiez ainsi. I forbid you to be absent like this.

(f) After superlatives and the words premier, first; dernier, last; seul, only; unique, only.

C'est la plus belle femme que j'aie jamais vue. She's the most beautiful woman I have ever seen.

(g) After impersonal verbs and expressions which do not express probability or certainty.

Il faut que vous soyez de retour avant neuf heures. It is necessary for you to be back before nine o'clock.

Il semble que j'aie tort. It seems that I am wrong.

* If a verb of fearing is used in the affirmative, an expletive ne is placed before the following verb:

Je crains qu'il ne vienne ici. I'm afraid that he will come here.

Imperfect or Present Subjunctive?

It is sometimes necessary to decide whether to use the Imperfect or Present Subjunctive. If the main verb is in the Present, Perfect, or Future of the Indicative, the Present Subjunctive is used after it; in other cases use the Imperfect Subjunctive.

Je préfère que vous arriviez à temps. I prefer you to arrive on time.

Je préférerais que vous arrivassiez à temps. I should prefer you to arrive on time.

However, even here, most Frenchmen would avoid the unpleasant-sounding Imperfect Subjunctive and say:

Je préférerais que vous arriviez à temps.

EÛT and FÛT

You will probably come across the Imperfect Subjunctive of avoir and être, especially the forms eût and fût, used in literary French for none of the above reasons. They are considered an elegant way of expressing aurait and serait.

S'il eût trouvé cela, il eût renvoyé tout le monde. If he had found that, he would have dismissed everyone.

The Subjunctive with QUEL QUE, QUELQUE QUE, QUI QUE, QUOI QUE

Whatever (adjective with être).

Quels que soient vos talents, vous ne réussirez pas sans travailler. Whatever your talents may be, you will not succeed without working.

Whatever (adjective with a noun).

Quelques talents que vous ayez, vous ne réussirez pas . . . Whatever talents you may have, you will not succeed . . .

However (adverb).

> Si
> Quelque } fatigués que vous soyez, marchez toujours!
> However tired you may be, keep on walking!

> Si
> Quelque } vite que nous marchions, nous ne serons pas
> là avant dix heures. However quickly we walk, we
> shall not be there before ten o'clock.

Whoever

> Qui que vous soyez . . . whoever you may be . . .

Whatever (pronoun).

> Quoi que vous disiez . . . whatever you may say . . .

CHAPTER V

ADVERBS

Adverbs are words that qualify or modify the meaning of a verb. In a sentence like "she sings sweetly", the word "sweetly" is an adverb: it tells us something about the verb "sings". Adverbs may also describe adjectives or other adverbs. "She sings very sweetly": in this sentence "very" is an adverb describing "sweetly", and if we say "he is extremely patient", "extremely" is an adverb describing the adjective "patient".

Position of Adverbs

Adverbs do not vary and can be spelt in one way only. In French the adverb generally follows the verb, but may be put for greater emphasis at the beginning of the sentence.

Elle pleure bien souvent. She cries very often.
Bien souvent elle pleure. Very often she cries.

What we must never do in French is to put the adverb between the subject and the verb as we do in English: "She very often comes here." This must be either **Elle vient ici bien souvent** or **Bien souvent elle vient ici** in French.

In a compound tense a short adverb generally comes before the Past Participle:

Nous y sommes souvent allés. We often went there.

Formation of Adverbs from Adjectives

1. Most adverbs are formed by adding **-ment** to the feminine of the adjective:

frais, (f.) fraîche: fraîchement, freshly.
heureux, (f.) heureuse: heureusement, happily.

97

2. If the adjective ends in a vowel, one simply adds -ment.

hardi, bold: **hardiment,** boldly.
vrai, true: **vraiment,** truly.

3. If the adjective ends in -ent or -ant, change these endings to -emment and -amment. Ardent, **ardemment,** ardently; constant, **constamment,** constantly. (N.B. **lent,** slow, becomes **lentement,** slowly.)

Some common exceptions to the above rules are: gentil, **gentiment,** nicely; **aveugle, aveuglément,** blindly; **confus, confusément,** confusedly; **énorme, énormément,** enormously; **précis, précisément,** precisely; **profond, profondément,** profoundly.

Adjectives Used as Adverbs

As sometimes happens in English, some adjectives may be used as adverbs. "That smells *good*", "Buy *British*!", etc. French examples are **aller droit,** to go straight; **voir rouge,** to see red; **coûter cher,** to cost a lot; **parler haut,** to speak up; **parler bas,** to speak in a whisper; **sentir bon,** to smell good; **sentir mauvais,** to smell bad; **travailler ferme,** to work hard; **travailler dur,** to work hard; **acheter français,** to buy French (goods made in France); **voir clair,** to see clear (-ly)

Comparison of Adverbs

Adverbs are compared like adjectives with the help of **plus,** more, and **le plus,** most; **moins,** less, and **le moins,** least; **aussi . . . que,** as . . . as. Thus:

Positive.	Comparative.	Superlative.
vite, quickly	plus vite, more quickly	le plus vite, most quickly
	moins vite, less quickly	le moins vite, least quickly

Il marche vite. He walks quickly.

Il marche plus vite que vous. He walks more quickly than you.

C'est lui qui marche le plus vite. It is he who walks most quickly (the fastest).

Il marche aussi vite que vous. He walks as quickly as you.

Il ne marche pas si vite que vous. He does not walk so quickly as you.

Il marche moins vite que vous. He walks less quickly than you.

Irregular Comparison

peu, little	moins, less	le moins, least
beaucoup, much	plus, more	le plus, most
mal, badly	plus mal ⎫ pis ⎭ worse*	le plus mal ⎫ le pis ⎭ worst
bien, well	mieux, better	le mieux, best

Je mange peu mais ma femme mange moins que moi. I eat little but my wife eats less than I.

Il chante beaucoup, mais c'est son frère qui chante le plus. He sings a lot, but it is his brother who sings most.

PLUS and MOINS with a Numeral

After plus and moins, de is used instead of que before numerals or when there is no real comparison.

Il a moins de vingt livres dans sa maison. He has fewer than twenty books in his house.

Il a mangé plus d'un kilo de pommes. He has eaten more than a kilo of apples.

* pis is used nowadays only in certain expressions: tant pis pour moi, so much the worse for me; de mal en pis, from bad to worse.

Expletive NE after a Comparative

If there is a verb after a comparative, it has an expletive or untranslated **ne** before it.

> **Il mange plus que vous *ne* croyez.** He eats more than you think.

The More . . . the Less . . .

Do not forget that in sentences like "The more he has, the more he wants"; "The less he works, the more he earns", the article is omitted in French:

> **Plus il a, plus il désire.**
> **Moins il travaille, plus il gagne.**

Adverbs of Affirmation—OUI and SI

There are two words for "yes": **oui** and **si**. **Oui** is more common; **si** being used only in a contradictory sense in answer to a negative question.

> **Vous allez faire cela? Oui!** You are going to do that? Yes!
>
> **Vous n'allez pas faire cela? Si!** You are not going to do that? Oh, yes, I am!

Note too **je crois que oui, je pense que oui,** I think so.

Adverbs of Negation—NON and NE . . . PAS

Negation is expressed by **NON** or by **NE . . . PAS** and a verb

Non is used to answer a question:

> **Vous aimez le café? Non!** You like coffee? No!

Non is also used when the negative comes immediately before a word which is not a verb.

> **Non loin de la forêt je vois une chaumière.** Not far from the forest I see a cottage.
>
> **Il est non seulement pauvre, mais aussi très malade.** Not only is he poor, he is also very ill.

Neither (Either)

Non is also used with **plus** to express "neither" or "either" with a negative:

> **Mon frère ne vient pas non plus.** My brother isn't coming either.
>
> **Vous n'aimez pas le poivre? Moi non plus.** You don't like pepper? Neither do I.

Negation with a Verb

The usual negative used with a verb is **NE** (placed before the verb) and **PAS** (placed after the verb): **j'accepte,** I accept; **je n'accepte pas,** I'm not accepting. In compound tenses, the **PAS** comes before the Past Participle: **Il a parlé,** he spoke; **il n'a pas parlé,** he did not speak.

Similar in use are **ne ... point,** not at all; **ne ... plus,** no more, no longer; **ne ... que,** only; **ne ... guère,** scarcely; **ne ... jamais,** never; **ne ... ni ... ni,** neither ... nor; **ne ... nulle part,** nowhere; **ne ... personne,** nobody; **ne ... rien,** nothing; **ne ... aucun, ne ... nul,** not ... any.

> **Je n'ai plus de pain.** I have no more bread.
>
> **Il ne sort que le soir.** He only* goes out in the evening.
>
> **Nous n'allons jamais au cinéma.** We never go to the cinema.
>
> **Vous n'avez ni plume ni encre.** You have neither pen nor ink.
>
> **Il n'a rien dit.** He said nothing.
>
> **Vous n'avez $\begin{Bmatrix} \text{aucune} \\ \text{nulle} \end{Bmatrix}$ idée.** You have $\begin{Bmatrix} \text{not any} \\ \text{no} \end{Bmatrix}$ idea.
>
> **Nous n'avons vu personne.** We have seen nobody.

---

* "Only" is rather difficult. When "only" describes a verb in sentences like "he only laughs at me", "he doesn't work, he only gives advice", we add the verb **faire**: **il ne fait que rire de moi; il ne travaille pas, il ne fait que conseiller.** "Not only" with a verb may be translated by **ne ... pas seulement:**

> **Il n'est pas seulement acteur, il est aussi auteur.** He is not only an actor, he is also an author.

In compound tenses **personne** comes after the Past Participle; **point, plus, guère, jamais, rien** come before it.

> Ils n'avaient rencontré personne en route. They had met no one on the way.
> Elle n'est jamais allée en France. She has never been to France.
> Il n'avait rien fait. He had done nothing.

Que, ni, aucun, nul come before the word that they modify:

> Il n'y est resté *qu*'un instant. He stayed there a moment only.
> Elle n'a fait *aucune* attention à moi. She paid no attention to me.

Of course, when the sentence begins with the negative, *nothing, nobody, never*, etc., the order of the words is similar to that in the corresponding English sentence:

> Nobody is there. **Personne n'est là.**
> Not a single soldier escaped. **Pas un seul soldat n'échappa.**

Two negatives may combine:

> Il n'en a jamais rien dit. He never said anything about it.

When the verb is not expressed, the ne is left out:

> Qu'avez-vous fait? **Rien!** What did you do? Nothing!
> A-t-il été à Nice? **Jamais.** Has he been to Nice? Never.

Pas may be omitted with the verbs **pouvoir, oser, savoir** and **cesser**:

> Ils n'osèrent entrer. They dared not enter.
> Je ne sais si vous pouvez y aller. I don't know if you can go there.
> Il ne cessa de pleurer. He did not stop crying.

TOUT (Quite, Completely)

This adverb, unlike others, can change. When it stands before a feminine adjective beginning with a *consonant* or *h aspirate*, it agrees with the noun like an adjective.

Elle est *toute* contente. She is quite pleased.

but Elle est *tout* étonnée. She is quite astonished.

Elles sont *toutes* confuses. They are quite confused.

but Ils sont *tout* heureux. They are quite happy.

Marie était *toute* honteuse (h aspirate). Mary was quite ashamed.

but Ils ont été *tout* surpris. They have been quite surprised.

C'est une *tout* autre proposition. It's quite a different proposition.

[If you find this too difficult, you may use, instead of **tout**, the adverb **tout à fait**, which means more or less the same thing and which never changes.]

Tout may also be used before an adjective in the sense of "however" (though).

Tout intelligents qu'ils sont, ils ne réussiront pas.

However intelligent they are ⎫
Intelligent though they may be ⎭ , they will not succeed.

COMME and COMMENT

Both can mean "how".

Comment is either an exclamation meaning "What!" or "What?"

Comment! Il a osé venir chez moi. What! He dared to come to my house.

Quel est le chemin le plus court? Comment? Which is the shortest way? What (did you say)?

or at the beginning of an interrogative sentence means "how?"

Comment expliquez-vous cela? How do you explain that?

Comme, which can also mean "like" or "as" (fort comme un taureau, strong as a bull), may also introduce a sentence but not an interrogative one.

Comme elle est belle! How beautiful she is!
Comme il fait beau! How fine the weather is!

Notice the word order in these sentences.

PLUTÔT AND PLUS TÔT

Plutôt means "rather".

Plutôt souffrir que mourir! Rather suffer than die!

Plus tôt means "earlier".

Deux jours plus tôt. Two days earlier.

ASSEZ, Enough, Rather, Fairly, Quite

Ce livre me semble assez intéressant. This book seems rather } quite } interesting.

Il est assez* grand pour voyager tout seul. He is big enough to travel on his own.

Expressions of Quantity

Assez, enough; beaucoup, much, many, a lot; tant, so much, so many; autant, as much, as many; trop, too much, too many; combien, how much, how many; peu, little, few; un peu, a little; plus, more; moins, less, fewer; pas mal, quite a lot (familiar), are followed by de when standing before a noun: assez de pain, enough bread; beaucoup de choses, a lot of things; tant de monde, so many people; trop de sucre, too much sugar; un peu de musique, a little music; peu de gens, few people.

* A similar construction is used with trop (too):
   Il n'est jamais trop tard, pour bien faire. It is never too late to do good.

Bien, also meaning "many, a lot", is followed by **des: bien des fois,** many times; so too is **la plupart,** most, the majority: **la plupart des hommes,** most (of the) men.

Encore, more, is followed by **du (de la, de l', des):**

> **Encore du pain, s'il vous plaît.** Some more bread, please.

Such (as an Adverb)

"Such" in English may be used as an adjective or an adverb. In French we have different words. In expressions like "such a man", "such books", "such" is an adjective and is rendered by **tel (telle, tels, telles): un tel homme, de tels livres.** When, however, we write "such a good man", "such interesting books", "such" in these cases is an adverb describing the adjectives "good" and "interesting" and is translated by **tellement** or **si.** Such a good book, **un si bon livre** or **un livre tellement bon;** such interesting films, **des films si intéressants** or **des films tellement intéressants.**

PEUT-ÊTRE, Perhaps

If **peut-être** is put at the beginning of the sentence it is followed by inversion of the verb and pronoun.

> **Il viendra peut-être demain.** He will come tomorrow perhaps.

but

> **Peut-être viendra-t-il demain.** Perhaps he will come tomorrow.

By adding **que** after **peut-être,** one can avoid inversion:

> **Peut-être qu'il viendra demain.**

AUSSI, and so

Aussi has a similar construction after it.

> **Elle était fatiguée; aussi se coucha-t-elle.** She was tired; (and) so she went to bed.

Aussi placed after a verb means "also", "too".

Elle va venir, elle aussi. She is coming also.

QUELQUE

Quelque may be used as an adverb:

Elle a quelque soixante ans. She is some sixty years old (about sixty).

Quelque vite que vous couriez . . . However quickly you may run . . .

DAVANTAGE, More

Davantage is used instead of **plus** when it stands on its own at the end of a clause.

Il a peu d'argent, vous en avez davantage. He has little money, you have more.

If anything is added, **plus** must be employed:

Il a peu d'argent, vous en avez plus que lui. He has little money, you have more than he.

DESSUS, DESSOUS, DEDANS, DEHORS

Do not confuse **dessus**, on it; **dessous**, under it; **dedans**, in it; **dehors**, outside, with the corresponding prepositions **sur,** on; **sous,** under; **dans,** in; **hors,** outside.

Les livres sont sur la table: ils sont dessus. The books are on the table: they are on it (on top).
Les fruits sont dans le buffet: ils sont dedans. The fruits are in the sideboard: they are in it (inside).

In this connection we must also mention the adverbs **là-dedans**, in there, within; **là-dehors**, outside; **là-dessous**, underneath; **là-dessus**, thereon, thereupon.

Là-dessus, elle est partie. Thereupon she went away.

Adverbs of Time

Avant-hier, the day before yesterday; **hier,** yesterday; **aujourd'hui,** today; **demain,** tomorrow; **après-demain,** the day after tomorrow, are all adverbs.

> **Demain il donne sa démission.** Tomorrow he is resigning.

The corresponding nouns are **l'avant-veille,** two days previously; **la veille,** the day before, the eve; **ce jour-là,** that day; **le lendemain,** the next day; **le surlendemain,** two days later.

> **La veille de Noël,** Christmas Eve
> **Le lendemain du bal, il se sentait bien fatigué.** The day after the dance he felt very tired.

CHAPTER VI

PRONOUNS

Pronouns are words that can replace nouns in a sentence. Instead of *"Mrs. Jones is still here"*, we can use a pronoun to write *"She is still here"*. Similarly for "I water *the plants*", we may say "I water *them*"; for "I talk to *the Director*", "I talk *to him*"; for "we go *to Paris*", "we go *there*".

Here is a reference table of Personal Pronouns:

Persons	Subject	Direct Object	Indirect Object	Reflexive (Direct and Indirect)	Disjunctive
Singular					
1st	je, I	me, me	me, to me	me, (to) myself	moi
2nd	tu, thou	te, thee	te, to thee	te, (to) thyself	toi
3rd Masc.	il, he, it	le, him, it	lui, to him	se, (to) himself	lui (soi)
3rd Fem.	elle, she, it	la, her, it	lui, to her	se, (to) herself	elle
Plural					
1st	nous, we	nous, us	nous, to us	nous, (to) our-selves	nous
2nd	vous, you	vous, you	vous, to you	vous, (to) your-self, yourselves	vous
3rd Masc.	ils, they	les, them	leur, to them	se, (to) them-selves	eux
3rd Fem.	elles, they	les, them	leur, to them	se, (to) them-selves	elles

The first type of pronouns we meet are those used as Subjects of verbs:

je donne, *I give*   *nous* donnons, *we give*
tu donnes, *thou givest*   *vous* donnez, *you give*
il donne, *he (it) gives*   *ils* donnent, *they give*
elle donne, *she (it) gives*   *elles* donnent, *they give*

1. **Tu** is used in French instead of **vous** when speaking to a child, a relative, a close friend or an animal. Its use is tending to spread, like Christian names in this country, with the increasing "familiarity" of modern times.

2. **Il** and **Elle** can also refer to things and mean "it".

> **Où est mon chapeau? Il est sur la table.** Where is my hat? It is on the table.

3. **Je** becomes **j'** before a vowel or mute **h: j'ai, j'habite,** etc., but not when used interrogatively:

> **Puis-je entrer?** May I come in?

OBJECT PRONOUNS (DIRECT AND INDIRECT OBJECTS)

These pronouns too are used with verbs and may be Direct or Indirect Objects.

Direct Objects.	Indirect Objects.
il *me* voit, he sees *me*	elle *me* parle, she speaks *to me*
il *te* voit, he sees *thee*	elle *te* parle, she speaks *to thee*
il *le* voit, he sees *him (it)*	elle *lui* parle, she speaks *to him*
il *la* voit, he sees *her (it)*	elle *lui* parle, she speaks *to her*
il *nous* voit, he sees *us*	elle *nous* parle, she speaks *to us*
il *vous* voit, he sees *you*	elle *vous* parle, she speaks *to you*
il *les* voit, he sees *them*	elle *leur* parle, she speaks *to them*

REFLEXIVE PRONOUNS (DIRECT AND INDIRECT OBJECTS)

Direct Object.	Indirect Object.
je *me* lave, I wash *myself*	je *me* dis, I say *to myself*
tu *te* laves, thou washes *thyself*	tu *te* dis, thou sayest *to thyself*
il *se* lave, he washes *himself*	il *se* dit, he says *to himself*
elle *se* lave, she washes *herself*	elle *se* dit, she says *to herself*
nous *nous* lavons, we wash *ourselves*	nous *nous* disons, we say *to ourselves*
vous *vous* lavez, you wash { *yourself* / *yourselves* }	vous *vous* dites, you say to { *yourself* / *yourselves* }
ils *se* lavent, they wash *themselves*	ils *se* disent, they say *to themselves*
elles *se* lavent, they wash *themselves*	elles *se* disent, they say *to themselves*

Uses of the Above Pronouns

1. **Le, la, les** may refer to things as well as to people, depending on the gender of the noun.

> **Où est ma plume? Je ne peux pas *la* trouver.** Where is my pen? I cannot find it.

2. **Le, la, les** are often used in French to complete the sense of a verb when the English equivalent is not needed:

> **Êtes-vous le père de cet enfant? Je *le* suis.** Are you the father of this child? I am (him).
>
> **Savez-vous qu'il est déjà arrivé? Je *le* sais.** Do you know that he has already arrived? I know (it).
>
> **Vous y allez aussi? Je *le* crois.** Are you going too? I think (so).

3. The Indirect Object is used after **dire**, to say, to tell; **demander**, to ask; **ordonner**, to order, etc.

> **Je *lui* ai dit de le faire.** I told him to do so.
>
> **Nous *leur* avons demandé de venir.** We asked them to come.

Y, there, to it, to them

Another important pronoun is **Y**, meaning "there", "to it", "to them". It stands instead of a thing or things, not for a person or persons: it is used for *à and a noun*.

> **Êtes-vous allé *à Paris*? J'*y* vais cet été.** Have you been to Paris? I'm going there this summer.
>
> **Elle pense déjà *à ses vacances*.** She is already thinking of (lit. "to") her holidays.
>
> **Elle *y* pense déjà.** She is already thinking of (lit. "to") them.

Je ne prête pas attention *à son discours.* I pay no attention to his speech.
Je n'*y* prête pas attention. I pay no attention to it.

EN, of it, of them, some, any

En, as you see, has many meanings. It stands instead of
de and a noun.

Combien *de beurre* désirez-vous? How much butter do
you want?
J'*en* désire un kilo. I want a kilo (of it).

Combien *de frères* avez-vous? How many brothers
have you?
J'*en* ai quatre. I have four (of them).

Avez-vous *des bonbons*? Have you any sweets?
Oui j'*en* ai. Yes I have (some).
Non, je n'*en* ai pas. No, I haven't (any).

Êtes-vous content *de mon travail*? Are you pleased
with (lit. "of") my work?
Oui, j'*en* suis bien content. Yes, I'm very pleased
(with it).

Notice that **en** must be used in French where in English
the corresponding pronoun may be omitted.

Position of the Object Pronouns

(*a*) These object pronouns are placed immediately before
a verb except in the Imperative Affirmative:

Il *me* voit. He sees me.
Il ne *la* voit pas. He does not see her.
Il ne *lui* a pas parlé. He did not speak to her. (The
Pronoun is placed before the auxiliary verb in com-
pound tenses.)

Elle n'*y* est jamais allée. She never went there.

***Les* avez-vous vus à la foire?** Did you see them at the fair?

Ne *le* regardez pas! Don't look at it!

N'*en* mangeons pas! Let us not eat any!

(*b*) In the Imperative Affirmative, the Pronouns come immediately after the verb and are joined to it by hyphens. **Me** and **te** change to **MOI** and **TOI**.

Allez-y! Go there!

Lavez-vous! Wash yourself!

Regardez-moi! Look at me!

Regarde-toi! Look at thyself!

Dépêchons-nous! Let us hurry (ourselves)!

Do not forget that in the Imperative *Negative*, the pronouns take their normal position *before* the verb:

N'y allez pas! Don't go there!

Ne vous lavez pas! Do not wash yourself!

Ne me regardez pas! Do not look at me!

Ne te regarde pas! Don't look at thyself!

Ne nous dépêchons pas! Let us not hurry (ourselves)!

(*c*) The pronouns come before **voici** and **voilà**.

Me voici. Here I am.

Le voilà. There he is.

Nous voici. Here we are.

(*d*) When two verbs come together, the pronoun precedes the verb which governs it:

Il vient *me* voir ce matin. He is coming to see me this morning.

Vous avez essayé de *l'*aider. You have tried to help him.

Order of the Object Pronouns

If we have two or more pronouns, in which order are they to be written? If the pronouns come *before* the verb the order of precedence is:

1	2	3	4	5
me te se nous vous	le la les	lui leur	y	en

Try to learn by heart this string of pronouns: **me, te, se, nous, vous, le, la, les, lui, leur, y, en.** If you know this and you have to decide whether **me** or **le** comes first, or choose between **lui** and **en**, you will make no mistakes.

Thus:

> Elle *me l'*envoie. She sends it to me.
>
> Vous *lui en* donnez. You give some to him.
>
> Nous *l'y* avons cherché. We looked for him there.

If you cannot remember the above list, try this rule: 1–2–3–Direct–Indirect–Y–EN. Thus a 1st Person (**me** or **nous**) will come before a 2nd Person (**te** or **vous**), which in turn will precede a 3rd (**le, la, les, lui, leur**). If the two pronouns are both in the 3rd Person, then the Direct Object (**le, la, les**) will have precedence over the Indirect (**lui, leur**). **Y** and **en** always come last in that order. **Y EN** sounds something like Hee Haw! so that even a donkey knows that **Y** comes before **EN**!

What happens when the pronouns come *after* the verb (i.e., in the Imperative Affirmative)? The order is much as it is in English: "Send them to me!" "Give it to him". The Direct Object comes before the Indirect with once again **y** and **en** bringing up the rear. Thus: 1. Direct Object, 2. Indirect Object, 3. **y**, 4. **en**.

Envoyez-les-moi! Send them to me!
Donnez-le-lui! Give it to him!

Before **y** and **en**, **moi** and **toi** become **m'** and **t'**:

Donnez-m'en! Give me some!
Va-t'en! Go away!

DISJUNCTIVE PRONOUNS

These are **moi, toi, lui, elle, nous, vous, eux, elles,** together with **soi.** As their name implies, these pronouns are used when the pronoun is not linked with a verb.

We find them:

1. After a preposition: **avec moi,** with me; **sans toi,** without thee; **derrière lui,** behind him; **avant elle,** before her; **après vous,** after you; **près d'eux,** near them; **chez elles,** to their house.

2. Standing alone in answer to a question or in an exclamation together with an infinitive:

Qui donc a parlé? Who spoke then?
Moi. Me (*or better* I did).

Moi, faire cela! I (Me) do that!
Jamais! Never!

3. After a comparative:

Elle est plus petite que lui. She is shorter than he.

4. Showing emphasis when combined with a subject pronoun or with **même, seul, aussi:**

Eux, ils sont innocents. *They* are innocent.
Lui seul ose le faire. He alone dares do it.
Moi aussi, je veux y aller. I too want to go there.
Je le ferai moi-même. I shall do it myself.

5. After c'est, ce sont: c'est moi, c'est toi, c'est lui, c'est elle, c'est nous, c'est vous *but* ce sont eux, ce sont elles, it is I, it is thou, it is he, etc.

> **C'est lui qui est arrivé le premier.** It's he who came in first.

6. When the subject of the verb is a double one:

> **Mon frère et moi, nous y allons souvent.** My brother and I often go there.
>
> **Vous et moi, nous sommes faits pour nous entendre.** You and I are made to understand each other.

7. After verbs of motion and the verb **penser**:

> **Il courut à moi.** He ran to me.
> **Il pensait à eux.** He was thinking of them.

8. Expressing possession with the verb être:

> **Ce livre est à lui.** This book belongs to him.

9. After reflexive verbs:

> **Elle s'est approchée de moi.** She approached me.
> **Je me suis fié à lui.** I trusted myself to him.

10. When the direct object pronoun is not in the 3rd Person. In that case a disjunctive pronoun is used for the indirect object:

> **Je le lui présente.** I introduce him to her.

but

> **Je vous présente à elle.** I introduce you to her.
> **Je me présente à eux.** I introduce myself to them.

Soi

What about **soi?** Soi is used when the subject is an indefinite pronoun like **chacun,** each one; **tout le monde,** everybody; **personne,** nobody; **on,** one.

> **Chacun pour soi.** Every man for himself.
> **On a souvent besoin d'un plus petit que soi.** One often needs someone smaller than oneself.

DEMONSTRATIVE PRONOUNS

celui (masc.), the one   celle (fem.), the one
ceux (masc.), the ones   celles (fem.), the ones

This is a most important pronoun with many uses:

1. **Mon crayon et celui de mon frère.** My pencil and my
    brother's (the one of my brother).

    Ma chambre et celle de mon oncle. My bedroom and my
    uncle's (the one of my uncle).

    Mes livres et ceux de votre tante. My books and your
    aunt's (the ones of your aunt).

    Je préfère mes fleurs à celles de mon voisin. I prefer my
    flowers to those (the ones) of my neighbour (to my
    neighbour's).

    Tous ceux qui viennent. All (those, the ones) who come.

    Celui qui hésite est perdu. He (the one) who hesitates,
    is lost.

2. Used in conjunction with -ci (here), -là (there): thus:

    celui-ci (masc.), the one here, this one, this
    celle-là (fem.), the one there, that one, that
    ceux-là (masc. plur.), the ones there, those ones, those
    celles-ci (fem. plur.), the ones here, these ones, these

    **J'aime les deux tableaux, mais celui-ci est plus beau
    que celui-là.** I like both pictures, but this (one) is
    finer than that (one).

Celui-ci (celle-ci) has also the sense of "the latter";
celui-là (celle-là) the meaning of "the former".

    **Corneille et La Fontaine vivaient au dix-septième siècle;
    celui-là était dramaturge, celui-ci était fabuliste.**
    Corneille and La Fontaine lived in the seventeenth
    century; the former was a dramatist, the latter a
    fabulist.

CECI, this; CELA, * that

Ceci and cela have only one form each. They are used when we are neither speaking of persons nor referring to particular nouns already mentioned. Ceci refers to something we are about to mention, cela to something already said.

> Écoutez ceci, mon ami! Listen to this, my friend!
>
> Mentir à son père! Je n'aime pas cela! Lie to one's father! I don't like that!

When cela is found with the verb être it is divided up into ce and là:

> Ce n'est pas là une belle action. That is not a nice deed.

RELATIVE PRONOUNS

Relative pronouns are words like "who","which","that", "whose", which join two clauses together to make a longer sentence.

> This is the house *that* Jack built.
>
> She is the girl *who* appeared on television.
>
> The man *whose* son won a "blue" at Cambridge is standing next to the vicar.
>
> Here's the pen with *which* he wrote the letter.

The first point to note is that the Relative Pronoun must never be left out in French. "The man I saw yesterday" may sound correct in English, but before you can translate it into French, you must rewrite it as "The man *whom* I saw yesterday". Secondly, where we may use in English a phrase such as "The pen I am writing with", we must recast it to "The pen *with which* I am writing" before turning it into French.

To make this as simple as possible, you would be wise to realise that there are really two main kinds of sentences in which Relative Pronouns appear:

* In conversation, cela is nearly always shortened to ça.

(1) *Relative Pronouns Used with Prepositions*

When the Relative Pronoun is used with a Preposition (i.e., with a word like "to", "of", "at", "on", "with", etc.).

> The man *with whom* you were speaking is my uncle.
> The boy *to whom* he is writing is ill.
> The chair *on which* you were sitting is broken.
> The houses *in which* they lived were very old.

In cases like this, we use **QUI** if we are referring to persons and **LEQUEL, LAQUELLE, LESQUELS, LESQUELLES** for things.* Thus the above sentences would be translated:

> L'homme avec *qui* vous parliez est mon oncle.
> Le garçon à *qui* il écrit est malade.
> La chaise sur *laquelle* vous étiez assis est cassée.
> Les maisons dans *lesquelles* ils demeuraient étaient très vieilles.

The prepositions de and à combine with lequel, laquelle, lesquels, lesquelles to form:

> with de: duquel, de laquelle, desquels, desquelles
> with à: auquel, à laquelle, auxquels, auxquelles

> Le chien au courage duquel je dois la vie . . . The dog to whose courage (the courage of which) I owe my life . . .
> La rue au coin de laquelle elle demeure . . . The street at the corner of which she lives . . .
> Le livre auquel il faisait allusion . . . The book to which he was alluding . . .

DONT, of whom, of which, whose.

However, if the Relative Pronoun stands next to its antecedent (the noun to which it refers) it is better to use

---

* After **parmi** (among) and **entre** (between) we use **lequel**, etc., even of persons:

> Les prisonniers parmi lesquels il se trouvait. The prisoners amongst whom he found himself.

the invariable **DONT** instead of **de qui, duquel, de laquelle, desquels** or **desquelles.**

> **Les livres dont vous parlez** . . . The books of which you speak . . .
>
> **L'homme dont le fils mourut en Algérie** . . . The man whose (of whom the) son died in Algeria . . .
>
> **La femme dont il connaissait le frère** . . . The woman whose brother he knew (of whom he knew the brother) . . .
>
> **Les journaux dont il lisait les articles** . . . The newspapers whose articles he read (of which he read the articles) . . .

Notice the word-order after **DONT:**

When the Relative Pronoun does not immediately follow its antecedent, **DONT** may not be used. We then have to employ **qui** or **lequel,** etc.

> **Cet homme** (antecedent) **à la bonté de qui** (relative pronoun) **je me fie** . . . This man in the goodness of whom I trust . . .
>
> **La maison dans le jardin de laquelle j'aime me reposer** . . . The house in the garden of which (in whose garden) I like to rest . . .

Quoi (what) may also serve as a relative pronoun in conjunction with a preposition when referring to something vague and indeterminate:

> **Trouvez-moi quelque chose sur quoi écrire.** Find me something on which to write.
>
> **Il se reposa un moment: après quoi il se remit à travailler.** He rested for a moment: after which he started to work again.

Où (where) may also replace with advantage **dans lequel** or **auquel,** etc.:

> **La maison où** (or **dans laquelle**) **je demeure** . . . The house where (in which) I live . . .

La ville d'où (or de laquelle) il vient . . . The town from which he comes (where he comes from).

(2) *Relative Pronouns Used without Prepositions*

In this case we use QUI, if the pronoun is the subject of the following verb and QUE (QU' before a vowel or mute h) if it is the object.

La lettre *qui* est sur la table . . . The letter which is on the table . . .

La lettre *que* vous écrivez . . . The letter which you are writing . . .

Le jeune homme *qui* passe devant la maison . . . The young man who passes the house . . .

Les personnes *que* je vois tous les jours . . . The people that I see every day . . .

The student is often puzzled when a French writer reverses the normal order of words in the sentence after que:

J'ai remarqué l'effet que produisit ce discours. I noticed the effect which this speech produced.

La maison qu'ont bâtie mes aïeux . . . The house which my ancestors built . . .

This inversion is frequent in this type of sentence, and the student must be on his guard.

CE QUI, CE QUE, CE DONT

"What" is expressed by ce qui or ce que: ce qui if the pronoun is the subject of the subsequent verb, ce que if it is the object:

Dites-moi ce qui vous intéresse. Tell me what interests you.

Dites-moi ce que vous préférez. Tell me what you prefer.

Racontez-moi ce dont il vous parlait. Tell me what he was speaking to you about (that of which he was speaking).

TOUT CE QUI, TOUT CE QUE

"All that", "everything" is **tout ce qui** (subject), or **tout ce que** (object).

> **Tout ce qui brille n'est pas or.** All that glitters is not gold.
>
> **Je sais tout ce que vous avez fait.** I know everything (that) you have done.

POSSESSIVE PRONOUNS

	Masc. Sing.	Fem. Sing.	Masc. Plur.	Fem. Plur.
mine	le mien	la mienne	les miens	les miennes
thine	le tien	la tienne	les tiens	les tiennes
his	le sien	la sienne	les siens	les siennes
hers	le sien	la sienne	les siens	les siennes
ours	le nôtre	la nôtre	les nôtres	les nôtres
yours	le vôtre	la vôtre	les vôtres	les vôtres
theirs	le leur	la leur	les leurs	les leurs

The gender of the Possessive Pronoun depends not on the gender of the owner but on that of the article possessed. Thus **cette montre est la sienne** could mean either "this watch is his" or "this watch is hers". A man talking of his house (**la maison**) might say, **La mienne est plus grande que la vôtre.** A woman referring to a book (**le livre**) may say, **Le mien n'est pas très intéressant.** Mine is not very interesting.

In the 3rd Person, when there is a need to distinguish between "his" and "hers" one says **le sien à lui, la sienne à lui** (his); **le sien à elle, la sienne à elle** (hers).

Of course, if you just want to express possession one may use the disjunctive pronouns:

> **Ce crayon est à lui.** This pencil is his.

Ce livre est à moi is much more common than **Ce livre est le mien.**

INTERROGATIVE PRONOUNS
Who? Whom?

(a) As subject of a sentence, "who?" is expressed by
Qui? or Qui est-ce qui?

Qui est à la porte? Who is at the door?

or

Qui est-ce qui est à la porte? Who is it who is at the door.

(b) "Whom?" as object of a verb is "qui?" or "qui est-ce
que?"

Qui voyez-vous? Whom do you see?
Qui est-ce que vous voyez? Who is it that you see?

(c) "Whom" with a preposition is expressed by qui.

À qui parliez-vous? To whom were you speaking?

À qui is also used to inquire about ownership.

À qui est ce livre? $\left\{\begin{array}{l}\text{Whose book is this?}\\ \text{To whom does this book belong?}\end{array}\right.$

Ce livre est à moi. This book $\left\{\begin{array}{l}\text{is mine.}\\ \text{belongs to me.}\end{array}\right.$

What? (Subject or Object)

(a) "What?" as subject of a sentence is Qu'est-ce qui?

Qu'est-ce qui est arrivé? $\left\{\begin{array}{l}\text{What has happened?}\\ \text{What is it that has}\\ \quad\text{happened?}\end{array}\right.$

(b) "What?" as object is que? or qu'est-ce que?

Que voyez-vous? What do you see?
Qu'est-ce que vous voyez? What is it that you see?

Note too:

Qu'est-ce? $\left.\begin{array}{l}\text{What is it?}\\ \end{array}\right\}$
Qu'est-ce que c'est? $\quad$ (What is it that it is?)
Qu'est-ce que c'est que cela? What is that?

C'est un bouton. It's a button.
Que faire? What's to be done?
Qu'importe? What does it matter?

Que may also be used with **de** as an exclamation with the sense of "What a lot of!"

Que d'eau! What a lot of water!

(c) *"What?"* (*with a preposition*). "What?" after a preposition is translated by "quoi".

De quoi avez-vous parlé? What did you talk about?
Avec quoi l'a-t-il fait? What did he do it with?
À quoi pensiez-vous? What were you thinking of?

In French the preposition must not end the sentence, but must be carried forward to join with **quoi**: *of what, with what*, etc.

Quoi may also stand on its own to show surprise or indignation:

Quoi! vous êtes encore là! What! you are still there!

In familiar and impolite language it is used when one has not heard another person's remark.

Marie, viens ici tout de suite! Marie, come here at
   once!
Quoi? What (did you say)?

Quoi is also found with **de** and an adjective:

Quoi de nouveau? What news?
Quoi d'autre? What else?
Quoi de plus beau que cela? What could be finer than
   that?

Which? or Which one(s)?

Lequel (m.), laquelle (f.), lesquels (m. pl.), lesquelles (f. pl.), contracted with à and de to auquel, à laquelle, auxquel(le)s, duquel, de laquelle, desquel(le)s, is another interrogative pronoun.

Lequel de ces livres allez-vous prendre? Which (one) of these books are you going to take?

Auquel des professeurs a-t-il parlé? To which of the masters has he spoken?

As you can see from these examples, **lequel** is used to find out a person's choice.

INDEFINITE PRONOUNS

There are many of these. Below you will find a list together with their meanings and examples of their use:

quelqu'un(e), someone, somebody

Quelqu'un est entré dans cette chambre. Someone has entered this room.

quelques-uns, quelques-unes, some (people)

quelques-uns d'entre nous, some of us

quelque chose, something (masculine)

Cela me fait quelque chose! That does something to me!

J'ai vu quelque chose à la fenêtre. I saw something at the window.

Quelque chose de nouveau, something new

Quelque chose, whatever (thing) (f.)

Quelque chose qu'il ait faite ... Whatever (thing) he has done ...

grand'chose, much (nearly always after pas)

Les femmes ne valent pas grand'chose, les hommes ne valent rien du tout! Women aren't worth much, men are worth nothing at all!

autre chose, something else

Voudriez-vous voir autre chose, monsieur? Would you like to see something else?

peu de chose, little

Il a peu de chose de neuf à vous dire. He has little to tell you that is new.

on, one, they, you, etc. (often used to avoid Passive Voice)

On dit qu'il va mieux. It is said } that he is getting
They say } better.

Ici on parle français. Here they speak French. French is spoken here.

On doit manger pour vivre. One must eat to live.

In familiar language, **on** is often used for **je, nous** or **vous.**

Comment va-t-on? How are you?
On n'est pas fier. I'm not fussy.
On sort ce soir? Shall we go out tonight?

chacun, each one, everyone

chacun de vous, everyone of you
chacun son métier, each man (to) his trade

quiconque, whoever, whosoever

Quiconque fera cela, s'exposera à de grands dangers. Whoever does that will run great dangers.

n'importe qui, anybody (you like) (lit. no matter who)

N'importe qui pourrait le faire! Anybody could do it!

n'importe quoi, anything (you like) (lit. no matter what)

Il mange n'importe quoi! He eats anything!

n'importe où, anywhere

Pour gagner ma vie, j'irais n'importe où. To earn my living, I would go anywhere.

je ne sais qui, somebody or other (lit. I don't know who)

Je ne sais qui me l'a dit. Somebody or other told me.

je ne sais quoi, something or other

Il y a un je ne sais quoi dans sa manière de parler qui me choque. There's something in his way of speaking which shocks me.

tout, all, everything

> **Tout est perdu.** All is lost.
> **Nous avons tout vu.** We saw everything.
> **Tout ce que vous voyez ici m'appartient.** Everything you see here belongs to me.

tous, all (plural); **toutes**

> **Ils sont tous venus.** They all came.
> **Nous étions** $\begin{Bmatrix} \text{toutes} \\ \text{tous} \end{Bmatrix}$ **là.** All of us were there.

Notice that **tous** and **toutes** come immediately after the verb.

tous (toutes) les deux, both

> **Ils sont morts tous les deux.** Both of them died.

tout le monde, everyone, everybody

> **Tout le monde le connaît.** Everyone knows him.

plusieurs, several

> **Plusieurs d'entre eux s'échappèrent.** Several of them escaped.

l'un ... l'autre, one ... the other

> **Il a deux fils: l'un est brun, l'autre est blond.** He has two sons: one is dark, the other is fair.

l'un l'autre, l'un à l'autre (of two people); **les uns les autres, les uns aux autres** (of more than two people) are often used with reflexive verbs to remove ambiguity.

> **Ils s'aiment l'un l'autre.** They love each other.
> (**Ils s'aiment** on its own might mean "they love themselves".)
> **Les femmes se disaient les unes aux autres ...** The women were saying to each other ...

se, each other, one another

>Ils se détestent l'un l'autre. They hate each other.
>Ils se jetèrent des cailloux les uns aux autres. They
>threw stones at each other.

"It" as Subject of a Verb

1. To tell the time, use il.

>Il est une heure. It is one o'clock.

2. To describe weather, use il.

>Il fait du vent. It is windy.

3. To refer to a noun just mentioned, use il or elle according to the gender.

>Où est mon chapeau? Where is my hat?
>Il est sur la table. It is on the table.
>Où est l'église? Where is the church?
>Elle est près de la gare. It is near the station.

4. To explain what a thing is or who a person is, use c'est.

>Qu'est-ce? What is it?
>C'est un bouton. It is a button.
>Qui est-ce? Who is it?
>C'est un de mes cousins. It (he) is one of my cousins.

5. Before disjunctive pronouns use c'est or ce sont.

>C'est moi. It is I (me).
>C'est vous. It is you.

"It Is" (with an Adjective)

"It is dangerous", "it is pleasant", etc.

1. When the main part of the sentence comes later, use il est:

>Il m'est difficile d'accepter sa proposition. It is difficult
>for me to accept his proposal.

2. When the main part of the sentence precedes, use c'est:

> **Partir avant l'aube? C'est possible.** Leave before dawn? It's possible.

This rule does not apply to adjectives etc. of emotion:

> **C'est dommage de le voir si malade.** It's a pity to see him so ill.
>
> **C'est affreux qu'elle soit obligée de mendier.** It's awful that she should be forced to beg.

"He Is", "She Is", "They Are"

Il est and c'est can both mean "he is"; elle est and c'est, "she is": the plurals of il est, elle est are ils sont, elles sont, c'est becomes ce sont.

Il est. Elle est

Use il est or elle est when the verb is followed by an adjective or a preposition.

> **Elle est très sévère.** She is very strict.
> **Il est dans la cuisine.** He is in the kitchen.
> **Ils sont tous en vacances.** They are all on holidays.

Il est and elle est may be used also when followed immediately by a noun showing nationality, profession, religion etc.

> **Il est Anglais.** He is an Englishman.
> **Elle est institutrice.** She is a schoolmistress.
> **Mon frère? Il est catholique.** My brother? He is a Catholic.

(One may also say: **C'est un Anglais.** He is an Englishman. **C'est une institutrice.** She is a schoolmistress, etc. But in this case the noun is preceded by an indefinite article.)

C'est

We put c'est (plural ce sont) for "he is", "she is" when it is followed by a noun accompanied by an article or adjective.

C'est une très bonne institutrice. She is a very good
    schoolmistress.

C'est mon cousin. He is my cousin.

Ce sont des amis. They are friends.

   C'est may also serve to emphasise a particular part of the
sentence:

C'est moi qui suis arrivé le premier. It was I who came
    in first.

C'est à Londres que nous allons passer nos vacances.
    It's in London that we are going to spend our holi-
    days.

"There" (with Impersonal Verbs)

   Il can also have the sense of "there" when used before an
Impersonal Verb.

Il ne me reste que cent francs.

> There remains to me
> only a hundred
> francs.
> I have only a hundred
> francs left.

Il arriva un accident.

> There happened an accident.
> An accident happened.

Il était une fois une bergère.
Il y avait une fois une bergère.

> There was once upon a
> time a shepherdess.

CHAPTER VII

PREPOSITIONS

Prepositions are words which show the relationship between someone or something and another person or thing. Prepositions can be simple (i.e., consisting of one word) like **avec**, with, or compound like **au lieu de**, instead of.

Simple Prepositions

Here is a list of common simple prepositions:

à, at or to
après, after
avant, before (of time or order)
avec, with (accompanied by)
chez, at, to the house of
comme, like
contre, against
dans, in, into, inside
de, of, from
depuis, since (of time)
devant, in front of (place)
en, in
entre, between, among (two objects)
envers, towards (of emotions)

environ, about (with numbers)
excepté, except
malgré, in spite of
outre, besides
par, by, through
parmi, among
pendant, during
pour, for, in order to
sans, without
sauf, except
selon, according to
sous, under(neath)
sur, on, upon
vers, towards; about (of time)

Compound Prepositions

Here are some compound prepositions:

à cause de, because of
à côté de, beside, alongside of
à travers
au travers de }through, across
au dessous de, below
au dessus de, above
au lieu de, instead of
au milieu de, in the middle of
auprès de, near, compared with

au sujet de, about, concerning
autour de, (a)round
de peur de, for fear of
en face de, opposite
hors de, out of
jusqu'à, up to, until
le long de, along
près de, near
quant à, as for

Using these prepositions wrongly is a source of frequent mistakes for the student. Here are some points to watch:

Verbs which Require no Preposition

attendre, to wait for	écouter, to listen to
chercher, to look for	espérer, to hope for
demander, to ask for	payer, to pay for

Do not put any prepositions after the above verbs. **Attendre** means "to wait *for*"; the "for" being included in the verb. Thus:

> **Nous attendions le train.** We were waiting *for* the train.
> **Il va écouter la radio.** He is going to listen *to* the wireless.
> **Que cherchez-vous?** What are you looking *for*?
> **J'ai payé ma bicyclette.** I've paid *for* my bicycle.

Uses of the Common Prepositions

Below you will find some notes on some of the prepositions already mentioned:

À may mean "to", "at" or "in": **au jardin,** to the garden, in the garden; **à l'école,** at school, to school; **à mon retour,** at, on my return. We find it before the names of towns: **à Paris,** to, at or in Paris; before masculine names of countries, **au Pays de Galles,** in or to Wales; **au Portugal, au Japon, au Canada, aux États-Unis,** in or to Portugal, Japan, Canada, the United States; as well as in **aux Indes.** It also has some idiomatic uses: **à cheval,** on horseback; **à pied,** on foot; **à genoux,** kneeling; **à la main,** in one's hand; **au secours!,** help!; **au voleur!,** stop thief!; **au feu!,** fire!; **il a mal à la jambe,** he has a pain in his leg; following this pattern we can make innumerable sentences like:

> **Il a mal aux yeux.** His eyes hurt.
> **Il a mal au ventre.** He has a pain in the stomach.
> **Il a mal à la tête.** His head aches.

It may express distance from a point:

Sidcup est à douze milles de Londres. Sidcup is (at) twelve miles from London.

It is found with verbs of taking away, stealing, borrowing, etc.:

Il a emprunté l'argent à son frère. He borrowed the money from his brother.

Il lui a pris le livre. He took the book from him.

À, too, describes a person's characteristics where in English we should write "with":

L'homme à la barbe noire. The man with the black beard.

La fille aux cheveux de lin. The girl with the flaxen hair.

For playing games we say "à":

Il joue au football, au rugby, au tennis. He plays (at) football, rugby, tennis.

Notice too expressions like **un verre à vin,** a wineglass (a glass *for* wine); **une cuiller à thé,** a teaspoon, and contrast with **un verre de vin,** a glass (full) of wine.

Avant, before (of time and order)

Il ne va pas rentrer avant sept heures. He won't be home before seven.

Je suis arrivé à l'arrêt avant lui. I arrived at the stop before him.

Avec, with (in the sense of "accompanied by")

Il est entré avec sa mère. He came in with his mother.

It is left out in sentences like:

He came in with his book in his hand. **Il entra son livre à la main.**

With a noun, it gives it an adverbial force: **avec soin,**
with care, carefully; **avec patience,** patiently. It expresses
"with" in connection with the use of an instrument:

> **Il l'a écrit avec son crayon.** He wrote it with his pencil.
> **Elle m'a frappé avec un marteau.** She hit me with a
> hammer.

Chez, at or to the house (shop, etc.) of

> **Chez moi,** at, to my house, home.
> **Je vais chez le boulanger.** I'm going to the baker's.
> **Elle est chez le curé.** She's at the vicar's (house).

Also with authors' names.

> **Chez Racine, il y a beaucoup de passion.** In Racine's
> work, there is much passion.

Dans, in, into, inside. Generally followed by an article or
similar word: **dans le jardin, dans le livre, dans le sac.**
Dans la main means "inside the hand", and could refer
only to an object small enough to be enclosed in one's
clasped hand; otherwise it is better to use **à la main:**

> **Il portait son chapeau à la main.** He was carrying his
> hat in his hand.

Dans with an expression of time means "at the end of,
after":

> **Dans deux jours je vais partir pour l'Amérique.** In two
> days' time I'm leaving for America.

Dans is used before British counties, **dans le Kent,** in
Kent. Notice too:

> **Il boit dans mon verre.** He is drinking from my glass.
> **Il mange dans un bol.** He is eating from a bowl.

A curious but logical idiom is:

> **Il prend l'argent dans sa poche.** He takes the money
> from his pocket (the money was *in* his pocket when
> he took it!).

Dans is generally found after **entrer**:

Il entre dans la maison. He enters the house.

De, of, from, is the commonest French preposition, with a variety of meanings. Its most frequent occurrence is to translate the English apostrophe s; "John's book" is recast to "the book of John", **le livre de Jean.** Similarly, **le chien de mon ami,** my friend's dog. It also signifies origin—*from*; **il vient de Nantes,** he comes from Nantes. However, **la route de Paris** means "the road *to* Paris".

Most verbs of following, filling, covering, adorning, liking, etc., are followed by **de: chargé de blé,** laden with wheat; **couvert de boue,** covered with mud; **aimé de tout le monde,** loved by everyone; **suivi de sa femme,** followed by his wife. **De** generally translates "with" if followed by parts of the body:

Je l'ai vu de mes propres yeux. I saw it with my own eyes.

Many adjectives are followed by **de; content d'être venu,** pleased to have come; **sûr de gagner,** sure to win. When one verb is followed by the infinitive of another the most common preposition between them is **de:**

Je décidai de la suivre. I decided to follow her.
Nous avons offert de l'aider. We offered to help him.

De is used after superlatives; **la plus belle maison de la région,** the finest house in the region. One says too, **de cette façon,** in this fashion; **d'une manière élégante,** in an elegant manner; **d'un ton froid,** in a cold tone; **de ce côté,** in this direction; **de l'autre côté,** on the other side; **sept heures du matin, du soir,** seven o'clock in the morning, in the evening. **De** is also seen with musical instruments:

Il joue du piano, elle joue de la harpe. He plays the piano, she plays the harp.

It may also mean "about":

Il parle de ses aventures. He is speaking about his adventures.

Depuis, since: **depuis sa naissance,** since his birth; **depuis ce jour-là,** since that day. It is also used of place as well as of time: **depuis Paris jusqu'à Marseille,** from Paris to Marseilles. We have already mentioned its effect on tenses (see pages 77 and 78):

Je suis ici depuis trois jours. I have been here for three days (and I *am* still here).

Devant, before (of place): **devant l'hôtel de ville,** before the town hall; **devant le maire,** in front of the mayor. It is used with **passer** in sentences like this:

J'ai passé devant la maison ce matin. I passed the house this morning.

En, in, must not be confused with **dans.** En expresses "to" or "in" before the names of feminine countries: **en Italie,** to or in Italy. **En** is used for "in" when it is followed *immediately* by a noun: **en France,** in France; **en été,** in summer; **en danger,** in danger; **en colère,** in anger; **en prison,** in prison; **en janvier,** in January; **en mil huit cent soixante-quinze,** in 1875; **en voiture,** by car. There are only a few expressions where we see **en** with the article: **en l'absence de mon frère,** in my brother's absence; **en l'an 1960,** in the year 1960; **sauter en l'air,** to jump in the air.

En draws attention to the material something is made of:

Cette robe est en soie naturelle. This dress is made of genuine silk.

En with an expression of time means "within":

Je le ferai en trois jours. I shall do it in three days (i.e., sometime within the next three days, it will be finished).

En may sometimes signify "as":

Il s'est déguisé en paysan. He disguised himself as a peasant.

Entre, between, among

Entre vous et moi. Between you and me.

Entre onze heures et midi. Between eleven and twelve o'clock.

J'ai remis la lettre entre les mains du directeur. I gave the letter into the hands of the manager (see **dans** above).

Environ, about (of numbers): environ trente kilomètres, about thirty kilometres.

Jusqu'à, up to, until, as far as

Je vais continuer mes efforts jusqu'au bout. I'm going to continue my efforts right up to the end.

Je voyage jusqu'à Londres. I'm travelling as far as London.

Jusqu'ici tout va bien. Up to now, all's well.

Not until is often rendered more suitably by **pas avant** (not before):

Il ne rentrera pas avant sept heures. He won't be home until seven.

Malgré, in spite of, despite

Malgré tout, je ferai mon devoir. Despite everything I shall do my duty.

Par, by, through

J'irai par la forêt. I shall go through the forest.
Par ici, monsieur! This way, sir!

Il regardait par la fenêtre. He was looking through the window.

Par négligence. Through negligence.

Je l'ai jeté par la fenêtre. I threw it out of the window.

Par is used with the instrument or agent of an action:

Il a été mordu par un chien. He was bitten by a dog.

Par is employed when speaking of the weather; **par un beau jour d'été,** on a fine summer's day; **par un temps superbe,** in superb weather, and to replace the English "a" in phrases such as **trois fois par jour,** three times a day; **deux fois par an,** twice a year. Remember that a tree falls **par terre,** to the ground, along the ground, since its roots are already there, while a stone falls **à terre** because it falls from a height.

Parmi, among(st): **Parmi ceux qui étaient là** . . . among those who were there . . .; **parmi les arbres,** among the trees.

Pendant, during: **pendant le voyage,** during the journey; **pendant mes vacances,** during my holidays.

Pour, for, in order to

Faites-le pour moi! Do it for me!

Ils partent pour Bruxelles. They are leaving for Brussels.

Je l'ai fait pour vous faire plaisir. I did it in order to please you.

With expressions of time, if the occasion is present or past, omit **pour:**

Il est resté trois jours chez moi. He stayed with me for three days.

Of future time **pour** returns:

Pour toujours! For ever!

Il sera à Paris pour trois jours. He will be in Paris for three days.

Sans, without

> **Sans votre aide.** Without your help.
> **Il est sans pitié.** He is pitiless.
> **Sans moi, il serait tombé.** Had it not been for me, he
> would have fallen.

Sauf, save, except for, apart from

> **Nous sommes tous ici, sauf Henri.** We are all here,
> except for Henri.

Selon, according to

> **L'Évangile selon Saint Luc.** The Gospel according to
> Saint Luke.
> **Selon lui, nous devons suivre ce sentier.** According to
> him, we must follow this path.
> **C'est selon.** It's all according.

Sous, under

> **Le chien est sous le lit.** The dog is under the bed.
> **Sous le règne de Louis XIV.** In the reign of Louis XIV.

Sur, on, on top of

> **La tasse est sur la table.** The cup is on the table.
> **Il prit une tasse sur la table.** He took a cup *from* the
> table (the cup was *on* the table when he took it).

> Omit **sur** with expressions of time: **lundi,** on Monday;
> **le premier janvier,** on the first of January. **Dix sur vingt,**
> ten out of twenty.

> **La table a trois pieds de long sur deux de large.** The
> table is three feet long by two wide.

À travers, au travers de, through, across: **À travers le champ,**
across, through the field. Use **au travers de** when difficulties or obstacles are envisaged: **au travers des difficultés
de la guerre,** through the difficulties of war.

Vers, towards; about (with time of day)

> Je me dirigeai **vers** la maison. I moved towards the house.
>
> Nous y arriverons **vers trois heures.** We shall arrive there about three o'clock.

Repetition of Prepositions

The prepositions **de, à** and **en** are repeated before subsequent words:

> in Paris and London, **à Paris et à Londres**
> to France and Germany, **en France et en Allemagne**

Prepositions Used with Verbs

When two clauses have the same subject* a preposition and an infinitive may be used:

> **Après avoir consulté ma montre, je décidai de partir.** After consulting my watch, I decided to leave.
>
> **Je suis entré dans ma chambre sans faire de bruit.** I went into my bedroom without making a noise.
>
> **Avant de partir, je dis adieu à tout le monde.** Before going I said goodbye to everyone.
>
> **Pour réussir il faut bien travailler.** You must work hard in order to succeed.
>
> **Sans hésiter, il plongea dans la rivière.** Without hesitating he dived into the river.
>
> **De peur d'être pris, ils se sauvèrent.** For fear of being captured, they ran away.

Similar sentences may be made with the help of **à moins de,** unless; **de crainte de,** for fear of; **afin de,** in order to.

You will have noticed that these prepositions are all followed by an infinitive. In fact, only one preposition does

---

* If the two clauses have different subjects a conjunction must be used. See the chapter on Conjunctions, page 143.

not govern the infinitive of the verb, that is **EN**, which is followed by the Present Participle.

> **En faisant ceci vous vous ferez détester.** By doing this, you will make yourself hated.

Note too that **après**, unlike the others, takes the Perfect Infinitive:

> **Après avoir consulté ma montre** ... After consulting (having consulted) my watch ...
>
> **Après avoir fini sa lettre** ... After finishing (having finished) his letter ...
>
> **Après s'être lavée, elle descendit.** After washing, she went downstairs.

CHAPTER VIII
CONJUNCTIONS

Conjunctions are words which join simple sentences together to make longer and more interesting ones. "When I arrived home, I discovered that I had left my key at the office" sounds much better than "I arrived home. I discovered something. I had left my key at the office". "When" is a conjunction or joining word.

Here is a list of conjunctions:

Co-ordinating Conjunctions

et, and	ou, or	cependant, however
pourtant, however	donc, therefore	car, for
ainsi, thus	aussi, and so	puis, then

Conjunctions of Time

quand }
lorsque } when

après que, after
*avant que, before

aussitôt que }
dès que } as soon as

depuis que, since
au moment où, just as

à peine . . . que, scarcely . . . than

tandis que }
pendant que } while, whilst

tant que, as long as
*jusqu'à ce que, until
un jour que, one day when
le jour où, the day when

Conjunctions of Purpose

*afin que }
*pour que } in order that

*de crainte que . . . ne }
*de peur que . . . ne } lest

*sans que, without
*de sorte que, so that

141

Conditional

si, if   *à moins que . . . ne, unless
*pourvu que, provided that, if only

Concessive

*quoique } although   *soit que . . . soit que, whether . . . or
*bien que }   quand même, even though

Causal

comme, as   attendu que } seeing that
parce que, because   vu que }
puisque, since

Comparative

à mesure que, in proportion as   selon que, according as
ainsi que, as, just as

Notes on the Above Conjunctions

1. The conjunctions marked with an asterisk are followed by a verb in the Subjunctive Mood:

> Bien qu'il soit très pauvre, il est toujours heureux.
> Although he is very poor, he is always happy.

2. Some of the conjunctions have an expletive or untranslated ne which is put before the following verb:

> À moins qu'ils *n*'arrivent bientôt, nous sortirons sans eux. Unless they arrive soon, we shall go out without them.

3. You will have noticed that words like "after", "before", "since", "because" may be prepositions or conjunctions. When they are conjunctions a que is always added.

Prepositions.	Conjunctions.
après mon arrivée, after my arrival	après que je fus arrivé, after I had arrived
avant mon retour, before my return	avant que je sois revenu, before I returned
depuis sa naissance, since his birth	depuis qu'il est né, since he was born
à cause de lui, because of him	parce qu'il était absent, because he was absent

If the subject of both clauses is the same it is often preferable and easier to use a preposition with an infinitive or a noun. Thus say or write:

> Avant de revenir j'ai fait des emplettes (purchases).
> Avant mon retour j'ai fait des emplettes.

rather than

> Avant que je sois revenu, j'ai fait des emplettes.

Most of these conjunctions are quite simple to use. However, there are some points to note:

1. Be careful of the tenses after quand, lorsque, après que, dès que, aussitôt que, tant que.

(a) If any idea of future time is implied, the Future or Future Perfect must be employed in French:

> Tant que je vivrai . . . As long as I (shall) live . . .
> Quand vous serez vieux, vous comprendrez mieux. When you are (will be) old, you will understand better.
> Après que vous aurez fini votre travail, vous pourrez vous amuser. After you have (will have) finished your work, you will be able to enjoy yourself.
> Dès que vous serez mort, on vous oubliera bien vite. As soon as you are (will be) dead, you'll soon be forgotten.

(b) When quand, lorsque, après que, dès que, aussitôt que are used with a Past Tense, the Past Anterior follows the conjunction if the main verb in the other clause is in the Past Historic:

> Quand il *fut rentré*, il se coucha tout de suite. When he (had) got home, he went straight to bed.
>
> Après qu'il *eut* bien dîné, il résolut de lui écrire une lettre. After he had dined well, he determined to write him a letter.

A similar construction with à peine inverts the verb and pronoun:

> À peine l'eut-il fait qu'il se mit à regretter sa mauvaise action. Hardly had he done so than he began to regret his evil deed.

2. Puisque, depuis que, since. Puisque, since (because).

> Puisque vous êtes riche, il faut donner aux pauvres. Since you are rich, you must give to the poor.

Depuis que: since (from the time that). Be careful of the tense used after it. See the chapter on Verbs, pages 76–78.

> Depuis que vous êtes ici, tout va bien. Since you have been here, everything has been going well.

Here the Present Tense is employed since "you" *are* still here.

3. Quand même, even if, even though. Quand même is followed by a verb in the Conditional or Conditional Perfect:

> Quand même je l'aurais vu, je n'en aurais pas parlé. Even if I had seen it, I should not have spoken of it.

4. When a conjunction has two clauses under its influence, the conjunction need not be repeated if que is used in its place.

> Quand vous y arriverez et *que* vous verrez ma mère . . . When you get there and (when) you see my mother . . .

If the conjunction is **si** (if), the **que** is followed by the subjunctive:

> **S'il vient ici et qu'il vous voie** . . . If he comes here and (if he) sees you . . .

5. **Car,** for. **Car** means "for" in the sense of "because".

> **Vous pouvez tout faire car vous êtes le roi.** You can do anything, for you are the king.

Be careful not to use **pour** in cases like this.

6. **Aussi,*** so, and so, therefore. **Aussi** is followed by inversion of the verb and pronoun:

> **Aussi allez-vous revenir samedi.** So you are going to return on Saturday.

Another way of saying this is to put **donc** (therefore, then) either at the beginning of the sentence or after the verb:

> **Vous allez donc revenir samedi.**

7. **Tandis que, pendant que,** while, whilst. **Pendant que** is to be preferred to **tandis que** if the two actions described occur simultaneously:

> **Pendant qu'elle descendait la rue, la jeune fille lisait le journal.** While she was coming down the street, the girl was reading the paper.

Tandis que is best used when two statements are contrasted.

> **Vous, vous êtes riche, tandis que moi, je suis pauvre.** You are rich, whilst I am poor.

8. **Si** may mean both "if" and "whether". When it stands for "if" it is never followed by the Future or Conditional tenses:

> **S'il vient demain** . . . If he comes tomorrow . . . (Present).

---

* **Aussi** may also be an adverb meaning "also", "too".

S'il venait demain . . . If he $\left.\begin{array}{l}\text{came} \\ \text{were to come}\end{array}\right\}$ tomorrow . . . (Imperfect).

However, the Future and Conditional are allowed when si means "whether".

Je ne sais pas s'il viendra. I do not know whether (if) he will come.

Tenses after SI, If

At this stage, it is worth while considering the possible combinations of tenses when si, if, is used:

Present and Future:

S'il vient ce soir, je serai content. If he comes tonight, I shall be pleased.

Imperfect and Conditional:

S'il venait ce soir, je serais content. If he $\left.\begin{array}{l}\text{were to come} \\ \text{came}\end{array}\right\}$ tonight, I should be pleased.

Pluperfect and Conditional Perfect:

S'il était venu ce soir, j'aurais été content. If he had come tonight, I should have been pleased.

CHAPTER IX

THE WEATHER, TIME OF DAY, AGES, DATES, SEASONS, L'AN, ANNO DOMINI, MEASUREMENT, FRACTIONS, COLLECTIVE AND APPROXIMATE NUMBERS, PRICE, DISTANCE, FEELINGS

The Weather

In every discussion about the weather we generally find the verb **faire** and not the verb **être**. The usual pattern is to use impersonally the 3rd Person of the verb **faire** together with a descriptive adjective.

Il fait beau. It is fine, the weather is fine.
Il fait mauvais. The weather is bad.
Il fait froid. It is cold.
Il fait frais. It is cool.

All these answer the question:

Quel temps fait-il? What is the weather like?

It is, of course, possible to make use of this pattern in any tense:

Il fera froid demain. It will be cold tomorrow.
Il faisait froid hier. It was cold yesterday.
Il a fait froid en Suisse. The weather was cold in Switzerland.

Other idiomatic expressions of similar pattern are:

Il fait un temps merveilleux. The weather is marvellous.
Il fait doux. The weather is mild.
Il fait lourd. The weather is close.
Il fait sombre. It's dark, dull.
Il fait du vent. It's windy.
Il fait du soleil. It's sunny.
Il fait du brouillard. It's foggy.

Il fait jour. It's daylight.
Il fait nuit. It's dark (night-time).
Il fait clair de lune. There's moonlight.
Il pleut. It's raining.

One can also make sentences of the type:

Le temps est beau. The weather is fine.
Le temps est mauvais. The weather is bad.

The Time of Day: L'HEURE

The word for "time of day" is heure and not temps,* and so "What time is it?" must be translated as Quelle heure est-il?

The answer to this question is given in "heures" (hours):

Il est une heure. It's one o'clock (lit. one hour).
Il est deux heures. It's two o'clock.
Il est trois heures. It's three o'clock.

and so on until we get to:

Il est midi. It's twelve o'clock (noon).
Il est minuit. It's twelve o'clock (midnight).

Please do not say, "Il est douze heures"!

"Half past" is expressed by adding et demie (when heure is mentioned) and et demi (after midi and minuit, which are masculine):

Il est une heure et demie. It's half past one.
Il est deux heures et demie. It's half past two.
Il est trois heures et demie. It's half past three.

but

Il est midi et demi. It's half past twelve (noon).
Il est minuit et demi. It's half past twelve (midnight).

The word demi (half) is an adjective, and so will agree with heure (f.) or midi or minuit (m.).

* Avez-vous l'heure? Have you the time? With the answer "It's two o'clock, etc.". Avez-vous le temps? Have you time (to spare to do something for someone)?

A "quarter past" and a "quarter to" are expressed by adding **et quart** or **moins le (un) quart** respectively.

Il est quatre heures et quart. It's a quarter past four.

Il est quatre heures **moins le quart.** ⎫ It's a quarter to
                      moins un quart. ⎭ four.

Minutes past the hour are indicated by adding **une, deux, trois, quatre,** etc. The French word "minute" is feminine, and that is why we say **une.**

Il est onze heures une. It's a minute past eleven.
Il est onze heures cinq. It's five past eleven.
Il est trois heures vingt. It's twenty past three.

The usage is similar to our railway time-tables: 11.1, 11.5, 3.20, etc.

Minutes to the hour are shown by **moins une, moins deux,** etc. **Moins** really means "less", so we are doing a little subtraction; "five to eleven" becomes "eleven hours **minus** five (minutes)".

Il est quatre heures moins dix. It's ten to four.
Il est neuf heures moins vingt-cinq. It's twenty-five to nine.

Some idiomatic expressions of time worth learning are:

À trois heures précises, at three o'clock exactly
vers une heure, about one o'clock
Il est dix heures environ. It's about ten o'clock.
Il est près de cinq heures. It's nearly five o'clock.
dix heures du matin, 10 a.m.
six heures du soir, 6 p.m.
une heure, an hour
une demi-heure, half an hour
un quart d'heure, a quarter of an hour
trois quarts d'heure, three-quarters of an hour.

On railway time-tables a twenty-four-hour system is found:

Départ à 22 h. Departure at 10 p.m.

Ages

The important thing to remember is that in French one *has* an age: one uses the verb **avoir** and not **être**.

> **Quel âge avez-vous?** How old are you?
> **J'ai vingt ans.** I am twenty.

Notice that in the reply the word **ans**, years, must be given. If you say **J'ai vingt** a Frenchman would ask himself what you have twenty of!

Try to learn these useful expressions too:

> **un homme d'un certain âge,** a middle-aged man
> **une femme de trente ans,** a thirty-year-old woman
> **Je suis plus âgé que lui de six ans.** I am six years older than he (older by six years).
> **Elle a passé la cinquantaine.** She's past fifty.

Dates and Expressions of Time

Dates

> **Quelle date sommes-nous?**
> **Quel jour est-ce?** } What is the date?
> **Quel jour sommes-nous?**
> **Le combien sommes-nous?**

For the first day of the month we use **le premier**; for all the others we use the cardinal numbers, **deux, trois, quatre,** etc.

> **C'est (nous sommes) le premier mai.** It's the first of May.
> **le deux mars,** the second of March
> **le dix octobre,** the tenth of October
> **le vingt décembre,** the twentieth of December

The names of the months are **janvier, février, mars, avril, mai, juin, juillet, août, septembre, octobre, novembre, décembre,** all spelt with a small letter, as are also the days of the week, dimanche (Sunday), lundi, mardi, mercredi, jeudi, vendredi, samedi. If we want to give an exact date we can say something like this: le lundi onze janvier, Monday January 11 (notice the word order).

Useful Expressions of Time

en janvier, au mois de janvier, in January

Quel jour de la semaine est-ce? What day of the week is it?

C'est jeudi. It's Thursday.

samedi, on Saturday

le samedi, on Saturdays

mercredi soir, on Wednesday evening

tous les vendredis, every Friday

lundi prochain, next Monday

mardi dernier, last Tuesday

il y a huit jours, a week ago

il y a quinze jours, a fortnight ago

la semaine dernière, last week

la semaine prochaine, next week (of future time)

la semaine suivante, the following (next) week (of past time)

La semaine prochaine je vais en Bretagne. Next week I'm going to Brittany.

La semaine suivante il reçut une lettre de son père. The next (following) week he received a letter from his father.

hier soir, last night (yesterday evening)

cette nuit, last night (the time you slept!)

Hier soir j'ai regardé la télévision. Last night I watched television.

Cette nuit je n'ai pas bien dormi. Last night I did not sleep well.

ce soir, this evening, tonight

ce soir-là, that evening

le matin, in the morning

le soir, in the evening

Le matin je travaille, le soir je lis un livre. In the morning I work, in the evening I read a book.

Notice no preposition is needed with expressions of time: le matin, *in* the morning; jeudi, *on* Thursday; le deux septembre, *on* the second of September.

The Seasons: LES SAISONS (f.)

The names of the seasons, starting with Spring, are le printemps, l'été, l'automne, l'hiver: they are masculine. We say au printemps, in Spring but en été, en automne, en hiver; in Summer, in Autumn, in Winter.

Year: L'AN (m.), L'ANNÉE (f.)

"Year" is, in French, either l'an (m.) or l'année (f.). The distinction between them is often a matter of which sounds better in a sentence. This will not help a learner very much, so here are two points of difference. With a cardinal number use an: quatre ans, four years; with an ordinal it is better to put année; la quatrième année, the fourth year. Moreover, l'année not only marks a point in time but also emphasises the *content* of the year.

Toute cette année j'ai travaillé dur. I've worked hard all this year.

Similarly, jour, matin, soir have feminine forms journée, matinée, soirée.

Anno Domini

There is not much difficulty about this in French. If we wish to give the year we form it more or less as we do in English: in 1960, en dix-neuf cent soixante. However, we can also say en mil neuf cent soixante (in one thousand nine hundred and sixty). This is not the usual spelling of mille, but after the year 1000, l'an mille, the spelling mil and not mille is used for dates.

Dimensions

There are three ways of translating into French the sentence "This table is two metres long".:

(1) **Cette table est longue de deux mètres.** This table is long by two metres.

(2) **Cette table a deux mètres de long (de longueur).** This table has two metres of length.

(3) **Cette table a une longueur de deux mètres.** This table has a length of two metres (rarely used).

Similar constructions may be used for width and length. Thus "This table is two metres wide":

Cette table a deux mètres de large (de largeur).
Cette table est large de deux mètres.
Cette table a une largeur de deux mètres.

Now to combine length and width we use the preposition **sur**:

Cette table a deux mètres de long *sur* deux de large. This table is two metres long by two metres wide.

De is used before a numeral to express the measure of difference in comparisons of sizes, ages, etc.

Mon frère est plus grand que moi de dix centimètres. My brother is ten centimetres taller than I (taller by 10 centimetres).

Fractions

The most common fractions you are likely to need are **un demi**, a half; **un tiers**, a third; **un quart**, a quarter. With these we can make other fractions like **deux tiers**, two-thirds; **trois quarts**, three-quarters. For the remaining numbers we use the ordinals: **un cinquième**, a fifth; **un sixième**, a sixth; **un septième**, a seventh, etc. We can then form fractions like **quatre septièmes**, four-sevenths.

Notice these common expressions:

il est à moitié (à demi) mort, he is half dead
trois sur quatre, three out of four
dix sur vingt, ten out of twenty
neuf fois sur dix, nine times out of ten

Collective and Approximate Numbers

une paire de gants, a pair of gloves

To make a definite number like **vingt,** twenty, into an approximate one, add **-aine, une vingtaine,** about twenty.

cent livres, a hundred books
une centaine de livres, about a hundred books
des centaines de livres, hundreds of books
une vingtaine d'hommes, about a score of men
une femme d'une trentaine d'années, a woman of about thirty

All these collectives are feminine nouns and are followed by **de,** like other expressions of quantity:

une douzaine d'œufs, a dozen eggs

The indefinite number for **mille** (thousand) is **un millier** (about a thousand).

Des milliers de mouches. Thousands of flies. (You are not likely to know the exact number!)

Price

We have already mentioned in the chapter on the articles that the French use the Definite Article after a price:

trois francs la bouteille, le mètre, la douzaine, la pièce, three francs a bottle, a metre, a dozen, a piece (each)

There are also a few idiomatic expressions of buying and selling which are worth learning:

Le prix de ce chapeau est de quarante francs. The price of this hat is forty francs.

Nous l'avons payé dix francs. We paid ten francs for it.
Elle l'a vendu vingt francs. She sold it for twenty francs.
On m'en a demandé cent francs. They charged me 100
    francs for it.

Distance and Speed

One should, of course, be able to ask how far it is to a town
and to answer a similar question. Here is a pattern:

Quelle distance y a-t-il d'ici à Verneuil? How far is it
    from here to Verneuil.
D'ici à Verneuil il y a vingt kilomètres. It's twenty
    kilometres from here to Verneuil.
cent kilomètres à l'heure, a hundred kilometres an hour.
L'auto faisait du cent à l'heure. The car was doing a
    hundred (kilometres!).

Feelings

To describe personal feelings of heat, cold, etc., the verb
avoir is used in the following expressions:

avoir chaud: il a chaud. He is (feels) warm.
avoir froid: Nous avons froid. We are (feel) cold.
avoir sommeil: J'ai sommeil. I am (feel) sleepy.
avoir faim: J'avais faim. I was (felt) hungry.
avoir soif: Avez-vous soif? Are you thirsty?
avoir peur: Il a peur de moi. He's afraid of me.
avoir envie: J'ai envie d'y aller. I feel like going there.

With these expressions avoir froid, avoir chaud, when there
is no question of a feeling of cold or warmth but of actual
temperature, the verb être is substituted for avoir.

En hiver l'eau de la piscine est froide. In winter the
    water in the swimming-pool is cold.
Cette soupe est très chaude. This soup is very hot.

CHAPTER X
INTERJECTIONS

Interjections are words or sounds used to express feelings of joy, sorrow, amazement, annoyance, to give orders, attract attention or to imitate various noises. We give here but a few of them: the student will be able to collect many more if he keeps his ears open on his travels.

To show joy or displeasure you vary the tone of **Ah!** **Eh!** **Hi!** or **Oh!** while **Aïe** signifies disapproval (generally repeated three times!). To call someone or to elicit attention one says **Hé!** **Pst!** or **Holà!** Disgust is expressed by **Fi!** or **Pouah!** **Allons!** means "Come on now!" and gives encouragement as does also the word **Courage!** You cannot go far without coming across **Attention!**, Mind your step!, or **Halte!**, Stop!, or **Gare!**, Watch out! To enjoin silence one may try **Paix!** or **Silence!** If you wish to show special approval you can call **Bravo!** or **Très bien!**, while to encore a singer you can shout **Bis!** **Mon Dieu!**, **Parbleu!**, **Ma foi!**, **Dame** and **Pardi** (in the South) are mild swear words used to enforce something you want to say. When you are chopping wood you can make the noise **Han!** to show that you are working very hard.

To imitate sounds is not as easy as you might think. French guns go **Pan!** **Pan!** and not "Bang! Bang!"; a French fist as it strikes gives the sound **Toc!**, a slap on the face **Vlan!** After this, you will not be surprised to hear that Gallic ducks say **Coin!** **Coin!** (not "Quack! Quack!"), a French locomotive makes a noise like **Teuf!** and a cockerel sings **Coquerico!** Any student would find great interest in collecting a list of these interjections. Here are two to start with: **Oh là là!** (untranslatable!) and **Hein?** (used to make a statement into a question):

Vous aimez ça, hein? You like that, eh?

CHAPTER XI

WORD ORDER IN FRENCH

The Usual Order

As a general rule, the question of the order in which to arrange the words in a French sentence presents little difficulty. French and English are very similar in usage, and the exceptions to normal procedure have already been mentioned in previous chapters. However, we shall now try to bring together the more important deviations as a handy reference for the reader.

Inversion of Subject and Verb

The usual position of the subject is before the verb, but in the following cases there is inversion:

(a) *Questions, Exclamations, Wishes.* Here the subject follows the verb:

> **Où allez-vous?** Where are you going?
> **Jean, est-il arrivé?** Has John arrived?
> **Vive le roi!** Long live the King!
> **Puissiez-vous être heureux!** May you be happy!

(b) **Dit-il,** *etc.* After reported conversation there is inversion of such verbs as dire, répondre, crier, s'écrier, songer, penser, sembler.

> **«Comment vous portez-vous?»** demanda-t-elle. "How are you?" she asked.
> **«Très bien, merci»** répondit-il. "Very well, thank you," he replied.

Que, ce que, comme, lorsque, quand. You may sometimes find inversion of subject and verb after the relative pronouns **que** and **ce que,** and the conjunctions **que, comme, lorsque** and **quand:**

157

Le séjour qu'ont bâti mes aïeux ... The dwelling which my ancestors built ...

Comme dormait Jacob ... As Jacob slept ...

Quand on est jeune et que fleurit le printemps ... When one is young and when spring is in bloom ...

The inversion here is a matter of style only. It is quite correct not to make it.

À peine, aussi, peut-être. There is inversion of normal order after the conjunctions à peine, scarcely, hardly; aussi, and so, therefore; also after peut-être, perhaps, and sometimes after en vain, in vain.

Il était fatigué; aussi se coucha-t-il immédiatement. He was tired, so he went to bed straightaway.

Peut-être viendra-t-il vous voir demain. Perhaps he will come and see you tomorrow.

Object of an Infinitive Dependent on FAIRE

When an infinitive is used after the verbs faire, entendre, voir, laisser, if the object of these verbs is a noun, you should place it after the infinitive and not between the verbs as in English:

Il fait travailler *ses hommes*. He makes *his men* work.

Je vois venir *le docteur*. I see *the doctor* coming.

When the object is a pronoun we have the normal order:

Il les fait travailler. He makes them work.

Je le vois venir. I see him coming.

Preposition at the End of a Sentence or Clause

In French you may not finish with a preposition. A sentence like "Whom were you talking to?" must be changed to "To whom were you talking?" before it can be translated:

À qui parliez-vous? Whom were you talking to?

Avec quoi l'avez-vous fait? What did you make it with?

DONT

After **DONT** the subject, verb and complement must follow in that order. Thus a phrase like "the man whose son I saw yesterday" must be changed to "the man of whom I saw the son yesterday", **l'homme dont j'ai vu le fils hier.**

Now study carefully these sentences:

> **Mon frère dont vous lisez le livre . . .** My brother whose book you are reading (of whom you are reading the book) . . .
>
> **Un auteur dont j'aime les romans . . .** An author whose novels I like (of whom I like the novels).

JAMAIS

Even if **jamais** begins a sentence, the word order still remains subject, verb and the rest of the sentence:

> **Jamais enfant ne fut plus gâté que lui.** Never was a child more spoiled than he.

COMME and QUE

In a sentence beginning with "how" used in an exclamatory sense there is no such inversion as there is in English:

> **Comme elle est belle!** How beautiful she is!
> **Qu'il fait mauvais!** How wretched the weather is!

Position of Adverb

The adverb either follows the verb or, if there is need for emphasis, comes first in the sentence. It does not come between the subject and the verb. Always say "he walks slowly" or "slowly he walks" and never "he slowly walks".

> **Il vient bien souvent chez nous.** ⎫ He comes to us very
> **Bien souvent il vient chez nous.** ⎭ often.

In a compound tense short adverbs usually precede the Past Participle, others follow:

J'ai trop vu. I have seen too much.

Elle y est allée régulièrement. She went there regularly.

Word Order in Questions

(*a*) When the subject of the verb is a personal pronoun, the pronoun follows the verb:

Va-t-*il* chanter ce soir? Is he going to sing tonight?

Aimez-*vous* le café? Do you like coffee?

Êtes-*vous* allé en France? Did you go to France?

N'acceptent-*ils* pas? Are they not accepting?

(*b*) When the subject is a noun the subject is put first, then the verb followed by the corresponding personal pronoun:

Votre frère va-t-il nous aider? Is your brother going to help us?

Quand la lettre est-elle arrivée? When did the letter arrive?

Vous et votre ami êtes-vous allés en Suisse? Did you and your friend go to Switzerland?

Of course, in colloquial French the above inversion may be avoided by using est-ce que? In this way the normal order of subject, verb and the rest of the sentence is preserved. Here are the above examples rewritten, using est-ce que . . . :

Est-ce que votre frère va nous aider?

Quand est-ce que la lettre est arrivée?

Est-ce que vous et votre ami êtes allés en Suisse?

Questions containing pronouns may be turned the same way:

Est-ce qu'il va chanter ce soir?

Est-ce que vous aimez le café?

Est-ce qu'ils n'acceptent pas?

CHAPTER XII

CONSTRUCTIONS WITH FRENCH VERBS

Although French and English usage are often very similar, we cannot always assume that this is so. Let us give an example. In English the same verb may frequently be used transitively or intransitively.

The water *boils*. Intransitive (i.e., having no object).
I *boil* the water. Transitive (i.e., "water" is the object of "boil").

When we translate these two sentences into French, we notice at once a great difference:

L'eau bout. The water boils.
Je fais bouillir l'eau. I boil the water. (I make the water boil.)

Only a very compendious dictionary containing a host of examples will give complete satisfaction to the student. Failing this and even better from the learner's point of view, a careful note should be made of the construction employed with a verb every time any reading of French books takes place.

It is impossible to cover the whole range of French verbs in a chapter. We shall have to be content with an outline of the main points.

Completion of the Meaning of a Verb

In English we may use the word "open" in two ways:

I *open* the door (transitively).
The door *opens* (intransitively).

To the French the second sentence seems incomplete. A verb like "open" is generally used with an object; one opens something. The Frenchman expects an object: in the sentence "The door opens", he asks "The door opens what?"

To this question the only possible answer is "The door opens *itself*" and the verb becomes reflexive:

J'ouvre la porte. I open the door.
La porte s'ouvre. The door opens.

Here are some further examples of the same process:

Je vends l'article. I sell the article.
L'article se vend bien. The article sells (itself) well.
Il arrête l'auto. He stops the car.
L'auto s'arrête. The car stops (itself).
La mère lave le plancher. The mother washes the floor.
La mère se lave. The mother washes (herself).
Le barbier rasait un client. The barber was shaving a customer.
Le barbier se rasait. The barber was shaving (himself).

Verbs with Two Objects

Verbs like "teach", "show", "tell" have two objects:

"I teach him French."
"He showed me a card."
"I tell the children stories."

One of these objects must be indirect, and the word "to" has to be added. The sentences will now read:

"I teach French to him."
"He showed a card to me."
"I tell stories to the children."

Always remember to insert "to" before translating into French:

I teach him French. (I teach French to him.) **Je lui apprends le français.**
I wish the boy a good journey. (I wish a good journey to the boy.) **Je souhaite un bon voyage au garçon.**
We told them a good story. (We told a good story to them.) **Nous leur avons raconté une bonne histoire.**

They refuse him permission. (They refuse permission to him.) **Ils lui refusent la permission.**

I gave the girl a present. (I gave a present to the girl.) **J'ai donné un cadeau à la fillette.**

The following verbs are used similarly:

confier quelque chose à quelqu'un, to entrust something to someone

demander quelque chose à quelqu'un, to ask someone for something

Nous avons demandé un verre de lait au fermier. We asked the farmer for a glass of milk.

dire quelque chose à quelqu'un $\begin{cases} \text{to say something to someone} \\ \text{to tell someone something} \end{cases}$

Je lui ai dit adieu. I said farewell to him.
Elle m'a dit le mot. She told me the word.

pardonner quelque chose à quelqu'un, to forgive someone something

Pardonnez-nous nos offenses. Forgive us our trespasses.

rendre quelque chose à quelqu'un, to give something back to someone

Nous lui rendrons le cadeau. We shall give him back the present.

Verbs Which Require no Prepositions

Some verbs do not need to be followed by a preposition:

attendre, to wait for: **J'attends l'autobus.**
chercher, to look for: **Il cherchait la maison.**
demander, to ask for: **Nous demandons du sucre.**
écouter, to listen to: **Vous écoutez la radio.**
espérer, to hope for: **J'espérais la paix.**
payer, to pay for: **Mon père a payé la bicyclette.**
regarder, to look at: **Regardez cet arbre!**

Verbs Which Are Followed by À Before a Noun

jouer à, to play (a game): **J'ai joué au tennis.**

obéir à, to obey: **Obéissez à vos parents.**

penser à, to think of (turn one's thoughts to): **À quoi pensez-vous?**

répondre à, to answer: **Répondez à cette question!**

ressembler à, to resemble: **Il ressemblait à son oncle.**

Some Verbs Are Followed by DE

s'approcher de, to approach: **Ils s'approchèrent de la maison.**

changer de, to change: **Il a changé de caractère.**

jouer de, to play (a musical instrument): **Vous aimez jouer du piano.**

manquer de, to lack: **Elle manque de tact.**

penser de, to think (have an opinion): **Que pensez-vous de ce tableau?**

ENTRER DANS Before a Noun

Ils entrèrent dans la maison. They entered the house.

Verbs of "Taking Away"

These put à before the person interested:

acheter quelque chose à quelqu'un, to buy something from someone

eacher quelque chose à quelqu'un, to hide something from someone

emprunter quelque chose à quelqu'un, to borrow something from someone

ôter quelque chose à quelqu'un, to take away something from someone

prendre quelque chose à quelqu'un, to take something from someone

voler quelque chose à quelqu'un, to steal something from someone

Il m'a pris le livre. He took the book from me.

Ils ont volé de l'argent à leur ami. They stole money from their friend.

Il emprunta dix livres à son père. He borrowed £10 from his father.

During your reading you should keep a careful watch. Note carefully how each verb is used and if possible write the sentence down and learn it.

Government of Verbs

As we have already mentioned, when two verbs are used together in French the second is put into the Infinitive and the two verbs are linked by the prepositions **à, de, par.** There may even be no preposition at all between them. Here are a few examples:

Il aime à chanter. He loves singing.

Nous essayons de comprendre. We are trying to understand.

Il finira par accepter. He will end up by accepting.

Je voudrais bien entrer. I should like to come in.

On page 87 you will find a list of verbs together with the preposition required. Of course, it is not possible to include every possible verb. The student should keep his eyes open when reading French to note down each new construction.

"Come and See", "Go and Fetch"

Do not use **et** between a verb and the following infinitive when you are writing down verbs of motion.

Go and fetch the doctor. **Allez chercher le docteur.**

He came and saw me often. **Il venait souvent me voir.**

Demander à quelqu'un de faire quelque chose

A very common group is the one which follows the above pattern. Here is a useful list of these verbs:

commander à quelqu'un de faire quelque chose, to command someone to do something

conseiller à quelqu'un de faire quelque chose, to advise someone to do something

défendre à quelqu'un de faire quelque chose, to forbid someone to do something

demander à quelqu'un de faire quelque chose, to ask someone to do something

dire à quelqu'un de faire quelque chose, to tell someone to do something

ordonner à quelqu'un de faire quelque chose, to order someone to do something

permettre à quelqu'un de faire quelque chose, to permit someone to do something

persuader à quelqu'un de faire quelque chose, to persuade someone to do something

promettre à quelqu'un de faire quelque chose, to promise someone to do something

Il avait permis à ses enfants d'y aller. He had permitted his children to go there.

Vous avez déjà dit à ce monsieur de ne pas entrer. You have already told this gentleman not to come in.

Promettez-moi de ne pas le faire. Promise me not to do it.

"To go in, out, up, down, away, across, on"

to go in, entrer
  Il entra dans la maison. He went into the house.
to go out, sortir
  Elle sortait du cinéma. She was going out of the cinema.

to go up, **monter**
> **Montez dans votre chambre.** Go up to your room.

to go down, **descendre**
> **Il descendit dans le trou.** He went down into the hole.

to go away, **partir**
> **Elle partit sans me dire adieu.** She went away without
>   saying goodbye to me.

to go across, **traverser**
> **Nous traversons le pont.** We cross the bridge.

to go on, **continuer**
> **Il continua de parler.** He went on speaking.

MIDWINTER MURDER

AGATHA CHRISTIE

MIDWINTER MURDER

FIRESIDE MYSTERIES
FROM THE QUEEN OF CRIME

HarperCollinsPublishers

HarperCollins*Publishers*
1 London Bridge Street,
London SE1 9GF
www.harpercollins.co.uk

Published by HarperCollins*Publishers* 2020

2

The AC Monogram Logo is a trade mark and AGATHA CHRISTIE,
POIROT, MARPLE and the Agatha Christie Signature are
registered trademarks of Agatha Christie Limited in the UK and elsewhere.
Copyright © Agatha Christie Limited 2020. All rights reserved.
www.agathachristie.com

Cover and endpaper design by Holly Macdonald
© HarperCollins*Publishers* Ltd 2020
Illustrations © Shutterstock.com

A catalogue record for this book is
available from the British Library

ISBN 978-0-00-832896-2

Printed and bound in Great Britain by
CPI Group (UK) Ltd, Croydon, CR0 4YY

MIX
Paper from
responsible sources
FSC™ C007454

CONTENTS

Christmas at Abney Hall

Christmas we used to spend in Cheshire, going up to the Watts'. Jimmy usually got his yearly holiday about then, and he and Madge used to go to St. Moritz for three weeks. He was a very good skater, and so it was the kind of holiday he liked most. Mother and I used to go up to Cheadle, and since their newly built house, called Manor Lodge, was not ready yet, we spent Christmas at Abney Hall, with the old Wattses and their four children and Jack. It was a wonderful house to have Christmas in if you were a child. Not only was it enormous Victorian Gothic, with quantities of rooms, passages, unexpected steps, back staircases, front staircases, alcoves, niches—everything in the world that a child could want—but it also had three different pianos that you could play, as well as an organ. All it lacked was the light of day; it was remarkably dark, except for the big drawing-room with its green satin walls and its big windows.

Nan Watts and I were fast friends by now. We were not only friends but drinking companions—we both liked the same drink, *cream,* ordinary plain, neat cream. Although I had consumed an enormous amount of Devonshire cream since I lived in Devonshire, raw cream was really more of a treat. When Nan stayed with me at Torquay, we used to visit one of the dairies in the town, where we would have a glass of half milk and half cream. When I stayed with her at Abney we used to go down to the home farm and drink cream by the half-pint. We continued these drinking bouts all through our lives, and I still remember buying our cartons of cream in Sunningdale and coming up to the golf course and sitting outside the club house waiting for our respective husbands to finish their rounds of golf, each drinking our pinta cream.

Abney was a glutton's paradise. Mrs Watts had what was called her store-room off the hall. It was not like Grannie's store-room, a kind of securely-locked treasure house from which things were taken out. There was free access to it, and all round the walls were shelves covered with every kind of dainty. One side was entirely chocolates, boxes of them, all different, chocolate creams in labelled boxes ... There were biscuits, gingerbread, preserved fruits, jams and so on.

Christmas was the supreme Festival, something never to be forgotten. Christmas stockings in bed. Breakfast, when everyone had a separate chair heaped with presents. Then a rush to church and back to continue present opening. At two o'clock Christmas Dinner, the blinds drawn down and glittering ornaments and lights. First, oyster soup (not relished by me), turbot, then boiled turkey, roast turkey, and a large roast sirloin of beef. This was followed by plum pudding, mince pies, and a trifle full of sixpences, pigs, rings, bachelors' buttons and all the rest of it. After that, again, innumerable kinds of dessert. In a story I once wrote, *The Affair of the Christmas Pudding*, I have described just such a feast. It is one of those things that I am sure will never be seen again in this generation; indeed I doubt nowadays if anyone's digestion would stand it. However, *our* digestions stood it quite well then.

I usually had to vie in eating prowess with Humphrey Watts, the Watts son next to James in age. I suppose he must have been twenty-one or twenty-two to my twelve or thirteen. He was a very handsome young man, as well as being a good actor and a wonderful entertainer and teller of stories. Good as I always was at falling in love with people, I don't think I fell in love with him, though it is amazing to me that I should *not* have done so. I suppose I was still at the stage where my love affairs had to be romantically impossible—concerned with public characters, such as the Bishop of London and King Alfonso of Spain, and of course with various actors. I know I fell deeply in love with Henry Ainley when I saw him in *The Bondman,* and I must have been just getting ripe for the K.O.W.s (Keen on Wallers), who were all to a girl in love with Lewis Waller in *Monsieur Beaucaire.*

Humphrey and I ate solidly through the Christmas Dinner. He scored over me in oyster soup, but otherwise we were neck and neck. We both first had roast turkey, then boiled turkey, and finally four or five slashing slices of sirloin of beef. It is possible that our elders confined themselves to only one kind of turkey for this course, but as far as I remember old Mr Watts certainly had beef as well as turkey. We then ate plum pudding and mince pies and trifle—I rather sparingly of trifle, because I didn't like the taste of wine. After that there were the crackers, the grapes, the oranges, the Elvas plums, the Carlsbad plums, and the preserved fruits. Finally, during the afternoon, various handfuls of chocolates were fetched from the store-room to suit our taste. Do I remember being sick the next day? Having bilious attacks? No, never. The only bilious attacks I ever remember were those that seized me after eating unripe apples in September. I ate unripe apples practically every day, but occasionally I must have overdone it.

What I do remember was when I was about six or seven years old and had eaten mushrooms. I woke up with a pain about eleven o'clock in the evening, and came rushing down to the drawing-room, where mother and father were entertaining a party of people, and announced dramatically: 'I am going to die! I am poisoned by mushrooms!' Mother rapidly soothed me and administered a dose of ipecacuanha wine—always kept in the medicine cupboard in those days—and assured me that I was not due to die this time.

At any rate I never remember being ill at Christmas. Nan Watts was just the same as I was; she had a splendid stomach. In fact, really, when I remember those days, everyone seemed to have a pretty good stomach. I suppose people had gastric and duodenal ulcers and had to be careful, but I cannot remember anybody living on a diet of fish and milk. A coarse and gluttonous age? Yes, but one of great zest and enjoyment. Considering the amount that I ate in my youth (for I was always hungry) I cannot imagine how I managed to remain so thin—a scrawny chicken indeed.

After the pleasurable inertia of Christmas afternoon— pleasurable, that is, for the elders: the younger ones read books, looked at their presents, ate more chocolates, and so on—there was a terrific tea, with a great iced Christmas cake as well as everything else, and finally a supper of cold turkey and hot mince pies. About nine o'clock there was the Christmas Tree, with more presents hanging on it. A splendid day, and one to be remembered till next year, when Christmas came again.

Agatha Christie

MIDWINTER MURDER

The Chocolate Box

It was a wild night. Outside, the wind howled malevolently, and the rain beat against the windows in great gusts.

Poirot and I sat facing the hearth, our legs stretched out to the cheerful blaze. Between us was a small table. On my side of it stood some carefully brewed hot toddy; on Poirot's was a cup of thick, rich chocolate which I would not have drunk for a hundred pounds! Poirot sipped the thick brown mess in the pink china cup, and sighed with contentment.

'*Quelle belle vie!*' he murmured.

'Yes, it's a good old world,' I agreed. 'Here am I with a job, and a good job too! And here are you, famous—'

'Oh, *mon ami!*' protested Poirot.

'But you are. And rightly so! When I think back on your long line of successes, I am positively amazed. I don't believe you know what failure is!'

'He would be a droll kind of original who could say that!'

'No, but seriously, *have* you ever failed?'

'Innumerable times, my friend. What would you? *La bonne chance*, it cannot always be on your side. I have been called in too late. Very often another, working towards the same goal, has arrived there first. Twice have I been stricken down with illness just as I was on

1

the point of success. One must take the downs with the ups, my friend.'

'I didn't quite mean that,' I said. 'I meant, had you ever been completely down and out over a case through your own fault?'

'Ah, I comprehend! You ask if I have ever made the complete prize ass of myself, as you say over here? Once, my friend—' A slow, reflective smile hovered over his face. 'Yes, once I made a fool of myself.'

He sat up suddenly in his chair.

'See here, my friend, you have, I know, kept a record of my little successes. You shall add one more story to the collection, the story of a failure!'

He leaned forward and placed a log on the fire. Then, after carefully wiping his hands on a little duster that hung on a nail by the fireplace, he leaned back and commenced his story.

That of which I tell you (said M. Poirot) took place in Belgium many years ago. It was at the time of the terrible struggle in France between church and state. M. Paul Déroulard was a French deputy of note. It was an open secret that the portfolio of a Minister awaited him. He was among the bitterest of the anti-Catholic party, and it was certain that on his accession to power, he would have to face violent enmity. He was in many ways a peculiar man. Though he neither drank nor smoked, he was nevertheless not so scrupulous in other ways. You comprehend, Hastings, *c'était des femmes— toujours des femmes*!

He had married some years earlier a young lady from Brussels who had brought him a substantial *dot*. Undoubtedly the money was useful to him in his career, as his family was not rich, though on the other hand he was entitled to call himself M. le Baron if he chose.

There were no children of the marriage, and his wife died after two years—the result of a fall downstairs. Among the property which she bequeathed to him was a house on the Avenue Louise in Brussels.

It was in this house that his sudden death took place, the event coinciding with the resignation of the Minister whose portfolio he was to inherit. All the papers printed long notices of his career. His death, which had taken place quite suddenly in the evening after dinner, was attributed to heart-failure.

At that time, *mon ami*, I was, as you know, a member of the Belgian detective force. The death of M. Paul Déroulard was not particularly interesting to me. I am, as you also know, *bon catholique*, and his demise seemed to me fortunate.

It was some three days afterwards, when my vacation had just begun, that I received a visitor at my own apartments—a lady, heavily veiled, but evidently quite young; and I perceived at once that she was a *jeune fille tout à fait comme il faut*.

'You are Monsieur Hercule Poirot?' she asked in a low sweet voice.

I bowed.

'Of the detective service?'

Again I bowed. 'Be seated, I pray of you, mademoiselle,' I said.

She accepted a chair and drew aside her veil. Her face was charming, though marred with tears, and haunted as though with some poignant anxiety.

'Monsieur,' she said, 'I understand that you are now taking a vacation. Therefore you will be free to take up a private case. You understand that I do not wish to call in the police.'

I shook my head. 'I fear what you ask is impossible,

mademoiselle. Even though on vacation, I am still of the police.'

She leaned forward. '*Ecoutez, monsieur.* All that I ask of you is to investigate. The result of your investigations you are at perfect liberty to report to the police. If what I believe to be true *is* true, we shall need all the machinery of the law.'

That placed a somewhat different complexion on the matter, and I placed myself at her service without more ado.

A slight colour rose in her cheeks. 'I thank you, monsieur. It is the death of M. Paul Déroulard that I ask you to investigate.'

'*Comment?*' I exclaimed, surprised.

'Monsieur, I have nothing to go upon—nothing but my woman's instinct, but I am convinced—*convinced*, I tell you—that M. Déroulard did not die a natural death!'

'But surely the doctors—'

'Doctors may be mistaken. He was so robust, so strong. Ah, Monsieur Poirot, I beseech of you to help me—'

The poor child was almost beside herself. She would have knelt to me. I soothed her as best I could.

'I will help you, mademoiselle. I feel almost sure that your fears are unfounded, but we will see. First, I will ask you to describe to me the inmates of the house.'

'There are the domestics, of course, Jeannette, Félice, and Denise the cook. She has been there many years; the others are simple country girls. Also there is François, but he too is an old servant. Then there is Monsieur Déroulard's mother who lived with him, and myself. My name is Virginie Mesnard. I am a poor cousin of the late Madame Déroulard, M. Paul's wife, and I have been a

4

member of their ménage for over three years. I have now described to you the household. There were also two guests staying in the house.'

'And they were?'

'M. de Saint Alard, a neighbour of M. Déroulard's in France. Also an English friend, Mr John Wilson.'

'Are they still with you?'

'Mr Wilson, yes, but M. de Saint Alard departed yesterday.'

'And what is your plan, Mademoiselle Mesnard?'

'If you will present yourself at the house in half an hour's time, I will have arranged some story to account for your presence. I had better represent you to be connected with journalism in some way. I shall say you have come from Paris, and that you have brought a card of introduction from M. de Saint Alard. Madame Déroulard is very feeble in health, and will pay little attention to details.'

On mademoiselle's ingenious pretext I was admitted to the house, and after a brief interview with the dead deputy's mother, who was a wonderfully imposing and aristocratic figure though obviously in failing health, I was made free of the premises.

I wonder, my friend (continued Poirot), whether you can possibly figure to yourself the difficulties of my task? Here was a man whose death had taken place three days previously. If there *had* been foul play, only one possibility was admittable—*poison*! And I had no chance of seeing the body, and there was no possibility of examining, or analysing, any medium in which the poison could have been administered. There were no clues, false or otherwise, to consider. Had the man been poisoned? Had he died a natural death? I, Hercule Poirot, with nothing to help me, had to decide.

First, I interviewed the domestics, and with their aid, I recapitulated the evening. I paid especial notice to the food at dinner, and the method of serving it. The soup had been served by M. Déroulard himself from a tureen. Next a dish of cutlets, then a chicken. Finally, a compote of fruits. And all placed on the table, and served by Monsieur himself. The coffee was brought in a big pot to the dinner-table. Nothing there, *mon ami*— impossible to poison one without poisoning all!

After dinner Madame Déroulard had retired to her own apartments and Mademoiselle Virginie had accompanied her. The three men had adjourned to M. Déroulard's study. Here they had chatted amicably for some time, when suddenly, without any warning, the deputy had fallen heavily to the ground. M. de Saint Alard had rushed out and told François to fetch the doctor immediately. He said it was without doubt an apoplexy, explained the man. But when the doctor arrived, the patient was past help.

Mr John Wilson, to whom I was presented by Mademoiselle Virginie, was what was known in those days as a regular John Bull Englishman, middle-aged and burly. His account, delivered in very British French, was substantially the same.

'Déroulard went very red in the face, and down he fell.'

There was nothing further to be found out there. Next I went to the scene of the tragedy, the study, and was left alone there at my own request. So far there was nothing to support Mademoiselle Mesnard's theory. I could not but believe that it was a delusion on her part. Evidently she had entertained a romantic passion for the dead man which had not permitted her to take a normal view of the case. Nevertheless, I searched the study with meticulous care. It was just possible that a hypodermic needle might have been introduced into the dead man's chair in such a way as to allow of a fatal injection. The minute puncture it would cause was likely to remain unnoticed. But I could discover no sign to support the theory. I flung myself down in the chair with a gesture of despair.

'*Enfin*, I abandon it!' I said aloud. 'There is not a clue anywhere! Everything is perfectly normal.'

As I said the words, my eyes fell on a large box of chocolates standing on a table near by, and my heart gave a leap. It might not be a clue to M. Déroulard's death, but here at least was something that was *not* normal. I lifted the lid. The box was full, untouched; not a chocolate was missing—but that only made the peculiarity that had caught my eye more striking. For, see you, Hastings, while the box itself was pink, the lid was *blue*. Now, one often sees a blue ribbon on a pink box, and vice versa, but a box of one colour, and a lid of another— no, decidedly—*ça ne se voit jamais!*

I did not as yet see that this little incident was of any use to me, yet I determined to investigate it as being out of the ordinary. I rang the bell for François, and asked him if his late master had been fond of sweets. A faint melancholy smile came to his lips.

'Passionately fond of them, monsieur. He would always have a box of chocolates in the house. He did not drink wine of any kind, you see.'

'Yet this box has not been touched?' I lifted the lid to show him.

'Pardon, monsieur, but that was a new box purchased on the day of his death, the other being nearly finished.'

'Then the other box was finished on the day of his death,' I said slowly.

'Yes, monsieur, I found it empty in the morning and threw it away.'

'Did M. Déroulard eat sweets at all hours of the day?'

'Usually after dinner, monsieur.'

I began to see light.

'François,' I said, 'you can be discreet?'

'If there is need, monsieur.'

'*Bon!* Know, then, that I am of the police. Can you find me that other box?'

'Without doubt, monsieur. It will be in the dustbin.'

He departed, and returned in a few minutes with a dust-covered object. It was the duplicate of the box I held, save for the fact that this time the box was *blue* and the lid was *pink*. I thanked François, recommended him once more to be discreet, and left the house in the Avenue Louise without more ado.

Next I called upon the doctor who had attended M. Déroulard. With him I had a difficult task. He entrenched himself prettily behind a wall of learned phraseology, but I fancied that he was not quite as sure about the case as he would like to be.

'There have been many curious occurrences of the kind,' he observed, when I had managed to disarm him somewhat. 'A sudden fit of anger, a violent emotion— after a heavy dinner, *c'est entendu*—then, with an access of rage, the blood flies to the head, and *pst!*—there you are!'

'But M. Déroulard had had no violent emotion.'

'No? I made sure that he had been having a stormy altercation with M. de Saint Alard.'

'Why should he?'

'*C'est évident!*' The doctor shrugged his shoulders. 'Was not M. de Saint Alard a Catholic of the most fanatical? Their friendship was being ruined by this

8

question of church and state. Not a day passed without discussions. To M. de Saint Alard, Déroulard appeared almost as Antichrist.'

This was unexpected, and gave me food for thought.

'One more question, Doctor: would it be possible to introduce a fatal dose of poison into a chocolate?'

'It would be possible, I suppose,' said the doctor slowly. 'Pure prussic acid would meet the case if there were no chance of evaporation, and a tiny globule of anything might be swallowed unnoticed—but it does not seem a very likely supposition. A chocolate full of morphine or strychnine—' He made a wry face. 'You comprehend, M. Poirot—one bite would be enough! The unwary one would not stand upon ceremony.'

'Thank you, M. le Docteur.'

I withdrew. Next I made inquiries of the chemists, especially those in the neighbourhood of the Avenue Louise. It is good to be of the police. I got the information I wanted without any trouble. Only in one case could I hear of any poison having been supplied to the house in question. This was some eye drops of atropine sulphate for Madame Déroulard. Atropine is a potent poison, and for the moment I was elated, but the symptoms of atropine poisoning are closely allied to those of ptomaine, and bear no resemblance to those I was studying. Besides, the prescription was an old one. Madame Déroulard had suffered from cataract in both eyes for many years.

I was turning away discouraged when the chemist's voice called me back.

'*Un moment, M. Poirot.* I remember, the girl who brought that prescription, she said something about having to go on to the *English* chemist. You might try there.'

9

I did. Once more enforcing my official status, I got the information I wanted. On the day before M. Déroulard's death they had made up a prescription for Mr John Wilson. Not that there was any making up about it. They were simply little tablets of trinitrine. I asked if I might see some. He showed me them, and my heart beat faster—for the tiny tablets were of *chocolate*.

'Is it a poison?' I asked.

'No, monsieur.'

'Can you describe to me its effect?'

'It lowers the blood-pressure. It is given for some forms of heart trouble—angina pectoris for instance. It relieves the arterial tension. In arteriosclerosis—'

I interrupted him. '*Ma foi*! This rigmarole says nothing to me. Does it cause the face to flush?'

'Certainly it does.'

'And supposing I ate ten—twenty of your little tablets, what then?'

'I should not advise you to attempt it,' he replied drily.

'And yet you say it is not poison?'

'There are many things not called poison which can kill a man,' he replied as before.

I left the shop elated. At last, things had begun to march!

I now knew that John Wilson had the means for the crime—but what about the motive? He had come to Belgium on business, and had asked M. Déroulard, whom he knew slightly, to put him up. There was apparently no way in which Déroulard's death could benefit him. Moreover, I discovered by inquiries in England that he had suffered for some years from that painful form of heart disease known as angina. Therefore he had a genuine right to have those tablets in his possession. Nevertheless, I was convinced that someone had gone to the chocolate box, opening the full one first by mistake, and had abstracted the contents of the last chocolate, cramming in instead as many little trinitrine tablets as it would hold. The chocolates were large ones. Between twenty or thirty tablets, I felt sure, could have been inserted. But who had done this?

There were two guests in the house. John Wilson had the means. Saint Alard had the motive. Remember, he was a fanatic, and there is no fanatic like a religious fanatic. Could he, by any means, have got hold of John Wilson's trinitrine?

Another little idea came to me. Ah, you smile at my little ideas! Why had Wilson run out of trinitrine? Surely he would bring an adequate supply from England. I called once more at the house in the Avenue Louise. Wilson was out, but I saw the girl who did his room, Félicie. I demanded of her immediately whether it was not true that M. Wilson had lost a bottle from his washstand some little time ago. The girl responded eagerly. It was quite true. She, Félicie, had been blamed for it. The English gentleman had evidently thought that she had broken it, and did not like to say so. Whereas she had never even touched it. Without doubt it was Jeannette always nosing round where she had no business to be—

I calmed the flow of words, and took my leave. I knew now all that I wanted to know. It remained for me to prove my case. That, I felt, would not be easy. *I* might be sure that Saint Alard had removed the bottle of trinitrine from John Wilson's washstand, but to convince others, I would have to produce evidence. And I had none to produce!

Never mind. I *knew*—that was the great thing. You remember our difficulty in the Styles case, Hastings?

11

There again, I *knew*—but it took me a long time to find the last link which made my chain of evidence against the murderer complete.

I asked for an interview with Mademoiselle Mesnard. She came at once. I demanded of her the address of M. de Saint Alard. A look of trouble came over her face.

'Why do you want it, monsieur?'

'Mademoiselle, it is necessary.'

She seemed doubtful—troubled.

'He can tell you nothing. He is a man whose thoughts are not in this world. He hardly notices what goes on around him.'

'Possibly, mademoiselle. Nevertheless, he was an old friend of M. Déroulard's. There may be things he can tell me—things of the past—old grudges—old love-affairs.'

The girl flushed and bit her lip. 'As you please—but—but I feel sure now that I have been mistaken. It was good of you to accede to my demand, but I was upset—almost distraught at the time. I see now that there is no mystery to solve. Leave it, I beg of you, monsieur.'

I eyed her closely.

'Mademoiselle,' I said, 'it is sometimes difficult for a dog to find a scent, but once he *has* found it, nothing on earth will make him leave it! That is if he is a good dog! And I, mademoiselle, I, Hercule Poirot, am a very good dog.'

Without a word she turned away. A few minutes later she returned with the address written on a sheet of paper. I left the house. François was waiting for me outside. He looked at me anxiously.

'There is no news, monsieur?'

'None as yet, my friend.'

'Ah! *Pauvre* Monsieur Déroulard!' he sighed. 'I too was of his way of thinking. I do not care for priests. Not that I would say so in the house. The women are all devout—a good thing perhaps. *Madame est très pieuse—et Mademoiselle Virginie aussi.*'

Mademoiselle Virginie? Was she '*très pieuse?*' Thinking of the tear-stained passionate face I had seen that first day, I wondered.

Having obtained the address of M. de Saint Alard, I wasted no time. I arrived in the neighbourhood of his château in the Ardennes but it was some days before I could find a pretext for gaining admission to the house. In the end I did—how do you think—as a plumber, *mon ami*! It was the affair of a moment to arrange a neat little gas leak in his bedroom. I departed for my tools, and took care to return with them at an hour when I knew I should have the field pretty well to myself. What I was searching for, I hardly knew. The one thing needful, I could not believe there was any chance of finding. He would never have run the risk of keeping it.

Still when I found the little cupboard above the washstand locked, I could not resist the temptation of seeing what was inside it. The lock was quite a simple one to pick. The door swung open. It was full of old bottles. I took them up one by one with a trembling hand. Suddenly, I uttered a cry. Figure to yourself, my friend, I held in my hand a little phial with an English chemist's label. On it were the words: '*Trinitrine Tablets. One to be taken when required. Mr John Wilson.*'

I controlled my emotion, closed the cupboard, slipped the bottle into my pocket, and continued to repair the gas leak! One must be methodical. Then I left the château, and took train for my own country as soon as possible. I arrived in Brussels late that night. I was writing out a report for the préfet in the morning, when a note was brought to me. It was from old Madame Déroulard, and it summoned me to the house in the Avenue Louise without delay.

François opened the door to me.

'Madame la Baronne is awaiting you.'

He conducted me to her apartments. She sat in state in a large armchair. There was no sign of Mademoiselle Virginie.

'M. Poirot,' said the old lady, 'I have just learned that you are not what you pretend to be. You are a police officer.'

'That is so, madame.'

'You came here to inquire into the circumstances of my son's death?'

Again I replied: 'That is so, madame.'

'I should be glad if you would tell me what progress you have made.'

I hesitated.

'First I would like to know how you have learned all this, madame.'

'From one who is no longer of this world.'

Her words, and the brooding way she uttered them, sent a chill to my heart. I was incapable of speech.

'Therefore, monsieur, I would beg of you most urgently to tell me exactly what progress you have made in your investigation.'

'Madame, my investigation is finished.'

'My son?'

'Was killed deliberately.'

'You know by whom?'

'Yes, madame.'

'Who, then?'

'M. de Saint Alard.'

'You are wrong. M. de Saint Alard is incapable of such a crime.'

'The proofs are in my hands.'

'I beg of you once more to tell me all.'

This time I obeyed, going over each step that had led me to the discovery of the truth. She listened attentively. At the end she nodded her head.

'Yes, yes, it is all as you say, all but one thing. It was not M. de Saint Alard who killed my son. It was I, his mother.'

I stared at her. She continued to nod her head gently.

'It is well that I sent for you. It is the providence of the good God that Virginie told me before she departed for the convent, what she had done. Listen, M. Poirot! My son was an evil man. He persecuted the church. He led a life of mortal sin. He dragged down the other souls beside his own. But there was worse than that. As I came out of my room in this house one morning, I saw my daughter-in-law standing at the head of the stairs. She was reading a letter. I saw my son steal up behind her. One swift push, and she fell, striking her head on the marble steps. When they picked her up she was dead. My son was a murderer, and only I, his mother, knew it.'

She closed her eyes for a moment. 'You cannot conceive, monsieur, of my agony, my despair. What was I to do? Denounce him to the police? I could not bring myself to do it. It was my duty, but my flesh was weak. Besides, would they believe me? My eyesight had been failing for some time—they would say I was mistaken. I kept silence. But my conscience gave me no peace. By keeping silence I too was a murderer. My son inherited his wife's money. He flourished as the green bay tree. And now he was to have a Minister's portfolio. His persecution of the church would be redoubled. And there was Virginie. She, poor child, beautiful, naturally pious, was fascinated by him. He had a strange and terrible power over women. I saw it coming. I was powerless to prevent it. He had no intention of marrying her. The time came when she was ready to yield everything to him.

'Then I saw my path clear. He was my son. I had given him life. I was responsible for him. He had killed one woman's body, now he would kill another's soul! I went to Mr Wilson's room, and took the bottle of tablets. He had once said laughingly that there were enough in it to kill a man! I went into the study and opened the big box of chocolates that always stood on the table. I opened a new box by mistake. The other was on the table also. There was just one chocolate left in it. That simplified things. No one ate chocolates except my son and Virginie. I would keep her with me that night. All went as I had planned—'

She paused, closing her eyes a minute then opened them again.

'M. Poirot, I am in your hands. They tell me I have not many days to live. I am willing to answer for my action before the good God. Must I answer for it on earth also?'

I hesitated. 'But the empty bottle, madame,' I said to gain time. 'How came that into M. de Saint Alard's possession?'

'When he came to say goodbye to me, monsieur, I slipped it into his pocket. I did not know how to get rid of it. You see, I cannot move about much without help, and finding it empty in my rooms might have caused suspicion. You understand, monsieur—' she drew herself up to her full height—'it was with no idea of casting suspicion on M. de Saint Alard! I never dreamed of such a thing. I thought his valet would find an empty bottle and throw it away without question.'

I bowed my head. 'I comprehend, madame,' I said.

'And your decision, monsieur?'

Her voice was firm and unfaltering, her head held as high as ever.

I rose to my feet.

'Madame,' I said, 'I have the honour to wish you good day. I have made my investigations—and failed! The matter is closed.'

He was silent for a moment, then said quietly: 'She died just a week later. Mademoiselle Virginie passed through her novitiate, and duly took the veil. That, my friend, is the story. I must admit that I do not make a fine figure in it.'

'But that was hardly a failure,' I expostulated. 'What else could you have thought under the circumstances?'

'Ah, sacré, mon ami,' cried Poirot, becoming suddenly animated. 'Is it that you do not see? But I was thirty-six times an idiot! My grey cells, they functioned not at all. The whole time I had the clue in my hands.'

'What clue?'

'The chocolate box! Do you not see? Would anyone in possession of their full eyesight make such a mistake? I knew Madame Déroulard had cataract—the atropine drops told me that. There was only one person in the household whose eyesight was such that she could not see which lid to replace. It was the chocolate box that started me on the track, and yet up to the end I failed consistently to perceive its real significance!

'Also my psychology was at fault. Had M. de Saint Alard been the criminal, he would never have kept an incriminating bottle. Finding it was a proof of his innocence. I had learned already from Mademoiselle Virginie that he was absent-minded. Altogether it was a miserable affair that I have recounted to you there! Only to you have I told the story. You comprehend, I do not figure well in it! An old lady commits a crime in such a simple and clever fashion that I, Hercule Poirot, am completely deceived. *Sapristi*! It does not bear thinking of! Forget it. Or no—remember it, and if you think at any time that I am growing conceited—it is not likely, but it might arise.'

I concealed a smile.

'*Eh bien*, my friend, you shall say to me, "Chocolate box". Is it agreed?'

'It's a bargain!'

'After all,' said Poirot reflectively, 'it was an experience! I, who have undoubtedly the finest brain in Europe at present, can afford to be magnanimous!'

'Chocolate box,' I murmured gently.

'*Pardon, mon ami?*'

I looked at Poirot's innocent face, as he bent forward inquiringly, and my heart smote me. I had suffered often at his hands, but I, too, though not possessing the finest brain in Europe, could afford to be magnanimous!

'Nothing,' I lied, and lit another pipe, smiling to myself.

A Christmas Tragedy

'I have a complaint to make,' said Sir Henry Clithering. His eyes twinkled gently as he looked round at the assembled company. Colonel Bantry, his legs stretched out, was frowning at the mantelpiece as though it were a delinquent soldier on parade, his wife was surreptitiously glancing at a catalogue of bulbs which had come by the late post, Dr Lloyd was gazing with frank admiration at Jane Helier, and that beautiful young actress herself was thoughtfully regarding her pink polished nails. Only that elderly, spinster lady, Miss Marple, was sitting bolt upright, and her faded blue eyes met Sir Henry's with an answering twinkle.

'A complaint?' she murmured.

'A very serious complaint. We are a company of six, three representatives of each sex, and I protest on behalf of the downtrodden males. We have had three stories told tonight—and told by the three men! I protest that the ladies have not done their fair share.'

'Oh!' said Mrs Bantry with indignation. 'I'm sure we have. We've listened with the most intelligent appreciation. We've displayed the true womanly attitude—not wishing to thrust ourselves in the limelight!'

'It's an excellent excuse,' said Sir Henry; 'but it won't do. And there's a very good precedent in the Arabian Nights! So, forward, Scheherazade.'

'Meaning me?' said Mrs Bantry. 'But I don't know anything to tell. I've never been surrounded by blood or mystery.'

'I don't absolutely insist upon blood,' said Sir Henry. 'But I'm sure one of you three ladies has got a pet mystery. Come now, Miss Marple—the "Curious Coincidence of the Charwoman" or the "Mystery of the Mothers' Meeting". Don't disappoint me in St Mary Mead.'

Miss Marple shook her head.

'Nothing that would interest you, Sir Henry. We have our little mysteries, of course—there was that gill of picked shrimps that disappeared so incomprehensibly; but that wouldn't interest you because it all turned out to be so trivial, though throwing a considerable light on human nature.'

'You have taught me to dote on human nature,' said Sir Henry solemnly.

'What about you, Miss Helier?' asked Colonel Bantry. 'You must have had some interesting experiences.'

'Yes, indeed,' said Dr Lloyd.

'Me?' said Jane. 'You mean—you want me to tell you something that happened to me?'

'Or to one of your friends,' amended Sir Henry.

'Oh!' said Jane vaguely. 'I don't think anything has ever happened to me—I mean not that kind of thing. Flowers, of course, and queer messages—but that's just men, isn't it? I don't think'—she paused and appeared lost in thought.

'I see we shall have to have that epic of the shrimps,' said Sir Henry. 'Now then, Miss Marple.'

'You're so fond of your joke, Sir Henry. The shrimps are only nonsense; but now I come to think of it, I *do* remember one incident—at least not exactly an incident, something very much more serious—a tragedy. And I was, in a way, mixed up in it; and for what I did, I have never had any regrets—no, no regrets at all. But it didn't happen in St Mary Mead.'

'That disappoints me,' said Sir Henry. 'But I will endeavour to bear up. I knew we should not rely upon you in vain.'

He settled himself in the attitude of a listener. Miss Marple grew slightly pink.

'I hope I shall be able to tell it properly,' she said anxiously. 'I fear I am very inclined to become *rambling*. One wanders from the point—altogether without knowing that one is doing so. And it is so hard to remember each fact in its proper order. You must all bear with me if I tell my story badly. It happened a very long time ago now.

'As I say, it was not connected with St Mary Mead. As a matter of fact, it had to do with a Hydro—'

'Do you mean a seaplane?' asked Jane with wide eyes.

'You wouldn't know, dear,' said Mrs Bantry, and explained. Her husband added his quota:

'Beastly places—absolutely beastly! Got to get up early and drink filthy-tasting water. Lot of old women sitting about. Ill-natured tittle tattle. God, when I think—'

'Now, Arthur,' said Mrs Bantry placidly. 'You know it did you all the good in the world.'

'Lot of old women sitting round talking scandal,' grunted Colonel Bantry.

'That I am afraid is true,' said Miss Marple. 'I myself—'

'My dear Miss Marple,' cried the Colonel, horrified. 'I didn't mean for one moment—'

With pink cheeks and a little gesture of the hand, Miss Marple stopped him.

'But it is *true*, Colonel Bantry. Only I should just like to say this. Let me recollect my thoughts. Yes. Talking scandal, as you say—well, it *is* done a good deal. And people are very down on it—especially young people. My nephew, who writes books—and very clever ones, I believe—has said some most *scathing* things about taking people's characters away without any kind of proof—and how wicked it is, and all that. But what I say is that none of these young people ever stop to *think*. They really don't examine the facts. Surely the whole crux of the matter is this: *How often is tittle tattle*, as you call it, *true*! And I think if, as I say, they really examined the facts they would find that it was true nine times out of ten! That's really just what makes people so annoyed about it.'

'The inspired guess,' said Sir Henry.

'No, not that, not that at all! It's really a matter of practice and experience. An Egyptologist, so I've heard, if you show him one of those curious little beetles, can tell you by the look and the feel of the thing what date bc it is, or if it's a Birmingham imitation. And he can't always give a definite rule for doing so. He just *knows*. His life has been spent handling such things.

'And that's what I'm trying to say (very badly, I know). What my nephew calls "superfluous women" have a lot of time on their hands, and their chief interest is usually *people*. And so, you see, they get to be what one might call *experts*. Now young people nowadays—they talk very freely about things that weren't mentioned in my young days, but on the other hand their minds are terribly innocent. They believe in everyone and everything. And if one tries to warn them, ever so gently, they tell one that one has a Victorian mind—and that, they say, is like a *sink*.'

'After all,' said Sir Henry, 'what is wrong with a *sink*?'

'Exactly,' said Miss Marple eagerly. 'It's the most necessary thing in any house; but, of course, not romantic. Now I must confess that I have my *feelings*, like everyone else, and I have sometimes been cruelly hurt by unthinking remarks. I know gentlemen are not interested in domestic matters, but I must just mention my maid Ethel—a very good-looking girl and obliging in every way. Now I realized as soon as I saw her that she was the same type as Annie Webb and poor Mrs Bruitt's girl. If the opportunity arose *mine* and *thine* would mean nothing to her. So I let her go at the month and I gave her a written reference saying she was honest and sober, but privately I warned old Mrs Edwards against taking her; and my nephew, Raymond, was exceedingly angry and said he had never heard of anything so wicked— yes, *wicked*. Well, she went to Lady Ashton, whom I felt no obligation to warn—and what happened? All the lace cut off her underclothes and two diamond brooches taken—and the girl departed in the middle of the night and never heard of since!'

Miss Marple paused, drew a long breath, and then went on.

'You'll be saying this has nothing to do with what went on at Keston Spa Hydro—but it has in a way. It explains why I felt no doubt in my mind the first moment I saw the Sanders together that he meant to do away with her.'

'Eh?' said Sir Henry, leaning forward.

Miss Marple turned a placid face to him.

'As I say, Sir Henry, I felt no doubt in my own mind. Mr Sanders was a big, good-looking, florid-faced man, very hearty in his manner and popular with all. And nobody could have been pleasanter to his wife than he was. But I knew! He meant to make away with her.'

'My dear Miss Marple—'

'Yes, I know. That's what my nephew, Raymond West, would say. He'd tell me I hadn't a shadow of proof. But I remember Walter Hones, who kept the Green Man. Walking home with his wife one night she fell into the river—and *he* collected the insurance money! And one or two other people that are walking about scot-free to this day—one indeed in our own class of life. Went to Switzerland for a summer holiday climbing with his wife. I warned her not to go—the poor dear didn't get angry with me as she might have done—she only laughed. It seemed to her funny that a queer old thing like me should say such things about her Harry. Well, well, there was an accident—and Harry is married to another woman now. But what could I *do*? I *knew*, but there was no proof.'

'Oh! Miss Marple,' cried Mrs Bantry. 'You don't really mean—'

'My dear, these things are very common—very common indeed. And gentlemen are especially tempted, being so much the stronger. So easy if a thing looks like an accident. As I say, I knew at once with the Sanders. It was on a tram. It was full inside and I had had to go on top. We all three got up to get off and Mr Sanders lost his balance and fell right against his wife, sending her headfirst down the stairs. Fortunately the conductor was a very strong young man and caught her.'

'But surely that must have been an accident.'

'Of course it was an accident—nothing could have looked more accidental! But Mr Sanders had been in the Merchant Service, so he told me, and a man who can keep his balance on a nasty tilting boat doesn't lose it on top of a tram if an old woman like me doesn't. Don't tell me!'

'At any rate we can take it that you made up your mind, Miss Marple,' said Sir Henry. 'Made it up then and there.'

The old lady nodded.

'I was sure enough, and another incident in crossing the street not long afterwards made me surer still. Now I ask you, what could I do, Sir Henry? Here was a nice contented happy little married woman shortly going to be murdered.'

'My dear lady, you take my breath away.'

'That's because, like most people nowadays, you won't face facts. You prefer to think such a thing couldn't be. But it was so, and I knew it. But one is so sadly handicapped! I couldn't, for instance, go to the police. And to warn the young woman would, I could see, be useless. She was devoted to the man. I just made it my business to find out as much as I could about them. One has a lot of opportunities doing one's needlework round the fire. Mrs Sanders (Gladys, her name was) was only too willing to talk. It seems they had not been married very long. Her husband had some property that was coming to him, but for the moment they were very badly off. In fact, they were living on her little income. One has heard that tale before. She bemoaned the fact that she could not touch the capital. It seems that somebody had had some sense somewhere! But the money was hers to will away—I found that out. And she and her husband had made wills in favour of each other directly after their marriage. Very touching. Of course, when Jack's affairs came right—That was the burden all day long, and in the meantime they were very hard up indeed—actually had a room on the top floor, all among the servants—and so dangerous in case of fire, though, as it happened, there was a fire escape just outside their window. I inquired carefully if there was a balcony—dangerous things, balconies. One push—you know!

'I made her promise not to go out on the balcony; I said I'd had a dream. That impressed her—one can do a lot with superstition sometimes. She was a fair girl, rather washed-out complexion, and an untidy roll of hair on her neck. Very credulous. She repeated what I had said to her husband, and I noticed him looking at me in a curious way once or twice. *He* wasn't credulous; and he knew I'd been on that tram.

'But I was very worried—terribly worried—because I couldn't see how to circumvent him. I could prevent anything happening at the Hydro, just by saying a few words to show him I suspected. But that only meant his putting off his plan till later. No, I began to believe that the only policy was a bold one—somehow or other to lay a trap for him. If I could induce him to attempt her life in a way of my own choosing—well, then he would be unmasked, and she would be forced to face the truth however much of a shock it was to her.'

'You take my breath away,' said Dr Lloyd. 'What conceivable plan could you adopt?'

'I'd have found one—never fear,' said Miss Marple. 'But the man was too clever for me. He didn't wait. He thought I might suspect, and so he struck before I could be sure. He knew I would suspect an accident. So he made it murder.'

A little gasp went round the circle. Miss Marple nodded and set her lips grimly together.

'I'm afraid I've put that rather abruptly. I must try and tell you exactly what occurred. I've always felt very bitterly about it—it seems to me that I ought, somehow, to have prevented it. But doubtless Providence knew best. I did what I could at all events.

'There was what I can only describe as a curiously eerie feeling in the air. There seemed to be something weighing on us all. A feeling of misfortune. To begin with, there was George, the hall porter. Had been there for years and knew everybody. Bronchitis and pneumonia, and passed away on the fourth day. Terribly sad. A real blow to everybody. And four days before Christmas too. And then one of the housemaids—such a nice girl—a septic finger, actually died in twenty-four hours.

'I was in the drawing-room with Miss Trollope and old Mrs Carpenter, and Mrs Carpenter was being positively ghoulish—relishing it all, you know.

'"Mark my words," she said. "*This isn't the end.* You know the saying? *Never two without three.* I've proved it true time and again. There'll be another death. Not a doubt of it. And we shan't have long to wait. *Never two without three.*"

'As she said the last words, nodding her head and clicking her knitting needles, I just chanced to look up and there was Mr Sanders standing in the doorway. Just for a minute he was off guard, and I saw the look in his face as plain as plain. I shall believe till my dying day that it was that ghoulish Mrs Carpenter's words that put the whole thing into his head. I saw his mind working.

'He came forward into the room smiling in his genial way.

'"Any Christmas shopping I can do for you ladies?" he asked. "I'm going down to Keston presently."

'He stayed a minute or two, laughing and talking, and then went out. As I tell you, I was troubled, and I said straight away:

'"Where's Mrs Sanders? Does anyone know?"

'Mrs Trollope said she'd gone out to some friends of hers, the Mortimers, to play bridge, and that eased my

27

mind for the moment. But I was still very worried and most uncertain as to what to do. About half an hour later I went up to my room. I met Dr Coles, my doctor, there, coming down the stairs as I was going up, and as I happened to want to consult him about my rheumatism, I took him into my room with me then and there. He mentioned to me then (in confidence, he said) about the death of the poor girl Mary. The manager didn't want the news to get about, he said, so would I keep it to myself. Of course I didn't tell him that we'd all been discussing nothing else for the last hour—ever since the poor girl breathed her last. These things are always known at once, and a man of his experience should know that well enough; but Dr Coles always was a simple unsuspicious fellow who believed what he wanted to believe and that's just what alarmed me a minute later. He said as he was leaving that Sanders had asked him to have a look at his wife. It seemed she'd been seedy of late—indigestion, etc.

'*Now that very self-same day Gladys Sanders had said to me that she'd got a wonderful digestion and was thankful for it.*

'You see? All my suspicions of that man came back a hundredfold. He was preparing the way—for what? Dr Coles left before I could make up my mind whether to speak to him or not—though really if I had spoken I shouldn't have known what to say. As I came out of my room, the man himself—Sanders—came down the stairs from the floor above. He was dressed to go out and he asked me again if he could do anything for me in the town. It was all I could do to be civil to the man! I went straight into the lounge and ordered tea. It was just on half past five, I remember.

'Now I'm very anxious to put clearly what happened next. I was still in the lounge at a quarter to seven when

Mr Sanders came in. There were two gentlemen with him and all three of them were inclined to be a little on the lively side. Mr Sanders left his two friends and came right over to where I was sitting with Miss Trollope. He explained that he wanted our advice about a Christmas present he was giving his wife. It was an evening bag.

'"And you see, ladies," he said. "I'm only a rough sailorman. What do I know about such things? I've had three sent to me on approval and I want an expert opinion on them."

'We said, of course, that we would be delighted to help him, and he asked if we'd mind coming upstairs, as his wife might come in any minute if he brought the things down. So we went up with him. I shall never forget what happened next—I can feel my little fingers tingling now.

'Mr Sanders opened the door of the bedroom and switched on the light. I don't know which of us saw it first . . .

'*Mrs Sanders was lying on the floor, face downwards—dead.*

'I got to her first. I knelt down and took her hand and felt for the pulse, but it was useless, the arm itself was cold and stiff. Just by her head was a stocking filled with sand—the weapon she had been struck down with. Miss Trollope, silly creature, was moaning and moaning by the door and holding her head. Sanders gave a great cry of "My wife, my wife," and rushed to her. I stopped him touching her. You see, I was sure at the moment he had done it, and there might have been something that he wanted to take away or hide.

'"Nothing must be touched," I said. "Pull yourself together, Mr Sanders. Miss Trollope, please go down and fetch the manager."

'I stayed there, kneeling by the body. I wasn't going to leave Sanders alone with it. And yet I was forced to admit that if the man was acting, he was acting marvellously. He looked dazed and bewildered and scared out of his wits.

'The manager was with us in no time. He made a quick inspection of the room then turned us all out and locked the door, the key of which he took. Then he went off and telephoned to the police. It seemed a positive age before they came (we learnt afterwards that the line was out of order). The manager had to send a messenger to the police station, and the Hydro is right out of the town, up on the edge of the moor; and Mrs Carpenter tried us all very severely. She was so pleased at her prophecy of "Never two without three" coming true so quickly. Sanders, I hear, wandered out into the grounds, clutching his head and groaning and displaying every sign of grief.

'However, the police came at last. They went upstairs with the manager and Mr Sanders. Later they sent down for me. I went up. The Inspector was there, sitting at a table writing. He was an intelligent-looking man and I liked him.

'"Miss Jane Marple?" he said.

'"Yes."

'"I understand, Madam, that you were present when the body of the deceased was found?"

'I said I was and I described exactly what had occurred. I think it was a relief to the poor man to find someone who could answer his questions coherently, having previously had to deal with Sanders and Emily Trollope, who, I gather, was completely demoralized—she would be, the silly creature! I remember my dear mother teaching me that a gentlewoman should always be able to control herself in public, however much she may give way in private.'

'An admirable maxim,' said Sir Henry gravely.

'When I had finished the Inspector said:

'"Thank you, Madam. Now I'm afraid I must ask you just to look at the body once more. Is that exactly the position in which it was lying when you entered the room? It hasn't been moved in any way?"

'I explained that I had prevented Mr Sanders from doing so, and the Inspector nodded approval.

'"The gentleman seems terribly upset," he remarked.

'"He seems so—yes," I replied.

'I don't think I put any special emphasis on the "seems", but the Inspector looked at me rather keenly.

'"So we can take it that the body is exactly as it was when found?" he said.

'"Except for the hat, yes," I replied.

'The Inspector looked up sharply.

'"What do you mean—the hat?"

'I explained that the hat had been on poor Gladys's head, whereas now it was lying beside her. I thought, of course, that the police had done this. The Inspector, however, denied it emphatically. Nothing had, as yet, been moved or touched. He stood looking down at that poor prone figure with a puzzled frown. Gladys was dressed in her outdoor clothes—a big dark-red tweed coat with a grey fur collar. The hat, a cheap affair of red felt, lay just by her head.

'The Inspector stood for some minutes in silence, frowning to himself. Then an idea struck him.

'"Can you, by any chance, remember, Madam, whether there were earrings in the ears, or whether the deceased habitually wore earrings?"

'Now fortunately I am in the habit of observing

31

closely. I remembered that there had been a glint of pearls just below the hat brim, though I had paid no particular notice to it at the time. I was able to answer his first question in the affirmative.

'"Then that settles it. The lady's jewel case was rifled—not that she had anything much of value, I understand—and the rings were taken from her fingers. The murderer must have forgotten the earrings, and come back for them after the murder was discovered. A cool customer! Or perhaps—" He stared round the room and said slowly, "He may have been concealed here in this room—all the time."

'But I negatived that idea. I myself, I explained, had looked under the bed. And the manager had opened the doors of the wardrobe. There was nowhere else where a man could hide. It is true the hat cupboard was locked in the middle of the wardrobe, but as that was only a shallow affair with shelves, no one could have been concealed there.

'The Inspector nodded his head slowly whilst I explained all this.

'"I'll take your word for it, Madam," he said. "In that case, as I said before, he must have come back. A very cool customer."

'"But the manager locked the door and took the key!"

'"That's nothing. The balcony and the fire escape— that's the way the thief came. Why, as likely as not, you actually disturbed him at work. He slips out of the window, and when you've all gone, back he comes and goes on with his business."

'"You are sure," I said, "that there *was* a thief?"

'He said drily:

'"Well, it looks like it, doesn't it?"

'But something in his tone satisfied me. I felt that he

wouldn't take Mr Sanders in the role of the bereaved widower too seriously.

'You see, I admit it frankly. I was absolutely under the opinion of what I believe our neighbours, the French, call the *idée fixe*. I knew that that man, Sanders, intended his wife to die. What I didn't allow for was that strange and fantastic thing, coincidence. My views about Mr Sanders were—I was sure of it—absolutely right and *true*. The man was a scoundrel. But although his hypocritical assumptions of grief didn't deceive me for a minute, I do remember feeling at the time that his *surprise* and *bewilderment* were marvellously well done. They seemed absolutely *natural*—if you know what I mean. I must admit that after my conversation with the Inspector, a curious feeling of doubt crept over me. Because if Sanders had done this dreadful thing, I couldn't imagine any conceivable reason why he should creep back by means of the fire escape and take the earrings from his wife's ears. It wouldn't have been a *sensible* thing to do, and Sanders was such a very sensible man—that's just why I always felt he was so dangerous.'

Miss Marple looked round at her audience.

'You see, perhaps, what I am coming to? It is, so often, the unexpected that happens in this world. I was so *sure*, and that, I think, was what blinded me. The result came as a shock to me. *For it was proved, beyond any possible doubt, that Mr Sanders could not possibly have committed the crime . . .*'

A surprised gasp came from Mrs Bantry. Miss Marple turned to her.

'I know, my dear, that isn't what you expected when I began this story. It wasn't what I expected either. But facts are facts, and if one is proved to be wrong, one must just be humble about it and start again. That Mr

Sanders was a murderer at heart I knew—and nothing ever occurred to upset that firm conviction of mine.

'And now, I expect, you would like to hear the actual facts themselves. Mrs Sanders, as you know, spent the afternoon playing bridge with some friends, the Mortimers. She left them at about a quarter past six. From her friends' house to the Hydro was about a quarter of an hour's walk—less if one hurried. She must have come in then about six-thirty. No one saw her come in, so she must have entered by the side door and hurried straight up to her room. There she changed (the fawn coat and skirt she wore to the bridge party were hanging up in the cupboard) and was evidently preparing to go out again, when the blow fell. Quite possibly, they say, she never even knew who struck her. The sandbag, I understand, is a very efficient weapon. That looks as though the attackers were concealed in the room, possibly in one of the big wardrobe cupboards—the one she didn't open.

'Now as to the movements of Mr Sanders. He went out, as I have said, at about five-thirty—or a little after. He did some shopping at a couple of shops and at about six o'clock he entered the Grand Spa Hotel where he encountered two friends—the same with whom he returned to the Hydro later. They played billiards and, I gather, had a good many whiskies and sodas together. These two men (Hitchcock and Spender, their names were) were actually with him the whole time from six o'clock onwards. They walked back to the Hydro with him and he only left them to come across to me and Miss Trollope. That, as I told you, was about a quarter to seven—at which time his wife must have been already dead.

'I must tell you that I talked myself to these two friends of his. I did not like them. They were neither pleasant nor gentlemanly men, but I was quite certain of one thing, that they were speaking the absolute truth when they said that Sanders had been the whole time in their company.

'There was just one other little point that came up. It seems that while bridge was going on Mrs Sanders was called to the telephone. A Mr Littleworth wanted to speak to her. She seemed both excited and pleased about something—and incidentally made one or two bad mistakes. She left rather earlier than they had expected her to do.

'Mr Sanders was asked whether he knew the name of Littleworth as being one of his wife's friends, but he declared he had never heard of anyone of that name. And to me that seems borne out by his wife's attitude— she too, did not seem to know the name of Littleworth. Nevertheless she came back from the telephone smiling and blushing, so it looks as though whoever it was did not give his real name, and that in itself has a suspicious aspect, does it not?

'Anyway, that is the problem that was left. The burglar story, which seems unlikely—or the alternative theory that Mrs Sanders was preparing to go out and meet somebody. Did that somebody come to her room by means of the fire escape? Was there a quarrel? Or did he treacherously attack her?'

Miss Marple stopped.

'Well?' said Sir Henry. 'What is the answer?'

'I wondered if any of you could guess.'

'I'm never good at guessing,' said Mrs Bantry. 'It seems a pity that Sanders had such a wonderful alibi; but if it satisfied you it must have been all right.'

Jane Helier moved her beautiful head and asked a question.

'Why,' she said, 'was the hat cupboard locked?'

'How very clever of you, my dear,' said Miss Marple, beaming. 'That's just what I wondered myself. Though the explanation was quite simple. In it were a pair of embroidered slippers and some pocket handkerchiefs that the poor girl was embroidering for her husband for Christmas. That's why she locked the cupboard. The key was found in her handbag.'

'Oh!' said Jane. 'Then it isn't very interesting after all.'

'Oh! but it is,' said Miss Marple. 'It's just the one really interesting thing—the thing that made all the murderer's plans go wrong.'

Everyone stared at the old lady.

'I didn't see it myself for two days,' said Miss Marple. 'I puzzled and puzzled—and then suddenly there it was, all clear. I went to the Inspector and asked him to try something and he did.'

'What did you ask him to try?'

'*I asked him to fit that hat on the poor girl's head*—and of course he couldn't. It wouldn't go on. *It wasn't her hat, you see.*'

Mrs Bantry stared.

'But it was on her head to begin with?'

'Not on *her* head—'

Miss Marple stopped a moment to let her words sink in, and then went on.

'We took it for granted that it was poor Gladys's body there; but we never looked at the face. She was face downwards, remember, and the hat hid everything.'

'But she *was* killed?'

'Yes, later. At the moment that we were telephoning to the police, Gladys Sanders was alive and well.'

'You mean it was someone pretending to be her? But surely when you touched her—'

'It was a dead body, right enough,' said Miss Marple gravely.

'But, dash it all,' said Colonel Bantry, 'you can't get hold of dead bodies right and left. What did they do with the—the first corpse afterwards?'

'He put it back,' said Miss Marple. 'It was a wicked idea—but a very clever one. It was our talk in the drawing-room that put it into his head. The body of poor Mary, the housemaid—why not use it? Remember, the Sanders' room was up amongst the servants' quarters. Mary's room was two doors off. The undertakers wouldn't come till after dark—he counted on that. He carried the body along the balcony (it was dark at five), dressed it in one of his wife's dresses and her big red coat. And then he found the hat cupboard locked! There was only one thing to be done, he fetched one of the poor girl's own hats. No one would notice. He put the sandbag down beside her. Then he went off to establish his alibi.

'He telephoned to his wife—calling himself Mr Littleworth. I don't know what he said to her—she was a credulous girl, as I said just now. But he got her to leave the bridge party early and not to go back to the Hydro, and arranged with her to meet him in the grounds of the Hydro near the fire escape at seven o'clock. He probably told her he had some surprise for her.

'He returns to the Hydro with his friends and arranges that Miss Trollope and I shall discover the crime with him. He even pretends to turn the body over—and I stop him! Then the police are sent for, and he staggers out into the grounds.

'Nobody asked him for an alibi *after* the crime. He meets his wife, takes her up the fire escape, they enter their room. Perhaps he has already told her some story

37

about the body. She stoops over it, and he picks up his sandbag and strikes ... Oh, dear! It makes me sick to think of, even now! Then quickly he strips off her coat and skirt, hangs them up, and dresses her in the clothes from the other body.

'*But the hat won't go on.* Mary's head is shingled— Gladys Sanders, as I say, had a great bun of hair. He is forced to leave it beside the body and hope no one will notice. Then he carries poor Mary's body back to her own room and arranges it decorously once more.'

'It seems incredible,' said Dr Lloyd. 'The risks he took. The police might have arrived too soon.'

'You remember the line was out of order,' said Miss Marple. 'That was a piece of *his* work. He couldn't afford to have the police on the spot too soon. When they did come, they spent some time in the manager's office before going up to the bedroom. That was the weakest point—the chance that someone might notice the difference between a body that had been dead two hours and one that had been dead just over half an hour; but he counted on the fact that the people who first discovered the crime would have no expert knowledge.'

Dr Lloyd nodded.

'The crime would be supposed to have been committed about a quarter to seven or thereabouts, I suppose,' he said. 'It was actually committed at seven or a few minutes after. When the police surgeon examined the body it would be about half past seven at the earliest. He couldn't possibly tell.'

'I am the person who should have known,' said Miss Marple. 'I felt the poor girl's hand and it was icy cold. Yet a short time later the Inspector spoke as though the murder must have been committed just before we arrived—and I saw nothing!'

'I think you saw a good deal, Miss Marple,' said Sir Henry. 'The case was before my time. I don't even remember hearing of it. What happened?'

'Sanders was hanged,' said Miss Marple crisply. 'And a good job too. I have never regretted my part in bringing that man to justice. I've no patience with modern humanitarian scruples about capital punishment.'

Her stern face softened.

'But I have often reproached myself bitterly with failing to save the life of that poor girl. But who would have listened to an old woman jumping to conclusions? Well, well—who knows? Perhaps it was better for her to die while life was still happy than it would have been for her to live on, unhappy and disillusioned, in a world that would have seemed suddenly horrible. She loved that scoundrel and trusted him. She never found him out.'

'Well, then,' said Jane Helier, 'she was all right. Quite all right. I wish—' she stopped.

Miss Marple looked at the famous, the beautiful, the successful Jane Helier and nodded her head gently.

'I see, my dear,' she said very gently. 'I see.'

The Coming of Mr Quin

It was New Year's Eve.

The elder members of the house party at Royston were assembled in the big hall.

Mr Satterthwaite was glad that the young people had gone to bed. He was not fond of young people in herds. He thought them uninteresting and crude. They lacked subtlety and as life went on he had become increasingly fond of subtleties.

Mr Satterthwaite was sixty-two—a little bent, dried-up man with a peering face oddly elf like, and an intense and inordinate interest in other people's lives. All his life, so to speak, he had sat in the front row of the stalls watching various dramas of human nature unfold before him. His role had always been that of the onlooker. Only now, with old age holding him in its clutch, he found himself increasingly critical of the drama submitted to him. He demanded now something a little out of the common.

There was no doubt that he had a flair for these things. He knew instinctively when the elements of drama were at hand. Like a war horse, he sniffed the scent. Since his arrival at Royston this afternoon, that strange inner sense of his had stirred and bid him be ready. Something interesting was happening or going to happen.

The house party was not a large one. There was Tom Evesham, their genial good-humoured host, and his serious political wife who had been before her marriage Lady Laura Keene. There was Sir Richard Conway, soldier, traveller and sportsman, there were six or seven young people whose names Mr Satterthwaite had not grasped and there were the Portals.

It was the Portals who interested Mr Satterthwaite.

He had never met Alex Portal before, but he knew all about him. Had known his father and his grandfather. Alex Portal ran pretty true to type. He was a man of close on forty, fair-haired, and blue-eyed like all the Portals, fond of sport, good at games, devoid of imagination. Nothing unusual about Alex Portal. The usual good sound English stock.

But his wife was different. She was, Mr Satterthwaite knew, an Australian. Portal had been out in Australia two years ago, had met her out there and had married her and brought her home. She had never been to England previous to her marriage. All the same, she wasn't at all like any other Australian woman Mr Satterthwaite had met.

He observed her now, covertly. Interesting woman—very. So still, and yet so—alive. Alive! That was just it! Not exactly beautiful—no, you wouldn't call her beautiful, but there was a kind of calamitous magic about her that you couldn't miss—that no man could miss. The masculine side of Mr Satterthwaite spoke there, but the feminine side (for Mr Satterthwaite had a large share of femininity) was equally interested in another question. *Why did Mrs Portal dye her hair?*

No other man would probably have known that she dyed her hair, but Mr Satterthwaite knew. He knew all those things. And it puzzled him. Many dark women

41

dye their hair blonde; he had never before come across a fair woman who dyed her hair black.

Everything about her intrigued him. In a queer intuitive way, he felt certain that she was either very happy or very unhappy—but he didn't know which, and it annoyed him not to know. Furthermore there was the curious effect she had upon her husband.

'He adores her,' said Mr Satterthwaite to himself, 'but sometimes he's—yes, afraid of her! That's very interesting. That's uncommonly interesting.'

Portal drank too much. That was certain. And he had a curious way of watching his wife when she wasn't looking.

'Nerves,' said Mr Satterthwaite. 'The fellow's all nerves. She knows it too, but she won't do anything about it.'

He felt very curious about the pair of them. Something was going on that he couldn't fathom.

He was roused from his meditations on the subject by the solemn chiming of the big clock in the corner.

'Twelve o'clock,' said Evesham. 'New Year's Day. Happy New Year—everybody. As a matter of fact that clock's five minutes fast ... I don't know why the children wouldn't wait up and see the New Year in?'

'I don't suppose for a minute they've really gone to bed,' said his wife placidly. 'They're probably putting hairbrushes or something in our beds. That sort of thing does so amuse them. I can't think why. We should never have been allowed to do such a thing in my young days.'

'*Autre temps, autres moeurs,*' said Conway, smiling.

He was a tall soldierly-looking man. Both he and Evesham were much of the same type—honest upright kindly men with no great pretensions to brains.

'In my young days we all joined hands in a circle and

42

sang "Auld Lang Syne",' continued Lady Laura. '"Should auld acquaintance be forgot"—so touching, I always think the words are.'

Evesham moved uneasily.

'Oh! drop it, Laura,' he muttered. '*Not here.*'

He strode across the wide hall where they were sitting, and switched on an extra light.

'Very stupid of me,' said Lady Laura, *sotto voce*. 'Reminds him of poor Mr Capel, of course. My dear, is the fire too hot for you?'

Eleanor Portal made a brusque movement.

'Thank you. I'll move my chair back a little.'

What a lovely voice she had—one of those low murmuring echoing voices that stay in your memory, thought Mr Satterthwaite. Her face was in shadow now. What a pity.

From her place in the shadow she spoke again.

'Mr—Capel?'

'Yes. The man who originally owned this house. He shot himself you know—oh! very well, Tom dear, I won't speak of it unless you like. It was a great shock for Tom, of course, because he was here when it happened. So were you, weren't you, Sir Richard?'

'Yes, Lady Laura.'

An old grandfather clock in the corner groaned, wheezed, snorted asthmatically, and then struck twelve.

'Happy New Year, Tom,' grunted Evesham perfunctorily.

Lady Laura wound up her knitting with some deliberation.

'Well, we've seen the New Year in,' she observed, and added, looking towards Mrs Portal, 'What do you think, my dear?'

Eleanor Portal rose quickly to her feet.

'Bed, by all means,' she said lightly.

'She's very pale,' thought Mr Satterthwaite, as he too rose, and began busying himself with candlesticks. 'She's not usually as pale as that.'

He lighted her candle and handed it to her with a funny little old-fashioned bow. She took it from him with a word of acknowledgment and went slowly up the stairs.

Suddenly a very odd impulse swept over Mr Satterthwaite. He wanted to go after her—to reassure her—he had the strangest feeling that she was in danger of some kind. The impulse died down, and he felt ashamed. *He* was getting nervy too.

She hadn't looked at her husband as she went up the stairs, but now she turned her head over her shoulder and gave him a long searching glance which had a queer intensity in it. It affected Mr Satterthwaite very oddly.

He found himself saying goodnight to his hostess in quite a flustered manner.

'I'm sure I hope it *will* be a happy New Year,' Lady Laura was saying. 'But the political situation seems to me to be fraught with grave uncertainty.'

'I'm sure it is,' said Mr Satterthwaite earnestly. 'I'm sure it is.'

'I only hope,' continued Lady Laura, without the least change of manner, 'that it will be a dark man who first crosses the threshold. You know that superstition, I suppose, Mr Satterthwaite? No? You surprise me. To bring luck to the house it must be a dark man who first steps over the door step on New Year's Day. Dear me, I hope I shan't find anything *very* unpleasant in my bed. I never trust the children. They have such very high spirits.'

44

Shaking her head in sad foreboding, Lady Laura moved majestically up the staircase.

With the departure of the women, chairs were pulled in closer round the blazing logs on the big open hearth.

'Say when,' said Evesham, hospitably, as he held up the whisky decanter.

When everybody had said when, the talk reverted to the subject which had been tabooed before.

'You knew Derek Capel, didn't you, Satterthwaite?' asked Conway.

'Slightly—yes.'

'And you, Portal?'

'No, I never met him.'

So fiercely and defensively did he say it, that Mr Satterthwaite looked up in surprise.

'I always hate it when Laura brings up the subject,' said Evesham slowly. 'After the tragedy, you know, this place was sold to a big manufacturer fellow. He cleared out after a year—didn't suit him or something. A lot of tommy rot was talked about the place being haunted of course, and it gave the house a bad name. Then, when Laura got me to stand for West Kidleby, of course it meant living up in these parts, and it wasn't so easy to find a suitable house. Royston was going cheap, and— well, in the end I bought it. Ghosts are all tommy rot, but all the same one doesn't exactly care to be reminded that you're living in a house where one of your own friends shot himself. Poor old Derek—we shall never know why he did it.'

'He won't be the first or the last fellow who's shot himself without being able to give a reason,' said Alex Portal heavily.

He rose and poured himself out another drink, splashing the whisky in with a liberal hand.

'There's something very wrong with him,' said Mr Satterthwaite, to himself. 'Very wrong indeed. I wish I knew what it was all about.'

'Gad!' said Conway. 'Listen to the wind. It's a wild night.'

'A good night for ghosts to walk,' said Portal with a reckless laugh. 'All the devils in Hell are abroad tonight.'

'According to Lady Laura, even the blackest of them would bring us luck,' observed Conway, with a laugh. 'Hark to that!'

The wind rose in another terrific wail, and as it died away there came three loud knocks on the big nailed doorway.

Everyone started.

'Who on earth can that be at this time of night?' cried Evesham.

They stared at each other.

'I will open it,' said Evesham. 'The servants have gone to bed.'

He strode across to the door, fumbled a little over the heavy bars, and finally flung it open. An icy blast of wind came sweeping into the hall.

Framed in the doorway stood a man's figure, tall and slender. To Mr Satterthwaite, watching, he appeared by some curious effect of the stained glass above the door, to be dressed in every colour of the rainbow. Then, as he stepped forward, he showed himself to be a thin dark man dressed in motoring clothes.

'I must really apologize for this intrusion,' said the stranger, in a pleasant level voice. 'But my car broke down. Nothing much, my chauffeur is putting it to rights, but it will take half an hour or so, and it is so confoundedly cold outside—'

He broke off, and Evesham took up the thread quickly.

'I should think it was. Come in and have a drink. We can't give you any assistance about the car, can we?'

'No, thanks. My man knows what to do. By the way, my name is Quin—Harley Quin.'

'Sit down, Mr Quin,' said Evesham. 'Sir Richard Conway, Mr Satterthwaite. My name is Evesham.'

Mr Quin acknowledged the introductions, and dropped into the chair that Evesham had hospitably pulled forward. As he sat, some effect of the firelight threw a bar of shadow across his face which gave almost the impression of a mask.

Evesham threw a couple more logs on the fire.

'A drink?'

'Thanks.'

Evesham brought it to him and asked as he did so:

'So you know this part of the world well, Mr Quin?'

'I passed through it some years ago.'

'Really?'

'Yes. This house belonged then to a man called Capel.'

'Ah! yes,' said Evesham. 'Poor Derek Capel. You knew him?'

'Yes, I knew him.'

Evesham's manner underwent a faint change, almost imperceptible to one who had not studied the English character. Before, it had contained a subtle reserve, now this was laid aside. Mr Quin had known Derek Capel. He was the friend of a friend, and, as such, was vouched for and fully accredited.

'Astounding affair, that,' he said confidentially. 'We were just talking about it. I can tell you, it went against the grain, buying this place. If there had been anything else suitable, but there wasn't you see. I was in the house the night he shot himself—so was Conway, and upon my word, I've always expected his ghost to walk.'

'A very inexplicable business,' said Mr Quin, slowly and deliberately, and he paused with the air of an actor who has just spoken an important cue.

'You may well say inexplicable,' burst in Conway. 'The thing's a black mystery—always will be.'

'I wonder,' said Mr Quin, non-committally. 'Yes, Sir Richard, you were saying?'

'Astounding—that's what it was. Here's a man in the prime of life, gay, light-hearted, without a care in the world. Five or six old pals staying with him. Top of his spirits at dinner, full of plans for the future. And from the dinner table he goes straight upstairs to his room, takes a revolver from a drawer and shoots himself. Why? Nobody ever knew. Nobody ever will know.'

'Isn't that rather a sweeping statement, Sir Richard?' asked Mr Quin, smiling.

Conway stared at him.

'What d'you mean? I don't understand.'

'A problem is not necessarily unsolvable because it has remained unsolved.'

'Oh! Come, man, if nothing came out at the time, it's not likely to come out now—ten years afterwards?'

Mr Quin shook his head gently.

'I disagree with you. The evidence of history is against you. The contemporary historian never writes such a true history as the historian of a later generation. It is a question of getting the true perspective, of seeing things in proportion. If you like to call it so, it is, like everything else, a question of relativity.'

Alex Portal leant forward, his face twitching painfully.

'You are right, Mr Quin,' he cried, 'you are right. Time does not dispose of a question—it only presents it anew in a different guise.'

Evesham was smiling tolerantly.

'Then you mean to say, Mr Quin, that if we were to hold, let us say, a Court of Inquiry tonight, into the circumstances of Derek Capel's death, we are as likely to arrive at the truth as we should have been at the time?'

'*More* likely, Mr Evesham. The personal equation has largely dropped out, and you will remember facts as facts without seeking to put your own interpretation upon them.'

Evesham frowned doubtfully.

'One must have a starting point, of course,' said Mr Quin in his quiet level voice. 'A starting point is usually a theory. One of you must have a theory, I am sure. How about you, Sir Richard?'

Conway frowned thoughtfully.

'Well, of course,' he said apologetically, 'we thought—naturally we all thought—that there must be a woman in it somewhere. It's usually either that or money, isn't it? And it certainly wasn't money. No trouble of that description. So—what else could it have been?'

Mr Satterthwaite started. He had leant forward to contribute a small remark of his own and in the act of doing so, he had caught sight of a woman's figure crouched against the balustrade of the gallery above. She was huddled down against it, invisible from everywhere but where he himself sat, and she was evidently listening with strained attention to what was going on below. So immovable was she that he hardly believed the evidence of his own eyes.

But he recognized the pattern of the dress easily enough—an old-world brocade. It was Eleanor Portal.

And suddenly all the events of the night seemed to fall into pattern—Mr Quin's arrival, no fortuitous chance, but the appearance of an actor when his cue was given. There was a drama being played in the big hall at Royston tonight—a drama none the less real in that one of the actors was dead. Oh! yes, Derek Capel had a part in the play. Mr Satterthwaite was sure of that.

And, again suddenly, a new illumination came to him. This was Mr Quin's doing. It was he who was staging the play—was giving the actors their cues. He was at the heart of the mystery pulling the strings, making the puppets work. He knew everything, even to the presence of the woman crouched against the woodwork upstairs. Yes, he knew.

Sitting well back in his chair, secure in his role of audience, Mr Satterthwaite watched the drama unfold before his eyes. Quietly and naturally, Mr Quin was pulling the strings, setting his puppets in motion.

'A woman—yes,' he murmured thoughtfully. 'There was no mention of any woman at dinner?'

'Why, of course,' cried Evesham. 'He announced his engagement. That's just what made it seem so absolutely mad. Very bucked about it he was. Said it wasn't to be announced just yet—but gave us the hint that he was in the running for the Benedick stakes.'

'Of course we all guessed who the lady was,' said Conway. 'Marjorie Dilke. Nice girl.'

It seemed to be Mr Quin's turn to speak, but he did not do so, and something about his silence seemed oddly provocative. It was as though he challenged the last statement. It had the effect of putting Conway in a defensive position.

'Who else could it have been? Eh, Evesham?'

'I don't know,' said Tom Evesham slowly. 'What did he say exactly now? Something about being in the running for the Benedick stakes—that he couldn't tell us the lady's name till he had her permission—it wasn't

50

to be announced yet. He said, I remember, that he was a damned lucky fellow. That he wanted his two old friends to know that by that time next year he'd be a happy married man. Of course, we assumed it was Marjorie. They were great friends and he'd been about with her a lot.'

'The only thing—' began Conway and stopped.

'What were you going to say, Dick?'

'Well, I mean, it was odd in a way, if it were Marjorie, that the engagement shouldn't be announced at once. I mean, why the secrecy? Sounds more as though it were a married woman—you know, someone whose husband had just died, or who was divorcing him.'

'That's true,' said Evesham. 'If that were the case, of course, the engagement couldn't be announced at once. And you know, thinking back about it, I don't believe he had been seeing much of Marjorie. All that was the year before. I remember thinking things seemed to have cooled off between them.'

'Curious,' said Mr Quin.

'Yes—looked almost as though someone had come between them.'

'Another woman,' said Conway thoughtfully.

'By jove,' said Evesham. 'You know, there was something almost indecently hilarious about old Derek that night. He looked almost drunk with happiness. And yet—I can't quite explain what I mean—but he looked oddly defiant too.'

'Like a man defying Fate,' said Alex Portal heavily.

Was it of Derek Capel he was speaking—or was it of himself? Mr Satterthwaite, looking at him, inclined to the latter view. Yes, that was what Alex Portal represented—a man defying Fate.

His imagination, muddled by drink, responded

suddenly to that note in the story which recalled his own secret preoccupation.

Mr Satterthwaite looked up. She was still there. Watching, listening—still motionless, frozen—like a dead woman.

'Perfectly true,' said Conway. 'Capel *was* excited—curiously so. I'd describe him as a man who had staked heavily and won against well nigh overwhelming odds.'

'Getting up courage, perhaps, for what he's made up his mind to do?' suggested Portal.

And as though moved by an association of ideas, he got up and helped himself to another drink.

'Not a bit of it,' said Evesham sharply. 'I'd almost swear nothing of that kind was in his mind. Conway's right. A successful gambler who has brought off a long shot and can hardly believe in his own good fortune. That was the attitude.'

Conway gave a gesture of discouragement.

'And yet,' he said. 'Ten minutes later—'

They sat in silence. Evesham brought his hand down with a bang on the table.

'Something must have happened in that ten minutes,' he cried. 'It must! But what? Let's go over it carefully. We were all talking. In the middle of it Capel got up suddenly and left the room—'

'Why?' said Mr Quin.

The interruption seemed to disconcert Evesham.

'I beg your pardon?'

'I only said: Why?' said Mr Quin.

Evesham frowned in an effort of memory.

'It didn't seem vital—at the time—Oh! of course—the Post. Don't you remember that jangling bell, and how excited we were. We'd been snowed up for three days, remember. Biggest snowstorm for years and years.

52

All the roads were impassable. No newspapers, no letters. Capel went out to see if something had come through at last, and got a great pile of things. Newspapers and letters. He opened the paper to see if there was any news, and then went upstairs with his letters. Three minutes afterwards, we heard a shot ... Inexplicable—absolutely inexplicable.'

'That's not inexplicable,' said Portal. 'Of course the fellow got some unexpected news in a letter. Obvious, I should have said.'

'Oh! Don't think we missed anything so obvious as that. It was one of the Coroner's first questions. *But Capel never opened one of his letters.* The whole pile lay unopened on his dressing-table.'

Portal looked crestfallen.

'You're sure he didn't open just one of them? He might have destroyed it after reading it?'

'No, I'm quite positive. Of course, that would have been the natural solution. No, every one of the letters was unopened. Nothing burnt—nothing torn up— There was no fire in the room.'

Portal shook his head.

'Extraordinary.'

'It was a ghastly business altogether,' said Evesham in a low voice. 'Conway and I went up when we heard the shot, and found him—It gave me a shock, I can tell you.'

'Nothing to be done but telephone for the police, I suppose?' said Mr Quin.

'Royston wasn't on the telephone then. I had it put in when I bought the place. No, luckily enough, the local constable happened to be in the kitchen at the time. One of the dogs—you remember poor old Rover, Conway?—had strayed the day before. A passing carter

53

had found it half buried in a snowdrift and had taken it to the police station. They recognized it as Capel's, and a dog he was particularly fond of, and the constable came up with it. He'd just arrived a minute before the shot was fired. It saved us some trouble.'

'Gad, that was a snowstorm,' said Conway reminiscently. 'About this time of year, wasn't it? Early January.'

'February, I think. Let me see, we went abroad soon afterwards.'

'I'm pretty sure it was January. My hunter Ned—you remember Ned?—lamed himself the end of January. That was just after this business.'

'It must have been quite the end of January then. Funny how difficult it is to recall dates after a lapse of years.'

'One of the most difficult things in the world,' said Mr Quin, conversationally. 'Unless you can find a landmark in some big public event—an assassination of a crowned head, or a big murder trial.'

'Why, of course,' cried Conway, 'it was just before the Appleton case.'

'Just after, wasn't it?'

'No, no, don't you remember—Capel knew the Appletons—he'd stayed with the old man the previous Spring—just a week before he died. He was talking of him one night—what an old curmudgeon he was, and how awful it must have been for a young and beautiful woman like Mrs Appleton to be tied to him. There was no suspicion then that she had done away with him.'

'By jove, you're right. I remember reading the paragraph in the paper saying an exhumation order had been granted. It would have been that same day—I remember only seeing it with half my mind, you know, the other half wondering about poor old Derek lying dead upstairs.'

'A common, but very curious phenomenon, that,' observed Mr Quin. 'In moments of great stress, the mind focuses itself upon some quite unimportant matter which is remembered long afterwards with the utmost fidelity, driven in, as it were, by the mental stress of the moment. It may be some quite irrelevant detail, like the pattern of a wallpaper, but it will never be forgotten.'

'Rather extraordinary, your saying that, Mr Quin,' said Conway. 'Just as you were speaking, I suddenly felt myself back in Derek Capel's room—with Derek lying dead on the floor—I saw as plainly as possible the big tree outside the window, and the shadow it threw upon the snow outside. Yes, the moonlight, the snow, and the shadow of the tree—I can see them again this minute. By Gad, I believe I could draw them, and yet I never realized I was looking at them at the time.'

'His room was the big one over the porch, was it not?' asked Mr Quin.

'Yes, and the tree was the big beech, just at the angle of the drive.'

Mr Quin nodded, as though satisfied. Mr Satterthwaite was curiously thrilled. He was convinced that every word, every inflection of Mr Quin's voice, was pregnant with purpose. He was driving at something— exactly what Mr Satterthwaite did not know, but he was quite convinced as to whose was the master hand.

There was a momentary pause, and then Evesham reverted to the preceding topic.

'That Appleton case, I remember it very well now. What a sensation it made. She got off, didn't she? Pretty woman, very fair—remarkably fair.'

Almost against his will, Mr Satterthwaite's eyes sought the kneeling figure up above. Was it his fancy, or did he see it shrink a little as though at a blow. Did he see a hand slide upwards to the table cloth—and then pause.

There was a crash of falling glass. Alex Portal, helping himself to whisky, had let the decanter slip.

'I say—sir, damn' sorry. Can't think what came over me.'

Evesham cut short his apologies.

'Quite all right. Quite all right, my dear fellow. Curious—That smash reminded me. That's what she did, didn't she? Mrs Appleton? Smashed the port decanter?'

'Yes. Old Appleton had his glass of port—only one— each night. The day after his death, one of the servants saw her take the decanter out and smash it deliberately. That set them talking, of course. They all knew she had been perfectly wretched with him. Rumour grew and grew, and in the end, months later, some of his relatives applied for an exhumation order. And sure enough, the old fellow had been poisoned. Arsenic, wasn't it?'

'No—strychnine, I think. It doesn't much matter. Well, of course, there it was. Only one person was likely to have done it. Mrs Appleton stood her trial. She was acquitted more through lack of evidence against her than from any overwhelming proof of innocence. In other words, she was lucky. Yes, I don't suppose there's much doubt she did it right enough. What happened to her afterwards?'

'Went out to Canada, I believe. Or was it Australia? She had an uncle or something of the sort out there who offered her a home. Best thing she could do under the circumstances.'

Mr Satterthwaite was fascinated by Alex Portal's right hand as it clasped his glass. How tightly he was gripping it.

56

'You'll smash that in a minute or two, if you're not careful,' thought Mr Satterthwaite. 'Dear me, how interesting all this is.'

Evesham rose and helped himself to a drink.

'Well, we're not much nearer to knowing why poor Derek Capel shot himself,' he remarked. 'The Court of Inquiry hasn't been a great success, has it, Mr Quin?'

Mr Quin laughed . . .

It was a strange laugh, mocking—yet sad. It made everyone jump.

'I beg your pardon,' he said. 'You are still living in the past, Mr Evesham. You are still hampered by your preconceived notion. But I—the man from outside, the stranger passing by, see only—facts!'

'Facts?'

'Yes—facts.'

'What do you mean?' said Evesham.

'I see a clear sequence of facts, outlined by yourselves but of which you have not seen the significance. Let us go back ten years and look at what we see— untrammelled by ideas or sentiment.'

Mr Quin had risen. He looked very tall. The fire leaped fitfully behind him. He spoke in a low compelling voice.

'You are at dinner. Derek Capel announces his engagement. You think then it was to Marjorie Dilke. You are not so sure now. He has the restlessly excited manner of a man who has successfully defied Fate— who, in your own words, has pulled off a big coup against overwhelming odds. Then comes the clanging of the bell. He goes out to get the long overdue mail. He doesn't open his letters, but you mention yourselves that *he opened the paper to glance at the news.* It is ten years ago—so we cannot know what the news was that

57

day—a far-off earthquake, a near at hand political crisis? The only thing we do know about the contents of that paper is that it contained one small paragraph—*a paragraph stating that the Home Office had given permission to exhume* the body of Mr Appleton three days ago.'

'What?'

Mr Quin went on.

'Derek Capel goes up to his room, and there he sees something out of the window. Sir Richard Conway has told us that the curtain was not drawn across it and further that it gave on to the drive. What did he see? What could he have seen that forced him to take his life?'

'What do you mean? What did he see?'

'I think,' said Mr Quin, 'that he saw a policeman. A policeman who had come about a dog—But Derek Capel didn't know that—he just saw—a policeman.'

There was a long silence—as though it took some time to drive the inference home.

'My God!' whispered Evesham at last. 'You can't mean that? Appleton? But he wasn't there at the time Appleton died. The old man was alone with his wife—'

'But he may have been there a week earlier. Strychnine is not very soluble unless it is in the form of hydrochloride. The greater part of it, put into the port, would be taken in the last glass, perhaps a week after he left.'

Portal sprung forward. His voice was hoarse, his eyes bloodshot.

'Why did she break the decanter?' he cried. 'Why did she break the decanter? Tell me that!'

For the first time that evening, Mr Quin addressed himself to Mr Satterthwaite.

'You have a wide experience of life, Mr Satterthwaite. Perhaps you can tell us that.'

Mr Satterthwaite's voice trembled a little. His cue

had come at last. He was to speak some of the most important lines in the play. He was an actor now—not a looker-on.

'As I see it,' he murmured modestly, 'she—cared for Derek Capel. She was, I think, a good woman—and she had sent him away. When her husband—died, she suspected the truth. And so, to save the man she loved, she tried to destroy the evidence against him. Later, I think, he persuaded her that her suspicions were unfounded, and she consented to marry him. But even then, she hung back—women, I fancy, have a lot of instinct.'

Mr Sattherthwaite had spoken his part.

Suddenly a long trembling sigh filled the air.

'My God!' cried Evesham, starting, 'what was that?'

Mr Satterthwaite could have told him that it was Eleanor Portal in the gallery above, but he was too artistic to spoil a good effect.

Mr Quin was smiling.

'My car will be ready by now. Thank you for your hospitality, Mr Evesham. I have, I hope, done something for my friend.'

They stared at him in blank amazement.

'That aspect of the matter has not struck you? He loved this woman, you know. Loved her enough to commit murder for her sake. When retribution overtook him, as he mistakenly thought, he took his own life. But unwittingly, he left her to face the music.'

'She was acquitted,' muttered Evesham.

'Because the case against her could not be proved. I fancy—it may be only a fancy—that she is still—facing the music.'

Portal had sunk into a chair, his face buried in his hands.

Quin turned to Satterthwaite.

'Goodbye, Mr Satterthwaite. You are interested in the drama, are you not?'

Mr Satterthwaite nodded—surprised.

'I must recommend the Harlequinade to your attention. It is dying out nowadays—but it repays attention, I assure you. Its symbolism is a little difficult to follow—but the immortals are always immortal, you know. I wish you all goodnight.'

They saw him stride out into the dark. As before, the coloured glass gave the effect of motley . . .

Mr Satterthwaite went upstairs. He went to draw down his window, for the air was cold. The figure of Mr Quin moved down the drive, and from a side door came a woman's figure, running. For a moment they spoke together, then she retraced her steps to the house. She passed just below the window, and Mr Satterthwaite was struck anew by the vitality of her face. She moved now like a woman in a happy dream.

'Eleanor!'

Alex Portal had joined her.

'Eleanor, forgive me—forgive me—You told me the truth, but God forgive me—I did not quite believe . . .'

Mr Satterthwaite was intensely interested in other people's affairs, but he was also a gentleman. It was borne in upon him that he must shut the window. He did so.

But he shut it very slowly.

He heard her voice, exquisite and indescribable.

'I know—I know. You have been in hell. So was I once. Loving—yet alternately believing and suspecting—thrusting aside one's doubts and having them spring up again with leering faces . . . I know, Alex, I know . . . But there is a worse hell than that, the hell I have lived in with you. I have seen your doubt—your

60

fear of me ... poisoning all our love. That man—that chance passer by, saved me. I could bear it no longer, you understand. Tonight—tonight I was going to kill myself ... Alex ... Alex ...'

The Mystery of the Baghdad Chest

The words made a catchy headline, and I said as much to my friend, Hercule Poirot. I knew none of the parties. My interest was merely the dispassionate one of the man in the street. Poirot agreed.

'Yes, it has a flavour of the Oriental, of the mysterious. The chest may very well have been a sham Jacobean one from the Tottenham Court Road; none the less the reporter who thought of naming it the Baghdad Chest was happily inspired. The word "mystery" is also thoughtfully placed in juxtaposition, though I understand there is very little mystery about the case.'

'Exactly. It is all rather horrible and macabre, but it is not mysterious.'

'Horrible and macabre,' repeated Poirot thoughtfully.

'The whole idea is revolting,' I said, rising to my feet and pacing up and down the room. 'The murderer kills this man—his friend—shoves him into the chest, and half an hour later is dancing in that same room with the wife of his victim. Think! If she had imagined for one moment—'

'True,' said Poirot thoughtfully. 'That much-vaunted possession, a woman's intuition—it does not seem to have been working.'

'The party seems to have gone off very merrily,' I said with a slight shiver. 'And all that time, as they danced and played poker, there was a dead man in the room with them. One could write a play about such an idea.'

'It has been done,' said Poirot. 'But console yourself, Hastings,' he added kindly. 'Because a theme has been used once, there is no reason why it should not be used again. Compose your drama.'

I had picked up the paper and was studying the rather blurred reproduction of a photograph.

'She must be a beautiful woman,' I said slowly. 'Even from this, one gets an idea.'

Below the picture ran the inscription:

A recent portrait of Mrs Clayton,
the wife of the murdered man

Poirot took the paper from me.

'Yes,' he said. 'She is beautiful. Doubtless she is of those born to trouble the souls of men.'

He handed the paper back to me with a sigh.

'*Dieu merci*, I am not of an ardent temperament. It has saved me from many embarrassments. I am duly thankful.'

I do not remember that we discussed the case further. Poirot displayed no special interest in it at the time. The facts were so clear, and there was so little ambiguity about them, that discussion seemed merely futile.

Mr and Mrs Clayton and Major Rich were friends of fairly long-standing. On the day in question, the tenth of March, the Claytons had accepted an invitation to spend the evening with Major Rich. At about seven-thirty, however, Clayton explained to another friend, a Major Curtiss, with whom he was having a drink, that he had been unexpectedly called to Scotland and was leaving by the eight o'clock train.

'I'll just have time to drop in and explain to old Jack,' went on Clayton. 'Marguerita is going, of course. I'm sorry about it, but Jack will understand how it is.'

Mr Clayton was as good as his word. He arrived at Major Rich's rooms about twenty to eight. The major was out at the time, but his manservant, who knew Mr Clayton well, suggested that he come in and wait. Mr Clayton said that he had no time, but that he would come in and write a note. He added that he was on his way to catch a train.

The valet accordingly showed him into the sitting-room.

About five minutes later Major Rich, who must have let himself in without the valet hearing him, opened the door of the sitting-room, called his man and told him to go out and get some cigarettes. On his return the man brought them to his master, who was then alone in the sitting-room. The man naturally concluded that Mr Clayton had left.

The guests arrived shortly afterwards. They comprised Mrs Clayton, Major Curtiss and a Mr and Mrs Spence. The evening was spent dancing to the phonograph and playing poker. The guests left shortly after midnight.

The following morning, on coming to do the sitting-room, the valet was startled to find a deep stain discolouring the carpet below and in front of a piece of furniture which Major Rich had brought from the East and which was called the Baghdad Chest.

Instinctively the valet lifted the lid of the chest and was horrified to find inside the doubled–up body of a man who had been stabbed to the heart.

Terrified, the man ran out of the flat and fetched the nearest policeman. The dead man proved to be Mr Clayton. The arrest of Major Rich followed very shortly afterward. The major's defence, it was understood, consisted of a sturdy denial of everything. He had not seen Mr Clayton the preceding evening and the first he had heard of his going to Scotland had been from Mrs Clayton.

Such were the bald facts of the case. Innuendoes and suggestions naturally abounded. The close friendship and intimacy of Major Rich and Mrs Clayton were so stressed that only a fool could fail to read between the lines. The motive for the crime was plainly indicated.

Long experience has taught me to make allowance for baseless calumny. The motive suggested might, for all the evidence, be entirely non-existent. Some quite other reason might have precipitated the issue. But one thing did stand out clearly—that Rich was the murderer.

As I say, the matter might have rested there, had it not happened that Poirot and I were due at a party given by Lady Chatterton that night.

Poirot, whilst bemoaning social engagements and declaring a passion for solitude, really enjoyed these affairs enormously. To be made a fuss of and treated as a lion suited him down to the ground.

On occasions he positively purred! I have seen him blandly receiving the most outrageous compliments as no more than his due, and uttering the most blatantly conceited remarks, such as I can hardly bear to set down.

Sometimes he would argue with me on the subject.

'But, my friend, I am not an Anglo-Saxon. Why should I play the hypocrite? *Si, si,* that is what you do, all of you. The airman who has made a difficult flight, the tennis champion—they look down their noses, they mutter inaudibly that "it is nothing". But do they really think that themselves? Not for a moment. They would admire the exploit in someone else. So, being reasonable men, they admire it in themselves. But their training prevents them from saying so. Me, I am not like that. The talents that I possess—I would salute them in another. As it happens, in my own particular line, there is no one to touch me. *C'est dommage!* As it is, I admit freely and without hypocrisy that I am a great man. I have the order, the method and the psychology in an unusual degree. I am, in fact, Hercule Poirot! Why should I turn red and stammer and mutter into my chin that really I am very stupid? It would not be true.'

'There is certainly only one Hercule Poirot,' I agreed—not without a spice of malice of which, fortunately, Poirot remained quite oblivious.

Lady Chatterton was one of Poirot's most ardent admirers. Starting from the mysterious conduct of a Pekingese, he had unravelled a chain which led to a noted burglar and housebreaker. Lady Chatterton had been loud in his praises ever since.

To see Poirot at a party was a great sight. His faultless evening clothes, the exquisite set of his white tie, the exact symmetry of his hair parting, the sheen of pomade on his hair, and the tortured splendour of his famous moustaches—all combined to paint the perfect picture of an inveterate dandy. It was hard, at these moments, to take the little man seriously.

It was about half-past eleven when Lady Chatterton, bearing down upon us, whisked Poirot neatly out of an admiring group, and carried him off—I need hardly say, with myself in tow.

'I want you to go into my little room upstairs,' said Lady Chatterton rather breathlessly as soon as she was out of earshot of her other guests. 'You know where it is, M. Poirot. You'll find someone there who needs your help very badly—and you will help her, I know. She's one of my dearest friends—so don't say no.'

Energetically leading the way as she talked, Lady Chatterton flung open a door, exclaiming as she did so, 'I've got him, Marguerita darling. And he'll do anything you want. You *will* help Mrs Clayton, won't you, M. Poirot?'

And taking the answer for granted, she withdrew with the same energy that characterized all her movements.

Mrs Clayton had been sitting in a chair by the window. She rose now and came toward us. Dressed in deep mourning, the dull black showed up her fair colouring. She was a singularly lovely woman, and there was about her a simple childlike candour which made her charm quite irresistible.

'Alice Chatterton is so kind,' she said. 'She arranged this. She said you would help me, M. Poirot. Of course I don't know whether you will or not—but I hope you will.'

She had held out her hand and Poirot had taken it. He held it now for a moment or two while he stood scrutinizing her closely. There was nothing ill-bred in his manner of doing it. It was more the kind but searching look that a famous consultant gives a new patient as the latter is ushered into his presence.

'Are you sure, madame,' he said at last, 'that I can help you?'

'Alice says so.'

'Yes, but I am asking you, madame.'

A little flush rose to her cheeks.

'I don't know what you mean.'

'What is it, madame, that you want me to do?'

'You—you—know who I am?' she asked.

'Assuredly.'

'Then you can guess what it is I am asking you to do, M. Poirot—Captain Hastings'—I was gratified that she realized my identity—'Major Rich did *not* kill my husband.'

'Why not?'

'I beg your pardon?'

Poirot smiled at her slight discomfiture.

'I said, "Why not?"' he repeated.

'I'm not sure that I understand.'

'Yet it is very simple. The police—the lawyers—they will all ask the same question: Why did Major Rich kill M. Clayton? I ask the opposite. I ask you, madame, why did Major Rich *not* kill Mr Clayton.'

'You mean—why I'm so sure? Well, but I *know*. I know Major Rich so well.'

'You know Major Rich so well,' repeated Poirot tonelessly.

The colour flamed into her cheeks.

'Yes, that's what they'll say—what they'll think! Oh, I know!'

'*C'est vrai*. That is what they will ask you about—how well you knew Major Rich. Perhaps you will speak the truth, perhaps you will lie. It is very necessary for a woman to lie, it is a good weapon. But there are three people, madame, to whom a woman should speak the truth. To her Father Confessor, to her hairdresser and to her private detective—if she trusts him. Do you trust me, madame?'

Marguerita Clayton drew a deep breath. 'Yes,' she said. 'I do. I must,' she added rather childishly.

'Then, how well do you know Major Rich?'

She looked at him for a moment in silence, then she raised her chin defiantly.

'I will answer your question. I loved Jack from the first moment I saw him—two years ago. Lately I think—I believe—he has come to love me. But he has never said so.'

'*Épatant!*' said Poirot. 'You have saved me a good quarter of an hour by coming to the point without beating the bush. You have the good sense. Now your husband—did he suspect your feelings?'

'I don't know,' said Marguerita slowly. 'I thought—lately—that he might. His manner has been different ... But that may have been merely my fancy.'

'Nobody else knew?'

'I do not think so.'

'And—pardon me, madame—you did not love your husband?'

There were, I think, very few women who would have answered that question as simply as this woman did. They would have tried to explain their feelings.

Marguerita Clayton said quite simply: 'No.'

'*Bien.* Now we know where we are. According to you, madame, Major Rich did not kill your husband, but you realize that all the evidence points to his having done so. Are you aware, privately, of any flaw in that evidence?'

'No. I know nothing.'

'When did your husband first inform you of his visit to Scotland?'

'Just after lunch. He said it was a bore, but he'd have to go. Something to do with land values, he said it was.'

'And after that?'

'He went out—to his club, I think. I—I didn't see him again.'

'Now as to Major Rich—what was his manner that evening? Just as usual?'

'Yes, I think so.'

'You are not sure?'

Marguerita wrinkled her brows.

'He was—a little constrained. With me—not with the others. But I thought I knew why that was. You understand? I am sure the constraint or—or—absent-mindedness perhaps describes it better—had nothing to do with Edward. He was surprised to hear that Edward had gone to Scotland, but not unduly so.'

'And nothing else unusual occurs to you in connection with that evening?'

Marguerita thought.

'No, nothing whatever.'

'You—noticed the chest?'

She shook her head with a little shiver.

'I don't even remember it—or what it was like. We played poker most of the evening.'

'Who won?'

'Major Rich. I had very bad luck, and so did Major Curtiss. The Spences won a little, but Major Rich was the chief winner.'

'The party broke up—when?'

'About half-past twelve, I think. We all left together.'

'Ah!'

Poirot remained silent, lost in thought.

'I wish I could be more helpful to you,' said Mrs Clayton. 'I seem to be able to tell you so little.'

'About the present—yes. What about the past, madame?'

'The past?'

'Yes. Have there not been incidents?'

She flushed.

'You mean that dreadful little man who shot himself. It wasn't my fault, M. Poirot. Indeed it wasn't.'

'It was not precisely of that incident that I was thinking.'

'That ridiculous duel? But Italians do fight duels. I was so thankful the man wasn't killed.'

'It must have been a relief to you,' agreed Poirot gravely.

She was looking at him doubtfully. He rose and took her hand in his.

'I shall not fight a duel for you, madame,' he said. 'But I will do what you have asked me. I will discover the truth. And let us hope that your instincts are correct—that the truth will help and not harm you.'

Our first interview was with Major Curtiss. He was a man of about forty, of soldierly build, with very dark hair and a bronzed face. He had known the Claytons for some years and Major Rich also. He confirmed the press reports.

Clayton and he had had a drink together at the club just before half-past seven, and Clayton had then announced his intention of looking in on Major Rich on his way to Euston.

'What was Mr Clayton's manner? Was he depressed or cheerful?'

The major considered. He was a slow-spoken man.

'Seemed in fairly good spirits,' he said at last.

'He said nothing about being on bad terms with Major Rich?'

'Good Lord, no. They were pals.'

'He didn't object to—his wife's friendship with Major Rich?'

The major became very red in the face.

'You've been reading those damned newspapers, with their hints and lies. Of course he didn't object. Why, he said to me: "Marguerita's going, of course."'

'I see. Now during the evening—the manner of Major Rich—was that much as usual?'

'I didn't notice any difference.'

'And madame? She, too, was as usual.'

'Well,' he reflected, 'now I come to think of it, she was a bit quiet. You know, thoughtful and faraway.'

'Who arrived first?'

'The Spences. They were there when I got there. As a matter of fact, I'd called round for Mrs Clayton, but found she'd already started. So I got there a bit late.'

'And how did you amuse yourselves? You danced? You played the cards?'

'A bit of both. Danced first of all.'

'There were five of you?'

'Yes, but that's all right, because I don't dance. I put on the records and the others danced.'

'Who danced most with whom?'

'Well, as a matter of fact the Spences like dancing together. They've got a sort of craze on it—fancy steps and all that.'

'So that Mrs Clayton danced mostly with Major Rich?'

'That's about it.'

'And then you played poker?'

'Yes.'

'And when did you leave?'

'Oh, quite early. A little after midnight.'

'Did you all leave together?'

'Yes. As a matter of fact, we shared a taxi, dropped Mrs Clayton first, then me, and the Spences took it on to Kensington.'

Our next visit was to Mr and Mrs Spence. Only Mrs Spence was at home, but her account of the evening

72

tallied with that of Major Curtiss except that she displayed a slight acidity concerning Major Rich's luck at cards.

Earlier in the morning Poirot had had a telephone conversation with Inspector Japp of Scotland Yard. As a result we arrived at Major Rich's rooms and found his manservant, Burgoyne, expecting us.

The valet's evidence was very precise and clear.

Mr Clayton had arrived at twenty minutes to eight. Unluckily Major Rich had just that very minute gone out. Mr Clayton had said that he couldn't wait, as he had to catch a train, but he would just scrawl a note. He accordingly went into the sitting-room to do so. Burgoyne had not actually heard his master come in, as he was running the bath, and Major Rich, of course, let himself in with his own key. In his opinion it was about ten minutes later that Major Rich called him and sent him out for cigarettes. No, he had not gone into the sitting-room. Major Rich had stood in the doorway. He had returned with the cigarettes five minutes later and on this occasion he had gone into the sitting-room, which was then empty, save for his master, who was standing by the window smoking. His master had inquired if his bath were ready and on being told it was had proceeded to take it. He, Burgoyne, had not mentioned Mr Clayton, as he assumed that his master had found Mr Clayton there and let him out himself. His master's manner had been precisely the same as usual. He had taken his bath, changed, and shortly after, Mr and Mrs Spence had arrived, to be followed by Major Curtiss and Mrs Clayton.

It had not occurred to him, Burgoyne explained, that Mr Clayton might have left before his master's return. To do so, Mr Clayton would have had to bang the front door behind him and that the valet was sure he would have heard.

Still in the same impersonal manner, Burgoyne proceeded to his finding of the body. For the first time my attention was directed to the fatal chest. It was a good-sized piece of furniture standing against the wall next to the phonograph cabinet. It was made of some dark wood and plentifully studded with brass nails. The lid opened simply enough. I looked in and shivered. Though well scrubbed, ominous stains remained.

Suddenly Poirot uttered an exclamation. 'Those holes there—they are curious. One would say that they had been newly made.'

The holes in question were at the back of the chest against the wall. There were three or four of them. They were about a quarter of an inch in diameter and certainly had the effect of having been freshly made.

Poirot bent down to examine them, looking inquiringly at the valet.

'It's certainly curious, sir. I don't remember ever seeing those holes in the past, though maybe I wouldn't notice them.'

'It makes no matter,' said Poirot.

Closing the lid of the chest, he stepped back into the room until he was standing with his back against the window. Then he suddenly asked a question.

'Tell me,' he said. 'When you brought the cigarettes into your master that night, was there not something out of place in the room?'

Burgoyne hesitated for a minute, then with some slight reluctance he replied, 'It's odd your saying that, sir. Now you come to mention it, there was. That screen there that cuts off the draught from the bedroom door—it was moved a bit more to the left.'

'Like this?'

Poirot darted nimbly forward and pulled at the screen. It was a handsome affair of painted leather. It already slightly obscured the view of the chest, and as Poirot adjusted it, it hid the chest altogether.

'That's right, sir,' said the valet. 'It was like that.'

'And the next morning?'

'It was still like that. I remember. I moved it away and it was then I saw the stain. The carpet's gone to be cleaned, sir. That's why the boards are bare.'

Poirot nodded.

'I see,' he said. 'I thank you.'

He placed a crisp piece of paper in the valet's palm.

'Thank you, sir.'

'Poirot,' I said when we were out in the street, 'that point about the screen—is that a point helpful to Rich?'

'It is a further point against him,' said Poirot ruefully. 'The screen hid the chest from the room. It also hid the stain on the carpet. Sooner or later the blood was bound to soak through the wood and stain the carpet. The screen would prevent discovery for the moment. Yes— but there is something there that I do not understand. The valet, Hastings, the valet.'

'What about the valet? He seemed a most intelligent fellow.'

'As you say, most intelligent. Is it credible, then, that Major Rich failed to realize that the valet would certainly discover the body in the morning? Immediately after the deed he had no time for anything—granted. He shoves the body into the chest, pulls the screen in front of it and goes through the evening hoping for the best. But after the guests are gone? Surely, then is the time to dispose of the body.'

'Perhaps he hoped the valet wouldn't notice the stain?'

'That, *mon ami*, is absurd. A stained carpet is the first thing a good servant would be bound to notice.

And Major Rich, he goes to bed and snores there comfortably and does nothing at all about the matter. Very remarkable and interesting, that.'

'Curtiss might have seen the stains when he was changing the records the night before?' I suggested.

'That is unlikely. The screen would throw a deep shadow just there, No, but I begin to see. Yes, dimly I begin to see.'

'See what?' I asked eagerly.

'The possibilities, shall we say, of an alternative explanation. Our next visit may throw light on things.'

Our next visit was to the doctor who had examined the body. His evidence was a mere recapitulation of what he had already given at the inquest. Deceased had been stabbed to the heart with a long thin knife something like a stiletto. The knife had been left in the wound. Death had been instantaneous. The knife was the property of Major Rich and usually lay on his writing table. There were no fingerprints on it, the doctor understood. It had been either wiped or held in a handkerchief. As regards time, any time between seven and nine seemed indicated.

'He could not, for instance, have been killed after midnight?' asked Poirot.

'No. That I can say. Ten o'clock at the outside—but seven-thirty to eight seems clearly indicated.'

'There *is* a second hypothesis possible,' Poirot said when we were back home. 'I wonder if you see it, Hastings. To me it is very plain, and I only need one point to clear up the matter for good and all.'

'It's no good,' I said. 'I'm not there.'

'But make an effort, Hastings. Make an effort.'

'Very well,' I said. 'At seven-forty Clayton is alive and well. The last person to see him alive is Rich—'

'So we assume.'

'Well, isn't it so?'

'You forget, *mon ami*, that Major Rich denies that. He states explicitly that Clayton had gone when he came in.'

'But the valet says that he would have heard Clayton leave because of the bang of the door. And also, if Clayton had left, when did he return? He couldn't have returned after midnight because the doctor says positively that he was dead at least two hours before that. That only leaves one alternative.'

'Yes, *mon ami*?' said Poirot.

'That in the five minutes Clayton was alone in the sitting-room, someone else came in and killed him. But there we have the same objection. Only someone with a key could come in without the valet's knowing, and in the same way the murderer on leaving would have had to bang the door, and that again the valet would have heard.'

'Exactly,' said Poirot. 'And therefore—'

'And therefore—nothing,' I said. 'I can see no other solution.'

'It is a pity,' murmured Poirot. 'And it is really so exceedingly simple—as the clear blue eyes of Madame Clayton.'

'You really believe—'

'I believe nothing—until I have got proof. One little proof will convince me.'

He took up the telephone and called Japp at Scotland Yard.

Twenty minutes later we were standing before a little

heap of assorted objects laid out on a table. They were the contents of the dead man's pockets.

There was a handkerchief, a handful of loose change, a pocketbook containing three pounds ten shillings, a couple of bills and a worn snapshot of Marguerita Clayton. There was also a pocketknife, a gold pencil and a cumbersome wooden tool.

It was on this latter that Poirot swooped. He unscrewed it and several small blades fell out.

'You see, Hastings, a gimlet and all the rest of it. Ah! it would be a matter of a very few minutes to bore a few holes in the chest with this.'

'Those holes we saw?'

'Precisely.'

'You mean it was Clayton who bored them himself?'

'*Mais, oui—mais, oui!* What did they suggest to you, those holes? They were not to *see* through, because they were at the back of the chest. What were they for, then? Clearly for air? But you do not make air holes for a dead body, so clearly they were *not* made by the murderer. They suggest one thing—and one thing only—that a man was going to *hide* in that chest. And at once, on that hypothesis, things become intelligible. Mr Clayton is jealous of his wife and Rich. He plays the old, old trick of pretending to go away. He watches Rich go out, then he gains admission, is left alone to write a note, quickly bores those holes and hides inside the chest. His wife is coming there that night. Possibly Rich will put the others off, possibly she will remain after the others have gone, or pretend to go and return. Whatever it is, Clayton will *know*. Anything is preferable to the ghastly torment of suspicion he is enduring.'

'Then you mean that Rich killed him *after* the others had gone? But the doctor said that was impossible.'

'Exactly. So you see, Hastings, he must have been killed *during* the evening.'

'But everyone was in the room!'

'Precisely,' said Poirot gravely. 'You see the beauty of that? "Everyone was in the room." What an alibi! What *sang-froid*—what nerve—what audacity!'

'I still don't understand.'

'Who went behind that screen to wind up the phonograph and change the records? The phonograph and the chest were side by side, remember. The others are dancing—the phonograph is playing. And the man who does not dance lifts the lid of the chest and thrusts the knife he has just slipped into his sleeve deep into the body of the man who was hiding there.'

'Impossible! The man would cry out.'

'Not if he were drugged first?'

'Drugged?'

'Yes. Who did Clayton have a drink with at seven-thirty? Ah! Now you see. Curtiss! Curtiss has inflamed Clayton's mind with suspicions against his wife and Rich. Curtiss suggests this plan—the visit to Scotland, the concealment in the chest, the final touch of moving the screen. Not so that Clayton can raise the lid a little and get relief—no, so that he, Curtiss, can raise that lid unobserved. The plan is Curtiss's, and observe the beauty of it, Hastings. If Rich had observed the screen was out of place and moved it back—well, no harm is done. He can make another plan. Clayton hides in the chest, the mild narcotic that Curtiss had administered takes effect. He sinks into unconsciousness. Curtiss lifts up the lid and strikes—and the phonograph goes on playing "Walking My Baby Back Home".'

I found my voice. 'Why? But why?'

Poirot shrugged his shoulders.

'Why did a man shoot himself? Why did two Italians fight a duel? Curtiss is of a passionate temperament. He wanted Marguerita Clayton. With her husband and Rich out of the way, she would, or so he thought, turn to him.'

He added musingly:

'These simple childlike women ... they are very dangerous. But *mon Dieu!* what an artistic masterpiece! It goes to my heart to hang a man like that. I may be a genius myself, but I am capable of recognizing genius in other people. A perfect murder, *mon ami.* I, Hercule Poirot, say it to you. A perfect murder. *Épatant!*'

The Clergyman's Daughter

'I wish,' said Tuppence, roaming moodily round the office, 'that we could befriend a clergyman's daughter.'

'Why?' asked Tommy.

'You may have forgotten the fact, but I was once a clergyman's daughter myself. I remember what it was like. Hence this altruistic urge—this spirit of thoughtful consideration for others—this—'

'You are getting ready to be Roger Sheringham, I see,' said Tommy. 'If you will allow me to make a criticism, you talk quite as much as he does, but not nearly so well.'

'On the contrary,' said Tuppence. 'There is a feminine subtlety about my conversation, a *je ne sais quoi* that no gross male could ever attain to. I have, moreover, powers unknown to my prototype—do I mean prototype? Words are such uncertain things, they so often sound well, but mean the opposite of what one thinks they do.'

'Go on,' said Tommy kindly.

'I was. I was only pausing to take breath. Touching these powers, it is my wish today to assist a clergyman's daughter. You will see, Tommy, the first person to enlist the aid of Blunt's Brilliant Detectives will be a clergyman's daughter.'

'I'll bet you it isn't,' said Tommy.

81

'Done,' said Tuppence. 'Hist! To your typewriters, Oh! Israel. One comes.'

Mr Blunt's office was humming with industry as Albert opened the door and announced:

'Miss Monica Deane.'

A slender, brown-haired girl, rather shabbily dressed, entered and stood hesitating. Tommy came forward.

'Good-morning, Miss Deane. Won't you sit down and tell us what we can do for you? By the way, let me introduce my confidential secretary, Miss Sheringham.'

'I am delighted to make your acquaintance, Miss Deane,' said Tuppence. 'Your father was in the Church, I think.'

'Yes, he was. But how *did* you know that?'

'Oh! we have our methods,' said Tuppence. 'You mustn't mind me rattling on. Mr Blunt likes to hear me talk. He always says it gives him ideas.'

The girl stared at her. She was a slender creature, not beautiful, but possessing a wistful prettiness. She had a quantity of soft mouse-coloured hair, and her eyes were dark blue and very lovely, though the dark shadows round them spoke of trouble and anxiety.

'Will you tell me your story, Miss Deane?' said Tommy.

The girl turned to him gratefully.

'It's such a long rambling story,' said the girl. 'My name is Monica Deane. My father was the rector of Little Hampsley in Suffolk. He died three years ago, and my mother and I were left very badly off. I went out as a governess, but my mother's physical condition deteriorated, and I had to come home to look after her. We were desperately poor, but one day we received a lawyer's letter telling us that an aunt of my father's had died and had left everything to me. I had often heard of

82

this aunt, who had quarrelled with my father many years ago, and I knew that she was very well off, so it really seemed that our troubles were at an end. But matters did not turn out quite as well as we had hoped. I inherited the house she had lived in, but after paying one or two small legacies, there was no money left. I suppose she must have lost it during the war, or perhaps she had been living on her capital. Still, we had the house, and almost at once we had a chance of selling it at quite an advantageous price. But, foolishly perhaps, I refused the offer. We were in tiny, but expensive lodgings, and I thought it would be much nicer to live in the Red House, where my mother could have comfortable rooms and take in paying guests to cover our expenses.

'I adhered to this plan, notwithstanding a further tempting offer from the gentleman who wanted to buy. We moved in, and I advertised for paying guests. For a time, all went well, we had several answers to our advertisement; my aunt's old servant remained on with us, and she and I between us did the work of the house. And then these unaccountable things began to happen.'

'What things?'

'The queerest things. The whole place seemed bewitched. Pictures fell down, crockery flew across the room and broke; one morning we came down to find all the furniture moved round. At first we thought someone was playing a practical joke, but we had to give up that explanation. Sometimes when we were all sitting down to dinner, a terrific crash would be heard overhead. We would go up and find no one there, but a piece of furniture thrown violently to the ground.'

'A *poltergeist*,' cried Tuppence, much interested.

'Yes, that's what Dr O'Neill said—though I don't know what it means.'

'It's a sort of evil spirit that plays tricks,' explained Tuppence, who in reality knew very little about the subject, and was not even sure that she had got the word *poltergeist* right.

'Well, at any rate, the effect was disastrous. Our visitors were frightened to death, and left as soon as possible. We got new ones, and they too left hurriedly. I was in despair, and, to crown all, our own tiny income ceased suddenly—the Company in which it was invested failed.'

'You poor dear,' said Tuppence sympathetically. 'What a time you have had. Did you want Mr Blunt to investigate this "haunting" business?'

'Not exactly. You see, three days ago, a gentleman called upon us. His name was Dr O'Neill. He told us that he was a member of the Society for Physical Research, and that he had heard about the curious manifestations that had taken place in our house and was much interested. So much so, that he was prepared to buy it from us, and conduct a series of experiments there.'

'Well?'

'Of course, at first, I was overcome with joy. It seemed the way out of all our difficulties. But—'

'Yes?'

'Perhaps you will think me fanciful. Perhaps I am. But—oh! I'm sure I haven't made a mistake. It was the same man!'

'What same man?'

'The same man who wanted to buy it before. Oh! I'm sure I'm right.'

'But why shouldn't it be?'

'You don't understand. The two men were quite different, different name and everything. The first man was quite young, a spruce, dark young man of thirty odd. Dr O'Neill is about fifty, he has a grey beard and wears glasses and stoops. But when he talked I saw a gold tooth one side of his mouth. It only shows when he laughs. The other man had a tooth in just the same position, and then I looked at his ears. I had noticed the other man's ears, because they were a peculiar shape with hardly any lobe. Dr O'Neill's were just the same. Both things couldn't be a coincidence, could they? I thought and thought and finally I wrote and said I would let him know in a week. I had noticed Mr Blunt's advertisement some time ago—as a matter of fact in an old paper that lined one of the kitchen drawers. I cut it out and came up to town.'

'You were quite right,' said Tuppence, nodding her head with vigour. 'This needs looking into.'

'A very interesting case, Miss Deane,' observed Tommy.

'We shall be pleased to look into this for you—eh, Miss Sheringham?'

'Rather,' said Tuppence, 'and we'll get to the bottom of it too.'

'I understand, Miss Deane,' went on Tommy, 'that the household consists of you and your mother and a servant. Can you give me any particulars about the servant?'

'Her name is Crockett. She was with my aunt about eight or ten years. She is an elderly woman, not very pleasant in manner, but a good servant. She is inclined to give herself airs because her sister married out of her station. Crockett has a nephew whom she is always telling us is "quite the gentleman".'

'H'm,' said Tommy, rather at a loss how to proceed.

Tuppence had been eyeing Monica keenly, now she spoke with sudden decision.

'I think the best plan would be for Miss Deane to come out and lunch with me. It's just one o'clock. I can get full details from her.'

'Certainly, Miss Sheringham,' said Tommy. 'An excellent plan.'

'Look here,' said Tuppence, when they were comfortably ensconced at a little table in a neighbouring restaurant, 'I want to know: Is there any special reason why you want to find out about all this?'

Monica blushed.

'Well, you see—'

'Out with it,' said Tuppence encouragingly.

'Well—there are two men who—who—want to marry me.'

'The usual story, I suppose? One rich, one poor, and the poor one is the one you like!'

'I don't know how you know all these things,' murmured the girl.

'That's a sort of law of Nature,' explained Tuppence. 'It happens to everybody. It happened to me.'

'You see, even if I sell the house, it won't bring us in enough to live on. Gerald is a dear, but he's desperately poor—though he's a very clever engineer; and if only he had a little capital, his firm would take him into partnership. The other, Mr Partridge, is a very good man, I am sure—and well off, and if I married him, it would be an end to all our troubles. But—but—'

'I know,' said Tuppence sympathetically. 'It isn't the same thing at all. You can go on telling yourself how good and worthy he is, and adding up his qualities as though they were an addition sum—and it all has a simply refrigerating effect.'

Monica nodded.

'Well,' said Tuppence, 'I think it would be as well

if we went down to the neighbourhood and studied matters upon the spot. What is the address?'

'The Red House, Stourton-in-the-Marsh.'

Tuppence wrote down the address in her note-book.

'I didn't ask you,' Monica began—'about terms—' she ended, blushing a little.

'Our payments are strictly by results,' said Tuppence gravely. 'If the secret of the Red House is a profitable one, as seems possible from the anxiety displayed to acquire the property, we should expect a small percentage, otherwise—nothing!'

'Thank you very much,' said the girl gratefully.

'And now,' said Tuppence, 'don't worry. Everything's going to be all right. Let's enjoy lunch and talk of interesting things.'

The Red House

'Well,' said Tommy, looking out of the window of the Crown and Anchor, 'here we are at Toad in the Hole— or whatever this blasted village is called.'

'Let us review the case,' said Tuppence.

'By all means,' said Tommy. 'To begin with, getting my say in first, *I* suspect the disabled mother!'

'Why?'

'My dear Tuppence, grant that this *poltergeist* business is all a put-up job, got up in order to persuade the girl to sell the house, someone must have thrown the things about. Now the girl said everyone was at dinner—but if the mother is disabled, she'd be upstairs in her room.'

'If she was disabled she could hardly throw furniture about.'

'Ah! but she wouldn't really be disabled. She'd be shamming.'

'Why?'

'There you have me,' confessed her husband. 'I was really going on the well-known principle of suspecting the most unlikely person.'

'You always make fun of everything,' said Tuppence severely. 'There must be *something* that makes these people so anxious to get hold of the house. And if you don't care about getting to the bottom of this matter, I do. I like that girl. She's a dear.'

Tommy nodded seriously enough.

'I quite agree. But I never can resist ragging you, Tuppence. Of course, there's something queer about the house, and whatever it is, it's something that's difficult to get at. Otherwise a mere burglary would do the trick. But to be willing to buy the house means either that you've got to take up floors or pull down walls, or else that there's a coal mine under the back garden.'

'I don't want it to be a coal mine. Buried treasure is much more romantic.'

'H'm,' said Tommy. 'In that case I think that I shall pay a visit to the local Bank Manager, explain that I am staying here over Christmas and probably buying the Red House, and discuss the question of opening an account.'

'But why—?'

'Wait and see.'

Tommy returned at the end of half an hour. His eyes were twinkling.

'We advance, Tuppence. Our interview proceeded on the lines indicated. I then asked casually whether he had had much gold paid in, as is often the case nowadays in these small country banks—small farmers who hoarded it during the war, you understand. From that we proceeded quite naturally to the extraordinary vagaries of old ladies. I invented an aunt who on the outbreak of war drove to the Army and Navy Stores in a four-wheeler, and returned with sixteen hams. He immediately mentioned a client of his own, who had insisted on drawing out every penny of money she had—in gold as far as possible, and who also insisted on having her securities, bearer bonds and such things, given into her own custody. I exclaimed on such an act of folly, and he mentioned casually that she was the former owner of the Red House. You see, Tuppence? She drew out all this money, and she hid it somewhere. You remember that Monica Deane mentioned that they were astonished at the small amount of her estate? Yes, she hid it in the Red House, and someone knows about it. I can make a pretty good guess who that someone is too.'

'Who?'

'What about the faithful Crockett? She would know all about her mistress's peculiarities.'

'And that gold-toothed Dr O'Neill?'

'The gentlemanly nephew, of course! That's it. But whereabouts did she hide it. You know more about old ladies than I do, Tuppence. Where do they hide things?'

'Wrapped up in stockings and petticoats, under mattresses.'

Tommy nodded.

'I expect you're right. All the same, she can't have done that because it would have been found when her things were turned over. It worries me—you see, an old lady like that can't have taken up floors or dug holes in the garden. All the same it's there in the Red House somewhere. Crockett hasn't found it, but she knows it's there, and once they get the house to themselves, she and her precious nephew, they can turn it upside down until they find what they're after. We've got to get ahead of them. Come on, Tuppence. We'll go to the Red House.'

Monica Deane received them. To her mother and Crockett they were represented as would-be purchasers of the Red House, which would account for their being taken all over the house and grounds. Tommy did not tell Monica of the conclusions he had come to, but he asked her various searching questions. Of the garments and personal belongings of the dead woman, some had been given to Crockett and the others sent to various poor families. Everything had been gone through and turned out.

'Did your aunt leave any papers?'

'The desk was full, and there were some in a drawer in her bedroom, but there was nothing of importance amongst them.'

'Have they been thrown away?'

'No, my mother is always very loath to throw away old papers. There were some old-fashioned recipes among them which she intends to go through one day.'

'Good,' said Tommy approvingly. Then, indicating an old man who was at work upon one of the flower beds in the garden, he asked: 'Was that old man the gardener here in your aunt's time?'

'Yes, he used to come three days a week. He lives in the village. Poor old fellow, he is past doing any really useful work. We have him just once a week to keep things tidied up. We can't afford more.'

Tommy winked at Tuppence to indicate that she was to keep Monica with her, and he himself stepped across to where the gardener was working. He spoke a few pleasant words to the old man, asked him if he had been there in the old lady's time, and then said casually.

'You buried a box for her once, didn't you?'

'No, sir, I never buried naught for her. What should she want to bury a box for?'

Tommy shook his head. He strolled back to the house frowning. It was to be hoped that a study of the old lady's papers would yield some clue—otherwise the problem was a hard one to solve. The house itself was old fashioned, but not old enough to contain a secret room or passage.

Before leaving, Monica brought them down a big cardboard box tied with string.

'I've collected all the papers,' she whispered. 'And they're in here. I thought you could take it away with you, and then you'll have plenty of time to go over them—but I'm sure you won't find anything to throw light on the mysterious happenings in this house—'

Her words were interrupted by a terrific crash overhead. Tommy ran quickly up the stairs. A jug and a basin in one of the front rooms was lying on the ground broken to pieces. There was no one in the room.

'The ghost up to its tricks again,' he murmured with a grin.

He went downstairs again thoughtfully.

'I wonder, Miss Deane, if I might speak to the maid, Crockett, for a minute.'

'Certainly. I will ask her to come to you.'

Monica went off to the kitchen. She returned with the elderly maid who had opened the door to them earlier.

'We are thinking of buying this house,' said Tommy pleasantly, 'and my wife was wondering whether, in that case, you would care to remain on with us?'

Crockett's respectable face displayed no emotion of any kind.

91

'Thank you, sir,' she said. 'I should like to think it over if I may.'

Tommy turned to Monica.

'I am delighted with the house, Miss Deane. I understand that there is another buyer in the market. I know what he has offered for the house, and I will willingly give a hundred more. And mind you, that is a good price I am offering.'

Monica murmured something noncommittal, and the Beresfords took their leave.

'I was right,' said Tommy, as they went down the drive, 'Crockett's in it. Did you notice that she was out of breath? That was from running down the backstairs after smashing the jug and basin. Sometimes, very likely, she has admitted her nephew secretly, and he has done a little poltergeisting, or whatever you call it, whilst she has been innocently with the family. You'll see Dr O'Neill will make a further offer before the day is out.'

True enough, after dinner, a note was brought. It was from Monica.

'I have just heard from Dr O'Neill. He raises his previous offer by £150.'

'The nephew must be a man of means,' said Tommy thoughtfully. 'And I tell you what, Tuppence, the prize he's after must be well worth while.'

'Oh! Oh! Oh! if only we could find it!'

'Well, let's get on with the spade work.'

They were sorting through the big box of papers, a wearisome affair, as they were all jumbled up pell mell without any kind of order or method. Every few minutes they compared notes.

'What's the latest, Tuppence?'

'Two old receipted bills, three unimportant letters, a

recipe for preserving new potatoes and one for making lemon cheesecake. What's yours?'

'One bill, a poem on Spring, two newspaper cuttings: "Why Women buy Pearls—a sound investment", and "Man with Four Wives—Extraordinary Story", and a recipe for Jugged Hare.'

'It's heart-breaking,' said Tuppence, and they fell to once more. At last the box was empty. They looked at each other.

'I put this aside,' said Tommy, picking up a half sheet of notepaper, 'because it struck me as peculiar. But I don't suppose it's got anything to do with what we're looking for.'

'Let's see it. Oh! it's one of these funny things, what do they call them? Anagrams, charades or something.' She read it:

> *'My first you put on glowing coal*
> *And into it you put my whole;*
> *My second really is the first;*
> *My third mislikes the winter blast.'*

'H'm,' said Tommy critically. 'I don't think much of the poet's rhymes.'

'I don't see what you find peculiar about it, though,' said Tuppence. 'Everybody used to have a collection of these sort of things about fifty years ago. You saved them up for winter evenings round the fire.'

'I wasn't referring to the verse. It's the words written below it that strike me as peculiar.'

'St Luke, xi, 9,' she read. 'It's a text.'

'Yes. Doesn't that strike you as odd? Would an old lady of a religious persuasion write a text just under a charade?'

'It is rather odd,' agreed Tuppence thoughtfully.

'I presume that you, being a clergyman's daughter, have got your Bible with you?'

'As a matter of fact, I have. Aha! you didn't expect that. Wait a sec.'

Tuppence ran to her suitcase, extracted a small red volume and returned to the table. She turned the leaves rapidly. 'Here we are. Luke, chapter xi, verse 9. Oh! Tommy, look.'

Tommy bent over and looked where Tuppence's small finger pointed to a portion of the verse in question.

'Seek and ye shall find.'

'That's it,' cried Tuppence. 'We've got it! Solve the cryptogram and the treasure is ours—or rather Monica's.'

'Well, let's get to work on the cryptogram, as you call it. *"My first* you put on glowing coal." What does that mean, I wonder? Then—"My *second* really is the first." That's pure gibberish.'

'It's quite simple, really,' said Tuppence kindly. 'It's just a sort of knack. Let *me* have it.'

Tommy surrendered it willingly. Tuppence ensconced herself in an armchair, and began muttering to herself with bent brows.

'It's quite simple, really,' murmured Tommy when half an hour had elapsed.

'Don't crow! We're the wrong generation for this. I've a good mind to go back to town tomorrow and call on some old dear who would probably read it as easy as winking. It's a knack, that's all.'

'Well, let's have one more try.'

'There aren't many things you can put on glowing coal,' said Tuppence thoughtfully. 'There's water, to put it out, or wood, or a kettle.'

'It must be one syllable, I suppose? What about *wood*, then?'

'You couldn't put anything *into* wood, though.'

'There's no one syllable word instead of *water*, but there must be one syllable things you can put on a fire in the kettle line.'

'Saucepans,' mused Tuppence. 'Frying pans. How about *pan?* or *pot?* What's a word beginning pan or pot that is something you cook?'

'Pottery,' suggested Tommy. 'You bake that in the fire. Wouldn't that be near enough?'

'The rest of it doesn't fit. Pancakes? No. Oh! bother.'

They were interrupted by the little serving-maid, who told them that dinner would be ready in a few minutes.

'Only Mrs Lumley, she wanted to know if you like your potatoes fried, or boiled in their jackets? She's got some of each.'

'Boiled in their jackets,' said Tuppence promptly. 'I love potatoes—' She stopped dead with her mouth open.

'What's the matter, Tuppence? Have you seen a ghost?'

'Tommy,' cried Tuppence. 'Don't you see? That's it! The word, I mean. *Potatoes!* "My first you put on glowing coal"—that's pot. "And into it you put my *whole*." "My *second* really is the first." That's A, the first letter of the alphabet. "My *third* mislikes the wintry blast"—cold *toes* of course!'

'You're right, Tuppence. Very clever of you. But I'm afraid we've wasted an awful lot of time over nothing. Potatoes don't fit in at all with missing treasure. Half a sec, though. What did you read out just now, when we were going through the box? Something about a recipe for New Potatoes. I wonder if there's anything in that.'

He rummaged hastily through the pile of recipes.

'Here it is. "To KEEP NEW POTATOES. Put the new potatoes into tins and bury them in the garden. Even in the middle of winter, they will taste as though freshly dug."'

'We've got it,' screamed Tuppence. 'That's it. The treasure is in the garden, buried in a tin.'

'But I asked the gardener. He said he'd never buried anything.'

'Yes, I know, but that's because people never really answer what you say, they answer what they think you mean. He knew he'd never buried anything out of the common. We'll go tomorrow and ask him where he buried the potatoes.'

The following morning was Christmas Eve. By dint of inquiry they found the old gardener's cottage. Tuppence broached the subject after some minutes' conversation.

'I wish one could have new potatoes at Christmas time,' she remarked. 'Wouldn't they be good with turkey? Do people round here ever bury them in tins? I've heard that keeps them fresh.'

'Ay, that they do,' declared the old man. 'Old Miss Deane, up to the Red House, she allus had three tins buried every summer, and as often as not forgot to have 'em dug up again!'

'In the bed by the house, as a rule, didn't she?'

'No, over against the wall by the fir tree.'

Having got the information they wanted, they soon took their leave of the old man, presenting him with five shillings as a Christmas box.

'And now for Monica,' said Tommy.

'Tommy! You have no sense of the dramatic. Leave it

to me. I've got a beautiful plan. Do you think you could manage to beg, borrow or steal a spade?'

Somehow or other, a spade was duly produced, and that night, late, two figures might have been seen stealing into the grounds of the Red House. The place indicated by the gardener was easily found, and Tommy set to work. Presently his spade rang on metal, and a few seconds later he had unearthed a big biscuit tin. It was sealed round with adhesive plaster and firmly fastened down, but Tuppence, by the aid of Tommy's knife, soon managed to open it. Then she gave a groan. The tin was full of potatoes. She poured them out, so that the tin was completely empty, but there were no other contents.

'Go on digging, Tommy.'

It was some time before a second tin rewarded their search. As before, Tuppence unsealed it.

'Well?' demanded Tommy anxiously.

'Potatoes again!'

'Damn!' said Tommy, and set to once more.

'The third time is lucky,' said Tuppence consolingly.

'I believe the whole thing's a mare's nest,' said Tommy gloomily, but he continued to dig.

At last a third tin was brought to light.

'Potatoes aga—' began Tuppence, then stopped. 'Oh, Tommy, we've got it. It's only potatoes on top. Look!'

She held up a big old-fashioned velvet bag.

'Cut along home,' cried Tommy. 'It's icy cold. Take the bag with you. I must shovel back the earth. And may a thousand curses light upon your head, Tuppence, if you open that bag before I come!'

'I'll play fair. Ouch! I'm frozen.' She beat a speedy retreat.

On arrival at the inn she had not long to wait. Tommy

was hard upon her heels, perspiring freely after his digging and the final brisk run.

'Now then,' said Tommy, 'the private inquiry agents make good! Open the loot, Mrs Beresford.'

Inside the bag was a package done up in oil silk and a heavy chamois leather bag. They opened the latter first. It was full of gold sovereigns. Tommy counted them.

'Two hundred pounds. That was all they would let her have, I suppose. Cut open the package.'

Tuppence did so. It was full of closely folded banknotes. Tommy and Tuppence counted them carefully. They amounted to exactly twenty thousand pounds.

'Whew!' said Tommy. 'Isn't it lucky for Monica that we're both rich and honest? What's that done up in tissue paper?'

Tuppence unrolled the little parcel and drew out a magnificent string of pearls, exquisitely matched.

'I don't know much about these things,' said Tommy slowly. 'But I'm pretty sure that those pearls are worth another five thousand pounds at least. Look at the size of them. Now I see why the old lady kept that cutting about pearls being a good investment. She must have realised all her securities and turned them into notes and jewels.'

'Oh, Tommy, isn't it wonderful? Darling Monica. Now she can marry her nice young man and live happily ever afterwards, like me.'

'That's rather sweet of you, Tuppence. So you *are* happy with me?'

'As a matter of fact,' said Tuppence, 'I am. But I didn't mean to say so. It slipped out. What with being excited, and Christmas Eve, and one thing and another—'

'If you really love me,' said Tommy, 'will you answer me one question?'

'I hate these catches,' said Tuppence, 'but—well—all right.'

'Then how did you know that Monica was a clergyman's daughter?'

'Oh, that was just cheating,' said Tuppence happily. 'I opened her letter making an appointment, and a Mr Deane was father's curate once, and he had a little girl called Monica, about four or five years younger than me. So I put two and two together.'

'You are a shameless creature,' said Tommy. 'Hullo, there's twelve o'clock striking. Happy Christmas, Tuppence.'

'Happy Christmas, Tommy. It'll be a Happy Christmas for Monica too—and all owing to US. I am glad. Poor thing, she has been so miserable. Do you know, Tommy, I feel all queer and choky about the throat when I think of it.'

'Darling Tuppence,' said Tommy.

'Darling Tommy,' said Tuppence. 'How awfully sentimental we are getting.'

'Christmas comes but once a year,' said Tommy sententiously. 'That's what our great-grandmothers said, and I expect there's a lot of truth in it still.'

The Plymouth Express

Alec Simpson, RN, stepped from the platform at Newton Abbot into a first-class compartment of the Plymouth Express. A porter followed him with a heavy suitcase. He was about to swing it up to the rack, but the young sailor stopped him.

'No—leave it on the seat. I'll put it up later. Here you are.'

'Thank you, sir.' The porter, generously tipped, withdrew.

Doors banged; a stentorian voice shouted: 'Plymouth only. Change for Torquay. Plymouth next stop.' Then a whistle blew, and the train drew slowly out of the station.

Lieutenant Simpson had the carriage to himself. The December air was chilly, and he pulled up the window. Then he sniffed vaguely, and frowned. What a smell there was! Reminded him of that time in hospital, and the operation on his leg. Yes, chloroform; that was it!

He let the window down again, changing his seat to one with its back to the engine. He pulled a pipe out of his pocket and lit it. For a little time he sat inactive, looking out into the night and smoking.

At last he roused himself, andopening the suitcase, took out some papers and magazines, then closed the

100

suitcase again and endeavoured to shove it under the opposite seat—without success. Some obstacle resisted it. He shoved harder with rising impatience, but it still stuck out half-way into the carriage.

'Why the devil won't it go in?' he muttered, and hauling it out completely, he stooped down and peered under the seat . . .

A moment later a cry rang out into the night, and the great train came to an unwilling halt in obedience to the imperative jerking of the communication cord.

'Mon ami,' said Poirot, 'you have, I know, been deeply interested in this mystery of the Plymouth Express. Read this.'

I picked up the note he flicked across the table to me. It was brief and to the point.

Dear Sir,

I shall be obliged if you will call upon me at your earliest convenience.

Yours faithfully,

EBENEZER HALLIDAY

The connection was not clear to my mind, and I looked inquiringly at Poirot.

For answer he took up the newspaper and read aloud: '"A sensational discovery was made last night. A young naval officer returning to Plymouth found under the seat of his compartment the body of a woman, stabbed through the heart. The officer at once pulled the communication cord, and the train was brought to a standstill. The woman, who was about thirty years of age, and richly dressed, has not yet been identified."

'And later we have this: "The woman found dead

in the Plymouth Express has been identified as the Honourable Mrs Rupert Carrington." You see now, my friend? Or if you do not I will add this—Mrs Rupert Carrington was, before her marriage, Flossie Halliday, daughter of old man Halliday, the steel king of America.'

'And he has sent for you? Splendid!'

'I did him a little service in the past—an affair of bearer bonds. And once, when I was in Paris for a royal visit, I had Mademoiselle Flossie pointed out to me. *La jolie petite pensionnaire*! She had the *joli dot* too! It caused trouble. She nearly made a bad affair.'

'How was that?'

'A certain Count de la Rochefour. *Un bien mauvais sujet*! A bad hat, as you would say. An adventurer pure and simple, who knew how to appeal to a romantic young girl. Luckily her father got wind of it in time. He took her back to America in haste. I heard of her marriage some years later, but I know nothing of her husband.'

'H'm,' I said. 'The Honourable Rupert Carrington is no beauty, by all accounts. He'd pretty well run through his own money on the turf, and I should imagine old man Halliday's dollars came along in the nick of time. I should say that for a good-looking, well-mannered, utterly unscrupulous young scoundrel, it would be hard to find his mate!'

'Ah, the poor little lady! *Elle n'est pas bien tombée*!'

'I fancy he made it pretty obvious at once that it was her money, and not she, that had attracted him. I believe they drifted apart almost at once. I have heard rumours lately that there was to be a definite legal separation.'

'Old man Halliday is no fool. He would tie up her money pretty tight.'

'I dare say. Anyway, I know as a fact that the

Honourable Rupert is said to be extremely hard up.'

'Aha! I wonder—'

'You wonder what?'

'My good friend, do not jump down my throat like that. You are interested, I see. Suppose you accompany me to see Mr Halliday. There is a taxi-stand at the corner.'

A few minutes sufficed to whirl us to the superb house in Park Lane rented by the American magnate. We were shown into the library, and almost immediately we were joined by a large stout man, with piercing eyes and an aggressive chin.

'M. Poirot?' said Mr Halliday. 'I guess I don't need to tell you what I want you for. You've read the papers, and I'm never one to let the grass grow under my feet. I happened to hear you were in London, and I remembered the good work you did over those bombs. Never forget a name. I've the pick of Scotland Yard, but I'll have my own man as well. Money no object. All the dollars were made for my little girl—and now she's gone, I'll spend my last cent to catch the damned scoundrel that did it! See? So it's up to you to deliver the goods.'

Poirot bowed.

'I accept, monsieur, all the more willingly that I saw your daughter in Paris several times. And now I will ask you to tell me the circumstances of her journey to Plymouth and any other details that seem to you to bear upon the case.'

'Well, to begin with,' responded Halliday, 'she wasn't going to Plymouth. She was going to join a house-party at Avonmead Court, the Duchess of Swansea's place. She left London by the twelve-fourteen from Paddington, arriving at Bristol (where she had to change) at two-fifty. The principal Plymouth expresses, of course, run via Westbury, and do not go near Bristol at all. The twelve-fourteen does a non-stop run to Bristol, afterwards stopping at Weston, Taunton, Exeter and Newton Abbot. My daughter travelled alone in her carriage, which was reserved as far as Bristol, her maid being in a third class carriage in the next coach.'

Poirot nodded, and Mr Halliday went on: 'The party at Avonmead Court was to be a very gay one, with several balls, and in consequence my daughter had with her nearly all her jewels—amounting in value, perhaps, to about a hundred thousand dollars.'

'*Un moment*,' interrupted Poirot. 'Who had charge of the jewels? Your daughter, or the maid?'

'My daughter always took charge of them herself, carrying them in a small blue morocco case.'

'Continue, monsieur.'

'At Bristol the maid, Jane Mason, collected her mistress's dressing-bag and wraps, which were with her, and came to the door of Flossie's compartment. To her intense surprise, my daughter told her that she was not getting out at Bristol, but was going on farther. She directed Mason to get out the luggage and put it in the cloakroom. She could have tea in the refreshment-room, but she was to wait at the station for her mistress, who would return to Bristol by an up-train in the course of the afternoon. The maid, although very much astonished, did as she was told. She put the luggage in the cloakroom and had some tea. But up-train after up-train came in, and her mistress did not appear. After the arrival of the last train, she left the luggage where it was, and went to a hotel near the station for the night. This morning she read of the tragedy, and returned to town by the first available train.'

'Is there nothing to account for your daughter's sudden change of plan?'

'Well there is this: According to Jane Mason, at Bristol, Flossie was no longer alone in her carriage. There was a man in it who stood looking out of the farther window so that she could not see his face.'

'The train was a corridor one, of course?'

'Yes.'

'Which side was the corridor?'

'On the platform side. My daughter was standing in the corridor as she talked to Mason.'

'And there is no doubt in your mind—excuse me!' He got up, and carefully straightened the inkstand which was a little askew. '*Je vous demande pardon*,' he continued, re-seating himself. 'It affects my nerves to see anything crooked. Strange, is it not? I was saying, monsieur, that there is no doubt in your mind as to this probably unexpected meeting being the cause of your daughter's sudden change of plan?'

'It seems the only reasonable supposition.'

'You have no idea as to who the gentleman in question might be?'

The millionaire hesitated for a moment, and then replied: 'No—I do not know at all.'

'Now—as to the discovery of the body?'

'It was discovered by a young naval officer who at once gave the alarm. There was a doctor on the train. He examined the body. She had been first chloroformed, and then stabbed. He gave it as his opinion that she had been dead about four hours, so it must have been done not long after leaving Bristol—probably between there and Weston, possibly between Weston and Taunton.'

'And the jewel-case?'

'The jewel-case, M. Poirot, was missing.'

'One thing more, monsieur. Your daughter's fortune—to whom does it pass at her death?'

'Flossie made a will soon after her marriage, leaving everything to her husband.' He hesitated for a minute, and then went on: 'I may as well tell you, Monsieur Poirot, that I regard my son-in-law as an unprincipled scoundrel, and that, by my advice, my daughter was on the eve of freeing herself from him by legal means— no difficult matter. I settled her money upon her in such a way that he could not touch it during her lifetime, but although they have lived entirely apart for some years, she had frequently acceded to his demands for money, rather than face an open scandal. However, I was determined to put an end to this. At last Flossie agreed, and my lawyers were instructed to take proceedings.'

'And where is Monsieur Carrington?'

'In town. I believe he was away in the country yesterday, but he returned last night.'

Poirot considered a little while. Then he said: 'I think that is all, monsieur.'

'You would like to see the maid, Jane Mason?'

'If you please.'

Halliday rang the bell, and gave a short order to the footman.

A few minutes later Jane Mason entered the room, a respectable, hard-featured woman, as emotionless in the face of tragedy as only a good servant can be.

'You will permit me to put a few questions? Your mistress, she was quite as usual before starting yesterday morning? Not excited or flurried?'

'Oh no, sir!'

'But at Bristol she was quite different?'

'Yes, sir, regular upset—so nervous she didn't seem to know what she was saying.'

'What did she say exactly?'

'Well, sir, as near as I can remember, she said: "Mason, I've got to alter my plans. Something has happened—I mean, I'm not getting out here after all. I must go on. Get out the luggage and put it in the cloakroom; then have some tea, and wait for me in the station."

'"Wait for you here, ma'am?" I asked.

'"Yes, yes. Don't leave the station. I shall return by a later train. I don't know when. It mayn't be until quite late."

'"Very well, ma'am," I says. It wasn't my place to ask questions, but I thought it very strange.'

'It was unlike your mistress, eh?'

'Very unlike her, sir.'

'What do you think?'

'Well, sir, I thought it was to do with the gentleman in the carriage. She didn't speak to him, but she turned round once or twice as though to ask him if she was doing right.'

'But you didn't see the gentleman's face?'

'No, sir; he stood with his back to me all the time.'

'Can you describe him at all?'

'He had on a light fawn overcoat, and a travelling-cap. He was tall and slender, like and the back of his head was dark.'

'You didn't know him?'

'Oh no, I don't think so, sir.'

'It was not your master, Mr Carrington, by any chance?'

Mason looked rather startled.

'Oh, I don't think so, sir!'

'But you are not *sure*?'

'It was about the master's build, sir—but I never thought of it being him. We so seldom saw him ... I couldn't say it *wasn't* him!'

Poirot picked up a pin from the carpet, and frowned at it severely; then he continued: 'Would it be possible for the man to have entered the train at Bristol before you reached the carriage?'

Mason considered.

'Yes, sir, I think it would. My compartment was very crowded, and it was some minutes before I could get out—and then there was a very large crowd on the platform, and that delayed me too. But he'd only have had a minute or two to speak to the mistress, that way. I took it for granted that he'd come along the corridor.'

'That is more probable, certainly.'

He paused, still frowning.

'You know how the mistress was dressed, sir?'

'The papers give a few details, but I would like you to confirm them.'

'She was wearing a white fox fur toque, sir, with a white spotted veil, and a blue frieze coat and skirt—the shade of blue they call electric.'

'H'm, rather striking.'

'Yes,' remarked Mr Halliday. 'Inspector Japp is in hopes that that may help us to fix the spot where the crime took place. Anyone who saw her would remember her.'

'*Précisément!*—Thank you, mademoiselle.'

The maid left the room.

'Well!' Poirot got up briskly. 'That is all I can do here—except, monsieur, that I would ask you to tell me everything, but *everything*!'

'I have done so.'

'You are sure?'

'Absolutely.'

'Then there is nothing more to be said. I must decline the case.'

'Why?'

'Because you have not been frank with me.'

'I assure you—'

'No, you are keeping something back.'

There was a moment's pause, and then Halliday drew a paper from his pocket and handed it to my friend.

'I guess that's what you're after, Monsieur Poirot—though how you know about it fairly gets my goat!'

Poirot smiled, and unfolded the paper. It was a letter written in thin sloping handwriting. Poirot read it aloud.

'Chère Madame,

It is with infinite pleasure that I look forward to the felicity of meeting you again. After your so amiable reply to my letter, I can hardly restrain my impatience. I have never forgotten those days in Paris. It is most cruel that you should be leaving London tomorrow. However, before very long, and perhaps sooner than you think, I shall have the joy of beholding once more the lady whose image has ever reigned supreme in my heart.

Believe, chère madame, all the assurances of my most devoted and unaltered sentiments—

ARMAND DE LA ROCHEFOUR.'

Poirot handed the letter back to Halliday with a bow.

'I fancy, monsieur, that you did not know that your daughter intended renewing her acquaintance with the Count de la Rochefour?'

'It came as a thunderbolt to me! I found this letter

in my daughter's handbag. As you probably know, Monsieur Poirot, this so-called count is an adventurer of the worst type.'

Poirot nodded.

'But I want to know how you knew of the existence of this letter?'

My friend smiled. 'Monsieur, I did not. But to track footmarks and recognize cigarette-ash is not sufficient for a detective. He must also be a good psychologist! I knew that you disliked and mistrusted your son-in-law. He benefits by your daughter's death; the maid's description of the mysterious man bears a sufficient resemblance to him. Yet you are not keen on his track! Why? Surely because your suspicions lie in another direction. Therefore you were keeping something back.'

'You're right, Monsieur Poirot. I was sure of Rupert's guilt until I found this letter. It unsettled me horribly.'

'Yes. The Count says "Before very long, and perhaps sooner than you think." Obviously he would not want to wait until you should get wind of his reappearance. Was it he who travelled down from London by the twelve-fourteen, and came along the corridor to your daughter's compartment? The Count de la Rochefour is also, if I remember rightly, tall and dark!'

The millionaire nodded.

'Well, monsieur, I will wish you good day. Scotland Yard has, I presume, a list of the jewels?'

'Yes, I believe Inspector Japp is here now if you would like to see him.'

Japp was an old friend of ours, and greeted Poirot with a sort of affectionate contempt.

'And how are you, monsieur? No bad feeling between us, though we *have* got our different ways of looking at things. How are the "little grey cells", eh? Going strong?'

Poirot beamed upon him. 'They function, my good Japp; assuredly they do!'

'Then that's all right. Think it was the Honourable Rupert, or a crook? We're keeping an eye on all the regular places, of course. We shall know if the shiners are disposed of, and of course whoever did it isn't going to keep them to admire their sparkle. Not likely! I'm trying to find out where Rupert Carrington was yesterday. Seems a bit of a mystery about it. I've got a man watching him.'

'A great precaution, but perhaps a day late,' suggested Poirot gently.

'You always will have your joke, Monsieur Poirot. Well, I'm off to Paddington. Bristol, Weston, Taunton, that's my beat. So long.'

'You will come round and see me this evening, and tell me the result?'

'Sure thing, if I'm back.'

'The good inspector believes in matter in motion,' murmured Poirot as our friend departed. 'He travels; he measures footprints; he collects mud and cigarette-ash! He is extremely busy! He is zealous beyond words! And if I mentioned psychology to him, do you know what he would do, my friend? He would smile! He would say to himself: "Poor old Poirot! He ages! He grows senile!" Japp is the "younger generation knocking on the door." And *ma foi*! They are so busy knocking that they do not notice that the door is open!'

'And what are you going to do?'

'As we have *carte blanche*, I shall expend threepence in ringing up the Ritz—where you may have noticed our Count is staying. After that, as my feet are a little damp, and I have sneezed twice, I shall return to my rooms and make myself a *tisane* over the spirit lamp!'

I did not see Poirot again until the following morning. I found him placidly finishing his breakfast.

'Well?' I inquired eagerly. 'What has happened?'

'Nothing.'

'But Japp?'

'I have not seen him.'

'The Count?'

'He left the Ritz the day before yesterday.'

'The day of the murder?'

'Yes.'

'Then that settles it! Rupert Carrington is cleared.'

'Because the Count de la Rochefour has left the Ritz? You go too fast, my friend.'

'Anyway, he must be followed, arrested! But what could be his motive?'

'One hundred thousand dollars' worth of jewellery is a very good motive for anyone. No, the question to my mind is: why kill her? Why not simply steal the jewels? She would not prosecute.'

'Why not?'

'Because she is a woman, *mon ami*. She once loved this man. Therefore she would suffer her loss in silence. And the Count, who is an extremely good psychologist where women are concerned—hence his successes— would know that perfectly well! On the other hand, if Rupert Carrington killed her, why take the jewels which would incriminate him fatally?'

'As a blind.'

'Perhaps you are right, my friend. Ah, here is Japp! I recognize his knock.'

The inspector was beaming good-humouredly.

'Morning, Poirot. Only just got back. I've done some good work! And you?'

'Me, I have arranged my ideas,' replied Poirot placidly.

Japp laughed heartily.

'Old chap's getting on in years,' he observed beneath his breath to me. 'That won't do for us young folk,' he said aloud.

'*Quel dommage?*' Poirot inquired.

'Well, do you want to hear what I've done?'

'You permit me to make a guess? You have found the knife with which the crime was committed, by the side of the line between Weston and Taunton, and you have interviewed the paper-boy who spoke to Mrs Carrington at Weston!'

Japp's jaw fell. 'How on earth did you know? Don't tell me it was those almighty "little grey cells" of yours!'

'I am glad you admit for once that they are *all mighty*! Tell me, did she give the paper-boy a shilling for himself?'

'No, it was half a crown!' Japp had recovered his temper, and grinned. 'Pretty extravagant, these rich Americans!'

'And in consequence the boy did not forget her?'

'Not he. Half-crowns don't come his way every day. She hailed him and bought two magazines. One had a picture of a girl in blue on the cover. "That'll match me," she said. Oh, he remembered her perfectly. Well, that was enough for me. By the doctor's evidence, the crime *must* have been committed before Taunton. I guessed they'd throw the knife away at once, and I walked down the line looking for it; and sure enough, there it was. I made inquiries at Taunton about our man, but of course it's a big station, and it wasn't likely they'd notice him. He probably got back to London by a later train.'

Poirot nodded. 'Very likely.'

'But I found another bit of news when I got back. They're passing the jewels, all right! That large emerald was pawned last night—by one of the regular lot. Who do you think it was?'

'I don't know—except that he was a short man.'

Japp stared. 'Well, you're right there. He's short enough. It was Red Narky.'

'Who is Red Narky?' I asked.

'A particularly sharp jewel-thief, sir. And not one to stick at murder. Usually works with a woman—Gracie Kidd; but she doesn't seem to be in it this time—unless she's got off to Holland with the rest of the swag.'

'You've arrested Narky?'

'Sure thing. But mind you, it's the other man we want—the man who went down with Mrs Carrington in the train. He was the one who planned the job, right enough. But Narky won't squeal on a pal.'

I noticed Poirot's eyes had become very green.

'I think,' he said gently, 'that I can find Narky's pal for you, all right.'

'One of your little ideas, eh?' Japp eyed Poirot sharply. 'Wonderful how you manage to deliver the goods sometimes, at your age and all. Devil's own luck, of course.'

'Perhaps, perhaps,' murmured my friend. 'Hastings, my hat. And the brush. So! My galoshes, if it still rains! We must not undo the good work of that *tisane*. *Au revoir*, Japp!'

'Good luck to you, Poirot.'

Poirot hailed the first taxi we met, and directed the driver to Park Lane.

When we drew up before Halliday's house, he skipped out nimbly, paid the driver and rang the bell. To the footman who opened the door he made a request in a low voice, and we were immediately taken upstairs. We went up to the top of the house, and were shown into a small neat bedroom. Poirot's eyes roved round the room and fastened themselves on a small black trunk. He knelt in front of it, scrutinized the labels on it, and took a small twist of wire from his pocket.

'Ask Mr Halliday if he will be so kind as to mount to me here,' he said over his shoulder to the footman.

The man departed, and Poirot gently coaxed the lock of the trunk with a practised hand. In a few minutes the lock gave, and he raised the lid of the trunk. Swiftly he began rummaging among the clothes it contained, flinging them out on the floor.

There was a heavy step on the stairs, and Halliday entered the room.

'What in hell are you doing here?' he demanded, staring.

'I was looking, monsieur, for *this.*' Poirot withdrew from the trunk a coat and skirt of bright blue frieze, and a small toque of white fox fur.

'What are you doing with my trunk?' I turned to see that the maid, Jane Mason, had entered the room.

'If you will just shut the door, Hastings. Thank you. Yes, and stand with your back against it. Now, Mr Halliday, let me introduce you to Gracie Kidd, otherwise Jane Mason, who will shortly rejoin her accomplice, Red Narky, under the kind escort of Inspector Japp.'

Poirot waved a deprecating hand. 'It was of the most simple!' He helped himself to more caviar.

'It was the maid's insistence on the clothes that her mistress was wearing that first struck me. Why was she so anxious that our attention should be directed to them? I reflected that we had only the maid's word for the mysterious man in the carriage at Bristol. As far as the doctor's evidence went, Mrs Carrington might easily have been murdered *before* reaching Bristol. But if so, then the maid must be an accomplice. And if she were an accomplice, she would not wish this point to rest on her evidence alone. The clothes Mrs Carrington was wearing were of a striking nature. A maid usually has a good deal of choice as to what her mistress shall wear. Now if, after Bristol, anyone saw a lady in a bright blue coat and skirt, and a fur toque, he will be quite ready to swear he had seen Mrs Carrington.

'I began to reconstruct. The maid would provide herself with duplicate clothes. She and her accomplice chloroform and stab Mrs Carrington between London and Bristol, probably taking advantage of a tunnel. Her body is rolled under the seat; and the maid takes her place. At Weston she must make herself noticed. How? In all probability, a newspaper-boy will be selected. She will insure his remembering her by giving him a large tip. She also drew his attention to the colour of her dress by a remark about one of the magazines. After leaving Weston, she throws the knife out of the window to mark the place where the crime presumably occurred, and changes her clothes, or buttons a long mackintosh over them. At Taunton she leaves the train and returns to Bristol as soon as possible, where her accomplice has duly left the luggage in the cloakroom. He hands over the ticket and himself returns to London. She waits on the platform, carrying out her role, goes to a hotel for the night and returns to town in the morning, exactly as she said.

'When Japp returned from his expedition, he confirmed all my deductions. He also told me that a well-known crook was passing the jewels. I knew that whoever it was would be the exact opposite of the man Jane Mason described. When I heard that it was Red Narky, who always worked with Gracie Kidd—well, I knew just where to find her.'

'And the Count?'

'The more I thought of it, the more I was convinced that he had nothing to do with it. That gentleman is much too careful of his own skin to risk murder. It would be out of keeping with his character.'

'Well, Monsieur Poirot,' said Halliday, 'I owe you a big debt. And the cheque I write after lunch won't go near to settling it.'

Poirot smiled modestly, and murmured to me: 'The good Japp, he shall get the official credit, all right, but though he has got his Gracie Kidd, I think that I, as the Americans say, have got his goat!'

Problem at Pollensa Bay

The steamer from Barcelona to Majorca landed Mr
Parker Pyne at Palma in the early hours of the morning—and straightaway he met with disillusionment.
The hotels were full! The best that could be done for
him was an airless cupboard overlooking an inner court
in a hotel in the centre of the town—and with that Mr
Parker Pyne was not prepared to put up. The proprietor
of the hotel was indifferent to his disappointment.

'What will you?' he observed with a shrug.

Palma was popular now! The exchange was favour-
able! Everyone—the English, the Americans—they all
came to Majorca in the winter. The whole place was
crowded. It was doubtful if the English gentleman
would be able to get in anywhere—except perhaps at
Formentor where the prices were so ruinous that even
foreigners blenched at them.

Mr Parker Pyne partook of some coffee and a roll and
went out to view the cathedral, but found himself in no
mood for appreciating the beauties of architecture.

He next had a conference with a friendly taxi driver
in inadequate French interlarded with native Spanish,
and they discussed the merits and possibilities of Soller,
Alcudia, Pollensa and Formentor—where there were
fine hotels but very expensive.

Mr Parker Pyne was goaded to inquire how expensive.

They asked, said the taxi driver, an amount that it would be absurd and ridiculous to pay—was it not well known that the English came here because prices were cheap and reasonable?

Mr Parker Pyne said that that was quite so, but all the same what sums *did* they charge at Formentor?

A price incredible!

Perfectly—but WHAT PRICE EXACTLY?

The driver consented at last to reply in terms of figures.

Fresh from the exactions of hotels in Jerusalem and Egypt, the figure did not stagger Mr Parker Pyne unduly.

A bargain was struck, Mr Parker Pyne's suitcases were loaded on the taxi in a somewhat haphazard manner, and they started off to drive round the island, trying cheaper hostelries en route but with the final objective of Formentor.

But they never reached that final abode of plutocracy, for after they had passed through the narrow streets of Pollensa and were following the curved line of the seashore, they came to the Hotel Pino d'Oro—a small hotel standing on the edge of the sea looking out over a view that in the misty haze of a fine morning had the exquisite vagueness of a Japanese print. At once Mr Parker Pyne knew that this, and this only, was what he was looking for. He stopped the taxi, passed through the painted gate with the hope that he would find a resting place.

The elderly couple to whom the hotel belonged knew no English or French. Nevertheless the matter was concluded satisfactorily. Mr Parker Pyne was allotted a room overlooking the sea, the suitcases were unloaded, the driver congratulated his passenger upon avoiding the monstrous exigencies of 'these new hotels', received his fare and departed with a cheerful Spanish salutation.

Mr Parker Pyne glanced at his watch and perceiving that it was, even now, but a quarter to ten, he went out onto the small terrace now bathed in a dazzling morning light and ordered, for the second time that morning, coffee and rolls.

There were four tables there, his own, one from which breakfast was being cleared away and two occupied ones. At the one nearest him sat a family of father and mother and two elderly daughters—Germans. Beyond them, at the corner of the terrace, sat what were clearly an English mother and son.

The woman was about fifty-five. She had grey hair of a pretty tone—was sensibly but not fashionably dressed in a tweed coat and skirt—and had that comfortable self-possession which marks an Englishwoman used to much travelling abroad.

The young man who sat opposite her might have been twenty-five and he too was typical of his class and age. He was neither good-looking nor plain, tall nor short. He was clearly on the best of terms with his mother—they made little jokes together—and he was assiduous in passing her things.

As they talked, her eye met that of Mr Parker Pyne. It passed over him with well-bred nonchalance, but he knew that he had been assimilated and labelled.

He had been recognized as English and doubtless, in due course, some pleasant non-committal remark would be addressed to him.

Mr Parker Pyne had no particular objection. His own countrymen and women abroad were inclined to bore him slightly, but he was quite willing to pass the time of day in an amiable manner. In a small hotel it caused constraint if one did not do so. This particular woman, he felt sure, had excellent 'hotel manners', as he put it.

The English boy rose from his seat, made some laughing remark and passed into the hotel. The woman took her letters and bag and settled herself in a chair facing the sea. She unfolded a copy of the *Continental Daily Mail*. Her back was to Mr Parker Pyne.

As he drank the last drop of his coffee, Mr Parker Pyne glanced in her direction, and instantly he stiffened. He was alarmed—alarmed for the peaceful continuance of his holiday! That back was horribly expressive. In his time he had classified many such backs. Its rigidity—the tenseness of its poise—without seeing her face he knew well enough that the eyes were bright with unshed tears—that the woman was keeping herself in hand by a rigid effort.

Moving warily, like a much-hunted animal, Mr Parker Pyne retreated into the hotel. Not half an hour before he had been invited to sign his name in the book lying on the desk. There it was—a neat signature— C. Parker Pyne, London.

A few lines above Mr Parker Pyne noticed the entries: Mrs R. Chester, Mr Basil Chester—Holm Park, Devon.

Seizing a pen, Mr Parker Pyne wrote rapidly over his signature. It now read (with difficulty) Christopher Pyne.

If Mrs R. Chester was unhappy in Pollensa Bay, it was not going to be made easy for her to consult Mr Parker Pyne.

Already it had been a source of abiding wonder to that gentleman that so many people he had come across abroad should know his name and have noted his advertisements. In England many thousands of people read the *Times* every day and could have answered quite truthfully that they had never heard such a name in their lives. Abroad, he reflected, they read their newspapers more thoroughly. No item, not even the advertisement columns, escaped them.

Already his holidays had been interrupted on several occasions. He had dealt with a whole series of problems from murder to attempted blackmail. He was determined in Majorca to have peace. He felt instinctively that a distressed mother might trouble that peace considerably.

Mr Parker Pyne settled down at the Pino d'Oro very happily. There was a larger hotel not far off, the Mariposa, where a good many English people stayed. There was also quite an artist colony living all round. You could walk along by the sea to the fishing village where there was a cocktail bar where people met—there were a few shops. It was all very peaceful and pleasant. Girls strolled about in trousers with brightly coloured handkerchiefs tied round the upper halves of their bodies. Young men in berets with rather long hair held forth in 'Mac's Bar' on such subjects as plastic values and abstraction in art.

On the day after Mr Parker Pyne's arrival, Mrs Chester made a few conventional remarks to him on the subject of the view and the likelihood of the weather keeping fine. She then chatted a little with the German lady about knitting, and had a few pleasant words about the sadness of the political situation with two Danish gentlemen who spent their time rising at dawn and walking for eleven hours.

Mr Parker Pyne found Basil Chester a most likeable young man. He called Mr Parker Pyne 'sir' and listened most politely to anything the older man said. Sometimes the three English people had coffee together after dinner in the evening. After the third day, Basil left the party after ten minutes or so and Mr Parker Pyne was left tete-a-tete with Mrs Chester.

They talked about flowers and the growing of them, of the lamentable state of the English pound and of how expensive France had become, and of the difficulty of getting good afternoon tea.

Every evening when her son departed, Mr Parker Pyne saw the quickly concealed tremor of her lips, but immediately she recovered and discoursed pleasantly on the above-mentioned subjects.

Little by little she began to talk of Basil—of how well he had done at school—'he was in the First XI, you know'—of how everyone liked him, of how proud his father would have been of the boy had he lived, of how thankful she had been that Basil had never been 'wild'. 'Of course I always urge him to be with young people, but he really seems to prefer being with me.'

She said it with a kind of nice modest pleasure in the fact.

But for once Mr Parker Pyne did not make the usual tactful response he could usually achieve so easily. He said instead:

'Oh! well, there seem to be plenty of young people here—not in the hotel, but round about.'

At that, he noticed, Mrs Chester stiffened. She said: Of course there were a lot of *artists*. Perhaps she was very old-fashioned—*real* art, of course, was different, but a lot of young people just made that sort of thing an excuse for lounging about and doing nothing—and the girls drank a lot too much.

On the following day Basil said to Mr Parker Pyne:

'I'm awfully glad you turned up here, sir—especially for my mother's sake. She likes having you to talk to in the evenings.'

123

'What did you do when you were first here?'

'As a matter of fact we used to play piquet.'

'I see.'

'Of course one gets rather tired of piquet. As a matter of fact I've got some friends here—frightfully cheery crowd. I don't really think my mother approves of them—' He laughed as though he felt this ought to be amusing. 'The mater's very old-fashioned ... Even girls in trousers shock her!'

'Quite so,' said Mr Parker Pyne.

'What I tell her is—one's got to move with the times ... The girls at home round us are frightfully dull ...'

'I see,' said Mr Parker Pyne.

All this interested him well enough. He was a spectator of a miniature drama, but he was not called upon to take part in it.

And then the worst—from Mr Parker Pyne's point of view—happened. A gushing lady of his acquaintance came to stay at the Mariposa. They met in the tea shop in the presence of Mrs Chester.

The newcomer screamed:

'Why—if it isn't Mr Parker Pyne—the one and only Mr Parker Pyne! And Adela Chester! Do you know each other? Oh, you do? You're staying at the same hotel? He's the one and only original wizard, Adela—the marvel of the century—all your troubles smoothed out while you wait! Didn't you *know*? You must have *heard* about him? Haven't you read his advertisements? *"Are you in trouble? Consult Mr Parker Pyne."* There's just nothing he can't do. Husbands and wives flying at each other's throats and he brings 'em together—if you've lost interest in life he gives you the most thrilling adventures. As I say the man's just a *wizard*!'

It went on a good deal longer—Mr Parker Pyne at intervals making modest disclaimers. He disliked the look that Mrs Chester turned upon him. He disliked even more seeing her return along the beach in close confabulation with the garrulous singer of his praises.

The climax came quicker than he expected. That evening, after coffee, Mrs Chester said abruptly,

'Will you come into the little salon, Mr Pyne? There is something I want to say to you.'

He could but bow and submit.

Mrs Chester's self-control had been wearing thin— as the door of the little salon closed behind them, it snapped. She sat down and burst into tears.

'My boy, Mr Parker Pyne. You must save him. *We* must save him. It's breaking my heart!'

'My dear lady, as a mere outsider—'

'Nina Wycherley says you can do *anything*. She said I was to have the utmost confidence in you. She advised me to tell you everything—and that you'd put the whole thing right.'

Inwardly Mr Parker Pyne cursed the obtrusive Mrs Wycherley. Resigning himself he said:

'Well, let us thrash the matter out. A girl, I suppose?'

'Did he tell you about her?'

'Only indirectly.'

Words poured in a vehement stream from Mrs Chester. 'The girl was dreadful. She drank, she swore—she wore no clothes to speak of. Her sister lived out here—was married to an artist—a Dutchman. The whole set was most undesirable. Half of them were living together without being married. Basil was completely changed. He had always been so quiet, so interested in serious subjects. He had thought at one time of taking up archaeology—'

125

'Well, well,' said Mr Parker Pyne. 'Nature will have her revenge.'

'What do you mean?'

'It isn't healthy for a young man to be interested in serious subjects. He ought to be making an idiot of himself over one girl after another.'

'Please be serious, Mr Pyne.'

'I'm perfectly serious. Is the young lady, by any chance, the one who had tea with you yesterday?'

He had noticed her—her grey flannel trousers—the scarlet handkerchief tied loosely around her breast—the vermilion mouth and the fact that she had chosen a cocktail in preference to tea.

'You saw her? Terrible! Not the kind of girl Basil has ever admired.'

'You haven't given him much chance to admire a girl, have you?'

'I?'

'He's been too fond of *your* company! Bad! However, I daresay he'll get over this—if you don't precipitate matters.'

'You don't understand. He wants to marry this girl— Betty Gregg—they're *engaged.*'

'It's gone as far as that?'

'Yes. Mr Parker Pyne, you *must* do something. You must get my boy out of this disastrous marriage! His whole life will be ruined.'

'Nobody's life can be ruined except by themselves.'

'Basil's will be,' said Mrs Chester positively.

'I'm not worrying about Basil.'

'You're not worrying about the *girl?*'

'No, I'm worrying about *you.* You've been squandering your birthright.'

Mrs Chester looked at him, slightly taken aback.

'What are the years from twenty to forty? Fettered and bound by personal and emotional relationships. That's bound to be. That's living. But later there's a new stage. You can think, observe life, discover something about other people and the truth about yourself. Life becomes real—significant. You see it as a whole. Not just one scene—the scene you, as an actor, are playing. No man or woman is actually himself (or herself) till after forty-five. That's when individuality has a chance.'

Mrs Chester said:

'I've been wrapped up in Basil. He's been *everything* to me.'

'Well, he shouldn't have been. That's what you're paying for now. Love him as much as you like—but you're Adela Chester, remember, a person—not just Basil's mother.'

'It will break my heart if Basil's life is ruined,' said Basil's mother.

He looked at the delicate lines of her face, the wistful droop of her mouth. She was, somehow, a lovable woman. He did not want her to be hurt. He said:

'I'll see what I can do.'

He found Basil Chester only too ready to talk, eager to urge his point of view.

'This business is being just hellish. Mother's hopeless—prejudiced, narrow-minded. If only she'd let herself, she'd *see* how fine Betty is.'

'And Betty?'

He sighed.

'Betty's being damned difficult! If she'd just conform a bit—I mean leave off the lipstick for a day—it might make all the difference. She seems to go out of her way to be—well—modern—when Mother's about.'

Mr Parker Pyne smiled.

'Betty and Mother are two of the dearest people in the world, I should have thought they would have taken to each other like hot cakes.'

'You have a lot to learn, young man,' said Mr Parker Pyne.

'I wish you'd come along and see Betty and have a good talk about it all.'

Mr Parker Pyne accepted the invitation readily.

Betty and her sister and her husband lived in a small dilapidated villa a little way back from the sea. Their life was of a refreshing simplicity. Their furniture comprised three chairs, a table and beds. There was a cupboard in the wall that held the bare requirements of cups and plates. Hans was an excitable young man with wild blond hair that stood up all over his head. He spoke very odd English with incredible rapidity, walking up and down as he did so. Stella, his wife, was small and fair. Betty Gregg had red hair and freckles and a mischievous eye. She was, he noticed, not nearly so made-up as she had been the previous day at the Pino d'Oro.

She gave him a cocktail and said with a twinkle:

'You're in on the big bust-up?'

Mr Parker Pyne nodded.

'And whose side are you on, big boy? The young lovers—or the disapproving dame?'

'May I ask you a question?'

'Certainly.'

'Have you been very tactful over all this?'

'Not at all,' said Miss Gregg frankly. 'But the old cat put my back up.' (She glanced round to make sure that Basil was out of earshot) 'That woman just makes me feel mad. She's kept Basil tied to her apron strings all these years—that sort of thing makes a man look a fool. Basil isn't a fool really. Then she's so terribly *pukka sahib*.'

128

'That's not really such a bad thing. It's merely "unfashionable" just at present.'

Betty Gregg gave a sudden twinkle.

'You mean it's like putting Chippendale chairs in the attic in Victorian days? Later you get them down again and say, "Aren't they marvellous?" '

'Something of the kind.'

Betty Gregg considered.

'Perhaps you're right. I'll be honest. It was Basil who put my back up—being so anxious about what impression I'd make on his mother. It drove me to extremes. Even now I believe he might give me up—if his mother worked on him good and hard.'

'He might,' said Mr Parker Pyne. 'If she went about it the right way.'

'Are you going to tell her the right way? She won't think of it herself, you know. She'll just go on disapproving and that won't do the trick. But if you prompted her—'

She bit her lip—raised frank blue eyes to his.

'I've heard about you, Mr Parker Pyne. You're supposed to know something about human nature.

Do you think Basil and I could make a go of it—or not?'

'I should like an answer to three questions.'

'Suitability test? All right, go ahead.'

'Do you sleep with your window open or shut?'

'Open. I like lots of air.'

'Do you and Basil enjoy the same kind of food?'

'Yes.'

'Do you like going to bed early or late?'

'Really, under the rose, early. At half past ten I yawn—and I secretly feel rather hearty in the mornings—but of course I daren't admit it.'

129

'You ought to suit each other very well,' said Mr Parker Pyne.

'Rather a superficial test.'

'Not at all. I have known seven marriages at least, entirely wrecked, because the husband liked sitting up till midnight and the wife fell asleep at half past nine and vice versa.'

'It's a pity,' said Betty, 'that everybody can't be happy. Basil and I, and his mother giving us her blessing.'

Mr Parker Pyne coughed.

'I think,' he said, 'that that could possibly be managed.'

She looked at him doubtfully.

'Now I wonder,' she said, 'if you're double-crossing me?'

Mr Parker Pyne's face told nothing.

To Mrs Chester he was soothing, but vague. An engagement was not marriage. He himself was going to Soller for a week. He suggested that her line of action should be non-committal. Let her appear to acquiesce.

He spent a very enjoyable week at Soller.

On his return he found that a totally unexpected development had arisen.

As he entered the Pino d'Oro the first thing he saw was Mrs Chester and Betty Gregg having tea together. Basil was not there. Mrs Chester looked haggard. Betty, too, was looking off colour. She was hardly made-up at all, and her eyelids looked as though she had been crying.

They greeted him in a friendly fashion, but neither of them mentioned Basil.

Suddenly he heard the girl beside him draw in her breath sharply as though something had hurt her. Mr Parker Pyne turned his head.

Basil Chester was coming up the steps from the sea front. With him was a girl so exotically beautiful that it quite took your breath away. She was dark and her figure was marvellous. No one could fail to notice the fact since she wore nothing but a single garment of pale blue crêpe. She was heavily made-up with ochre powder and an orange scarlet mouth—but the unguents only displayed her remarkable beauty in a more pronounced fashion. As for young Basil, he seemed unable to take his eyes from her face.

'You're very late, Basil,' said his mother. 'You were to have taken Betty to Mac's.'

'My fault,' drawled the beautiful unknown. 'We just drifted.' She turned to Basil. 'Angel—get me something with a kick in it!'

She tossed off her shoe and stretched out her mani-cured toenails which were done emerald green to match her fingernails.

She paid no attention to the two women, but she leaned a little towards Mr Parker Pyne.

'Terrible island this,' she said. 'I was just dying with boredom before I met Basil. He is rather a pet!'

'Mr Parker Pyne—Miss Ramona,' said Mrs Chester.

The girl acknowledged the introduction with a lazy smile.

'I guess I'll call you Parker almost at once,' she mur-mured. 'My name's Dolores.'

Basil returned with the drinks. Miss Ramona divided her conversation (what there was of it—it was mostly glances) between Basil and Mr Parker Pyne. Of the two women she took no notice whatever. Betty attempted once or twice to join in the conversation but the other girl merely stared at her and yawned.

Suddenly Dolores rose.

'Guess I'll be going along now. I'm at the other hotel. Anyone coming to see me home?'

131

Basil sprang up.

'I'll come with you.'

Mrs Chester said: 'Basil, my dear—'

'I'll be back presently, Mother.'

'Isn't he the mother's boy?' Miss Ramona asked of the world at large. 'Just toots round after her, don't you?'

Basil flushed and looked awkward. Miss Ramona gave a nod in Mrs Chester's direction, a dazzling smile to Mr Parker Pyne and she and Basil moved off together.

After they had gone there was rather an awkward silence. Mr Parker Pyne did not like to speak first. Betty Gregg was twisting her fingers and looking out to sea. Mrs Chester looked flushed and angry.

Betty said: 'Well, what do you think of our new acquisition in Pollensa Bay?' Her voice was not quite steady.

Mr Parker Pyne said cautiously:

'A little—er—exotic.'

'Exotic?' Betty gave a short bitter laugh.

Mrs Chester said: 'She's terrible—terrible. Basil must be quite mad.'

Betty said sharply: 'Basil's all right.'

'Her toenails,' said Mrs Chester with a shiver of nausea.

Betty rose suddenly.

'I think, Mrs Chester, I'll go home and not stay to dinner after all.'

'Oh, my dear—Basil will be so disappointed.'

'Will he?' asked Betty with a short laugh. 'Anyway, I think I will. I've got rather a headache.'

She smiled at them both and went off. Mrs Chester turned to Mr Parker Pyne.

'I wish we had never come to this place—never!'

Mr Parker Pyne shook his head sadly.

'You shouldn't have gone away,' said Mrs Chester. 'If you'd been here this wouldn't have happened.'

Mr Parker Pyne was stung to respond.

'My dear lady, I can assure you that when it comes to a question of a beautiful young woman, I should have no influence over your son whatever. He—er—seems to be of a very susceptible nature.'

'He never used to be,' said Mrs Chester tearfully.

'Well,' said Mr Parker Pyne with an attempt at cheerfulness, 'this new attraction seems to have broken the back of his infatuation for Miss Gregg. That must be some satisfaction to you.'

'I don't know what you mean,' said Mrs Chester. 'Betty is a dear child and devoted to Basil. She is behaving extremely well over this. I think my boy must be mad.'

Mr Parker Pyne received this startling change of face without wincing. He had met inconsistency in women before. He said mildly:

'Not exactly mad—just bewitched.'

'She's impossible.'

'But extremely good-looking.'

Mrs Chester snorted.

Basil ran up the steps from the sea front.

'Hullo, Mater, here I am. Where's Betty?'

'Betty's gone home with a headache. I don't wonder.'

'Sulking, you mean.'

'I consider, Basil, that you are being extremely unkind to Betty.'

'For God's sake, Mother, don't jaw. If Betty is going to make this fuss every time I speak to another girl a nice sort of life we'll lead together.'

'You *are* engaged.'

'Oh, we're engaged all right. That doesn't mean that we're not going to have any friends of our own.

Nowadays people have to lead their own lives and try to cut out jealousy.'

He paused.

'Look here, if Betty isn't going to dine with us—I think I'll go back to the Mariposa. They did ask me to dine . . .'

'Oh, Basil—'

The boy gave her an exasperated look, then ran off down the steps.

Mrs Chester looked eloquently at Mr Parker Pyne.

'You see,' she said.

He saw.

Matters came to a head a couple of days later. Betty and Basil were to have gone for a long walk, taking a picnic lunch with them. Betty arrived at the Pino d'Oro to find that Basil had forgotten the plan and gone over to Formentor for the day with Dolores Ramona's party.

Beyond a tightening of the lips the girl made no sign. Presently, however, she got up and stood in front of Mrs Chester (the two women were alone on the terrace).

'It's quite all right,' she said. 'It doesn't matter. But I think—all the same—that we'd better call the whole thing off.'

She slipped from her finger the signet ring that Basil had given her—he would buy the real engagement ring later.

'Will you give him back this Mrs Chester? And tell him it's all right—not to worry . . .'

'Betty dear, don't! He *does* love you—really.'

'It looks like it, doesn't it?' said the girl with a short laugh. 'No—I've got some pride. Tell him everything's all right and that I—I wish him luck.'

When Basil returned at sunset he was greeted by a storm.

He flushed a little at the sight of his ring.

'So that's how she feels, is it? Well, I daresay it's the best thing.'

'Basil!'

'Well, frankly, Mother, we don't seem to have been hitting it off lately.'

'Whose fault was that?'

'I don't see that it was mine particularly. Jealousy's beastly and I really don't see why *you* should get all worked up about it. You begged me yourself not to marry Betty.'

'That was before I knew her. Basil—my dear—you're not thinking of marrying this other creature.'

Basil Chester said soberly:

'I'd marry her like a shot if she'd have me—but I'm afraid she won't.'

Cold chills went down Mrs Chester's spine. She sought and found Mr Parker Pyne, placidly reading a book in a sheltered corner.

'You must *do* something! You *must* do something! My boy's life will be ruined.'

Mr Parker Pyne was getting a little tired of Basil Chester's life being ruined.

'What can I do?'

'Go and see this terrible creature. If necessary buy her off.'

'That may come very expensive.'

'I don't care.'

'It seems a pity. Still there are, possibly, other ways.'

She looked a question. He shook his head.

'I'll make no promises—but I'll see what I can do. I have handled that kind before. By the way, not a word to Basil—that would be fatal.'

'Of course not.'

Mr Parker Pyne returned from the Mariposa at midnight. Mrs Chester was sitting up for him.

'Well?' she demanded breathlessly.

His eyes twinkled.

'The Señorita Dolores Ramona will leave Pollensa tomorrow morning and the island tomorrow night.'

'Oh, Mr Parker Pyne! How did you manage it?'

'It won't cost a cent,' said Mr Parker Pyne. Again his eyes twinkled. 'I rather fancied I might have a hold over her—and I was right.'

'You are wonderful. Nina Wycherley was quite right. You must let me know—er—your fees—'

Mr Parker Pyne held up a well-manicured hand.

'Not a penny. It has been a pleasure. I hope all will go well. Of course the boy will be very upset at first when he finds she's disappeared and left no address. Just go easy with him for a week or two.'

'If only Betty will forgive him—'

'She'll forgive him all right. They're a nice couple. By the way, I'm leaving tomorrow, too.'

'Oh, Mr Parker Pyne, we shall miss you.'

'Perhaps it's just as well I should go before that boy of yours gets infatuated with yet a third girl.'

Mr Parker Pyne leaned over the rail of the steamer and looked at the lights of Palma. Beside him stood Dolores Ramona. He was saying appreciatively:

'A very nice piece of work, Madeleine. I'm glad I wired you to come out. It's odd when you're such a quiet, stay-at-home girl really.'

Madeleine de Sara, alias Dolores Ramona, alias Maggie Sayers, said primly: 'I'm glad you're pleased, Mr Parker Pyne. It's been a nice little change. I think I'll go below now and get to bed before the boat starts. I'm such a bad sailor.'

A few minutes later a hand fell on Mr Parker Pyne's shoulder. He turned to see Basil Chester.

'Had to come and see you off, Mr Parker Pyne, and give you Betty's love and her and my best thanks. It was a grand stunt of yours. Betty and Mother are as thick as thieves. Seemed a shame to deceive the old darling—but she *was* being difficult. Anyway it's all right now. I must just be careful to keep up the annoyance stuff a couple of days longer. We're no end grateful to you, Betty and I.'

'I wish you every happiness,' said Mr Parker Pyne. 'Thanks.'

There was a pause, then Basil said with somewhat overdone carelessness:

'Is Miss—Miss de Sara—anywhere about? I'd like to thank her, too.'

Mr Parker Pyne shot a keen glance at him.

He said:

'I'm afraid Miss de Sara's gone to bed.'

'Oh, too bad—well, perhaps I'll see her in London sometime.'

'As a matter of fact she is going to America on business for me almost at once.'

'Oh!' Basil's tone was blank. 'Well,' he said. 'I'll be getting along ...'

Mr Parker Pyne smiled. On his way to his cabin he tapped on the door of Madeleine's.

'How are you, my dear? All right? Our young friend has been along. The usual slight attack of Madeleinitis. He'll get over it in a day or two, but you are rather distracting.'

Sanctuary

The vicar's wife came round the corner of the vicarage with her arms full of chrysanthemums. A good deal of rich garden soil was attached to her strong brogue shoes and a few fragments of earth were adhering to her nose, but of that fact she was perfectly unconscious.

She had a slight struggle in opening the vicarage gate which hung, rustily, half off its hinges. A puff of wind caught at her battered felt hat, causing it to sit even more rakishly than it had done before. 'Bother!' said Bunch.

Christened by her optimistic parents Diana, Mrs Harmon had become Bunch at an early age for somewhat obvious reasons and the name had stuck to her ever since. Clutching the chrysanthemums, she made her way through the gate to the churchyard, and so to the church door.

The November air was mild and damp. Clouds scudded across the sky with patches of blue here and there. Inside, the church was dark and cold; it was unheated except at service times.

'Brrrrrh!' said Bunch expressively. 'I'd better get on with this quickly. I don't want to die of cold.'

With the quickness born of practice she collected the necessary paraphernalia: vases, water, flower-holders. 'I wish we had lilies,' thought Bunch to herself. 'I get

138

so tired of these scraggy chrysanthemums.' Her nimble fingers arranged the blooms in their holders.

There was nothing particularly original or artistic about the decorations, for Bunch Harmon herself was neither original nor artistic, but it was a homely and pleasant arrangement. Carrying the vases carefully, Bunch stepped up the aisle and made her way towards the altar. As she did so the sun came out.

It shone through the east window of somewhat crude coloured glass, mostly blue and red—the gift of a wealthy Victorian churchgoer. The effect was almost startling in its sudden opulence. 'Like jewels,' thought Bunch. Suddenly she stopped, staring ahead of her. On the chancel steps was a huddled dark form.

Putting down the flowers carefully, Bunch went up to it and bent over it. It was a man lying there, huddled over on himself. Bunch knelt down by him and slowly, carefully, she turned him over. Her fingers went to his pulse—a pulse so feeble and fluttering that it told its own story, as did the almost greenish pallor of his face. There was no doubt, Bunch thought, that the man was dying.

He was a man of about forty-five, dressed in a dark, shabby suit. She laid down the limp hand she had picked up and looked at his other hand. This seemed clenched like a fist on his breast. Looking more closely she saw that the fingers were closed over what seemed to be a large wad or handkerchief which he was holding tightly to his chest. All round the clenched hand there were splashes of a dry brown fluid which, Bunch guessed, was dry blood. Bunch sat back on her heels, frowning.

Up till now the man's eyes had been closed but at this point they suddenly opened and fixed themselves on Bunch's face. They were neither dazed nor wandering.

They seemed fully alive and intelligent. His lips moved, and Bunch bent forward to catch the words, or rather the word. It was only one word that he said:

'Sanctuary.'

There was, she thought, just a very faint smile as he breathed out this word. There was no mistaking it, for after a moment he said it again, 'Sanctuary . . .'

Then, with a faint, long-drawn-out sigh, his eyes closed again. Once more Bunch's fingers went to his pulse. It was still there, but fainter now and more intermittent. She got up with decision.

'Don't move,' she said, 'or try to move. I'm going for help.'

The man's eyes opened again but he seemed now to be fixing his attention on the coloured light that came through the east window. He murmured something that Bunch could not quite catch. She thought, startled, that it might have been her husband's name.

'Julian?' she said. 'Did you come here to find Julian?' But there was no answer. The man lay with eyes closed, his breathing coming in slow, shallow fashion.

Bunch turned and left the church rapidly. She glanced at her watch and nodded with some satisfaction. Dr Griffiths would still be in his surgery. It was only a couple of minutes' walk from the church. She went in, without waiting to knock or ring, passing through the waiting room and into the doctor's surgery.

'You must come at once,' said Bunch. 'There's a man dying in the church.'

Some minutes later Dr Griffiths rose from his knees after a brief examination.

'Can we move him from here into the vicarage? I can attend to him better there—not that it's any use.'

'Of course,' said Bunch. 'I'll go along and get things

ready. I'll get Harper and Jones, shall I? To help you carry him.'

'Thanks. I can telephone from the vicarage for an ambulance, but I'm afraid—by the time it comes ...' He left the remark unfinished.

Bunch said, 'Internal bleeding?'

Dr Griffiths nodded. He said, 'How on earth did he come here?'

'I think he must have been here all night,' said Bunch, considering. 'Harper unlocks the church in the morning as he goes to work, but he doesn't usually come in.'

It was about five minutes later when Dr Griffiths put down the telephone receiver and came back into the morning-room where the injured man was lying on quickly arranged blankets on the sofa. Bunch was moving a basin of water and clearing up after the doctor's examination.

'Well, that's that,' said Griffiths. 'I've sent for an ambulance and I've notified the police.' He stood, frowning, looking down on the patient who lay with closed eyes. His left hand was plucking in a nervous, spasmodic way at his side.

'He was shot,' said Griffiths. 'Shot at fairly close quarters. He rolled his handkerchief up into a ball and plugged the wound with it so as to stop the bleeding.'

'Could he have gone far after that happened?' Bunch asked.

'Oh, yes, it's quite possible. A mortally wounded man has been known to pick himself up and walk along a street as though nothing had happened, and then suddenly collapse five or ten minutes later. So he needn't have been shot in the church. Oh no. He may have been shot some distance away. Of course, he may have shot himself and then dropped the revolver and staggered blindly towards the church. I don't quite know why he made for the church and not for the vicarage.'

'Oh, I know *that*,' said Bunch. 'He said it: "Sanctuary."'

The doctor stared at her. 'Sanctuary?'

'Here's Julian,' said Bunch, turning her head as she heard her husband's steps in the hall. 'Julian! Come here.'

The Reverend Julian Harmon entered the room. His vague, scholarly manner always made him appear much older than he really was. 'Dear me!' said Julian Harmon, staring in a mild, puzzled manner at the surgical appliances and the prone figure on the sofa.

Bunch explained with her usual economy of words. 'He was in the church, dying. He'd been shot. Do you know him, Julian? I thought he said your name.'

The vicar came up to the sofa and looked down at the dying man. 'Poor fellow,' he said, and shook his head. 'No, I don't know him. I'm almost sure I've never seen him before.'

At that moment the dying man's eyes opened once more. They went from the doctor to Julian Harmon and from him to his wife. The eyes stayed there, staring into Bunch's face. Griffiths stepped forward.

'If you could tell us,' he said urgently.

But with eyes fixed on Bunch, the man said in a weak voice, 'Please—*please*—' And then, with a slight tremor, he died . . .

Sergeant Hayes licked his pencil and turned the page of his notebook.

'So that's all you can tell me, Mrs Harmon?'

'That's all,' said Bunch. 'These are the things out of his coat pockets.'

On a table at Sergeant Hayes's elbow was a wallet, a

rather battered old watch with the initials W.S. and the return half of a ticket to London. Nothing more.

'You've found out who he is?' asked Bunch.

'A Mr and Mrs Eccles phoned up the station. He's her brother, it seems. Name of Sandbourne. Been in a low state of health and nerves for some time. He's been getting worse lately. The day before yesterday he walked out and didn't come back. He took a revolver with him.'

'And he came out here and shot himself with it?' said Bunch. 'Why?'

'Well, you see, he'd been depressed . . .'

Bunch interrupted him. 'I don't mean *that*. I mean, why here?'

Since Sergeant Hayes obviously did not know the answer to that one, he replied in an oblique fashion, 'Come out here, he did, on the five-ten bus.'

'Yes,' said Bunch again. 'But *why*?'

'I don't know, Mrs Harmon,' said Sergeant Hayes. 'There's no accounting. If the balance of the mind is disturbed—'

Bunch finished for him. 'They may do it anywhere. But it still seems to me unnecessary to take a bus out to a small country place like this. He didn't know anyone here, did he?'

'Not so far as can be ascertained,' said Sergeant Hayes. He coughed in an apologetic manner and said, as he rose to his feet, 'It may be as Mr and Mrs Eccles will come out and see you, ma'am—if you don't mind, that is.'

'Of course I don't mind,' said Bunch. 'It's very natural. I only wish I had something to tell them.'

'I'll be getting along,' said Sergeant Hayes.

'I'm only so thankful,' said Bunch, going with him to the front door, 'that it wasn't murder.'

A car had driven up at the vicarage gate. Sergeant Hayes, glancing at it, remarked: 'Looks as though that's Mr and Mrs Eccles come here now, ma'am, to talk with you.'

Bunch braced herself to endure what, she felt, might be rather a difficult ordeal. 'However,' she thought, 'I can always call Julian to help me. A clergyman's a great help when people are bereaved.'

Exactly what she had expected Mr and Mrs Eccles to be like, Bunch could not have said, but she was conscious, as she greeted them, of a feeling of surprise. Mr Eccles was a stout florid man whose natural manner would have been cheerful and facetious. Mrs Eccles had a vaguely flashy look about her. She had a small, mean, pursed-up mouth. Her voice was thin and reedy.

'It's been a terrible shock, Mrs Harmon, as you can imagine,' she said.

'Oh, I know,' said Bunch. 'It must have been. Do sit down. Can I offer you—well, perhaps it's a little early for tea—'

Mr Eccles waved a pudgy hand. 'No, no, nothing for us,' he said. 'It's very kind of you, I'm sure. Just wanted to ... well ... what poor William said and all that, you know?'

'He's been abroad a long time,' said Mrs Eccles, 'and I think he must have had some very nasty experiences. Very quiet and depressed he's been, ever since he came home. Said the world wasn't fit to live in and there was nothing to look forward to. Poor Bill, he was always moody.'

Bunch stared at them both for a moment or two without speaking.

'Pinched my husband's revolver, he did,' went on Mrs Eccles. 'Without our knowing. Then it seems he come

144

here by bus. I suppose that was nice feeling on his part. He wouldn't have liked to do it in our house.'

'Poor fellow, poor fellow,' said Mr Eccles, with a sigh. 'It doesn't do to judge.'

There was another short pause, and Mr Eccles said, 'Did he leave a message? Any last words, nothing like that?'

His bright, rather pig-like eyes watched Bunch closely. Mrs Eccles, too, leaned forward as though anxious for the reply.

'No,' said Bunch quietly. 'He came into the church when he was dying, for sanctuary.'

Mrs Eccles said in a puzzled voice. 'Sanctuary? I don't think I quite . . .'

Mr Eccles interrupted. 'Holy place, my dear,' he said impatiently. 'That's what the vicar's wife means. It's a sin—suicide, you know. I expect he wanted to make amends.'

'He tried to say something just before he died,' said Bunch. 'He began, "Please," but that's as far as he got.'

Mrs Eccles put her handkerchief to her eyes and sniffed. 'Oh, dear,' she said. 'It's terribly upsetting, isn't it?'

'There, there, Pam,' said her husband. 'Don't take on. These things can't be helped. Poor Willie. Still, he's at peace now. Well, thank you very much, Mrs Harmon. I hope we haven't interrupted you. A vicar's wife is a busy lady, we know that.'

They shook hands with her. Then Eccles turned back suddenly to say, 'Oh yes, there's just one other thing. I think you've got his coat here, haven't you?'

'His coat?' Bunch frowned.

Mrs Eccles said, 'We'd like all his things, you know. Sentimental-like.'

'He had a watch and a wallet and a railway ticket in the pockets,' said Bunch. 'I gave them to Sergeant Hayes.'

'That's all right, then,' said Mr Eccles. 'He'll hand them over to us, I expect. His private papers would be in the wallet.'

'There was a pound note in the wallet,' said Bunch. 'Nothing else.'

'No letters? Nothing like that?'

Bunch shook her head.

'Well, thank you again, Mrs Harmon. The coat he was wearing—perhaps the sergeant's got that too, has he?'

Bunch frowned in an effort of remembrance.

'No,' she said. 'I don't think ... let me see. The doctor and I took his coat off to examine his wound.' She looked round the room vaguely. 'I must have taken it upstairs with the towels and basin.'

'I wonder now, Mrs Harmon, if you don't mind ... We'd like his coat, you know, the last thing he wore. Well, the wife feels rather sentimental about it.'

'Of course,' said Bunch. 'Would you like me to have it cleaned first? I'm afraid it's rather—well—stained.'

'Oh, no, no, no, that doesn't matter.'

Bunch frowned. 'Now I wonder where ... excuse me a moment.' She went upstairs and it was some few minutes before she returned.

'I'm so sorry,' she said breathlessly, 'my daily woman must have put it aside with other clothes that were going to the cleaners. It's taken me quite a long time to find it. Here it is. I'll do it up for you in brown paper.'

Disclaiming their protests she did so; then once more effusively bidding her farewell the Eccleses departed.

Bunch went slowly back across the hall and entered the study. The Reverend Julian Harmon looked up and his brow cleared. He was composing a sermon and was fearing that he'd been led astray by the interest of the political relations between Judaea and Persia, in the reign of Cyrus.

'Yes, dear?' he said hopefully.

'Julian,' said Bunch. 'What's *Sanctuary* exactly?'

Julian Harmon gratefully put aside his sermon paper.

'Well,' he said. 'Sanctuary in Roman and Greek temples applied to the *cella* in which stood the statue of a god. The Latin word for altar "*ara*" also means protection.' He continued learnedly: 'In three hundred and ninety-nine A.D. the right of sanctuary in Christian churches was finally and definitely recognized. The earliest mention of the right of sanctuary in England is in the Code of Laws issued by Ethelbert in A.D. six hundred . . .'

He continued for some time with his exposition but was, as often, disconcerted by his wife's reception of his erudite pronouncement.

'Darling,' she said. 'You *are* sweet.'

Bending over, she kissed him on the tip of his nose. Julian felt rather like a dog who has been congratulated on performing a clever trick.

'The Eccleses have been here,' said Bunch.

The vicar frowned. 'The Eccleses? I don't seem to remember . . .'

'You don't know them. They're the sister and her husband of the man in the church.'

'My dear, you ought to have called me.'

'There wasn't any need,' said Bunch. 'They were not in need of consolation. I wonder now . . .' She frowned. 'If I put a casserole in the oven tomorrow, can you manage, Julian? I think I shall go up to London for the sales.'

'The sails?' Her husband looked at her blankly. 'Do you mean a yacht or a boat or something?'

Bunch laughed. 'No, darling. There's a special white sale at Burrows and Portman's. You know, sheets, table cloths and towels and glass-cloths. I don't know what we do with our glass-cloths, the way they wear through. Besides,' she added thoughtfully, 'I think I ought to go and see Aunt Jane.'

That sweet old lady, Miss Jane Marple, was enjoying the delights of the metropolis for a fortnight, comfortably installed in her nephew's studio flat.

'So kind of dear Raymond,' she murmured. 'He and Joan have gone to America for a fortnight and they insisted I should come up here and enjoy myself. And now, dear Bunch, do tell me what it is that's worrying you.'

Bunch was Miss Marple's favourite godchild, and the old lady looked at her with great affection as Bunch, thrusting her best felt hat farther on the back of her head, started her story.

Bunch's recital was concise and clear. Miss Marple nodded her head as Bunch finished. 'I see,' she said. 'Yes, I see.'

'That's why I felt I had to see you,' said Bunch. 'You see, not being clever—'

'But you *are* clever, my dear.'

'No, I'm not. Not clever like Julian.'

'Julian, of course, has a very solid intellect,' said Miss Marple.

'That's it,' said Bunch. 'Julian's got the intellect, but on the other hand, I've got the *sense*.'

'You have a lot of common sense, Bunch, and you're very intelligent.'

'You see, I don't really know what I ought to do.

148

I can't ask Julian because—well, I mean, Julian's so full of rectitude . . .'

This statement appeared to be perfectly understood by Miss Marple, who said, 'I know what you mean, dear. We women—well, it's different.' She went on. 'You told me what happened, Bunch, but I'd like to know first exactly what you think.'

'It's all wrong,' said Bunch. 'The man who was there in the church, dying, knew all about Sanctuary. He said it just the way Julian would have said it. I mean, he was a well-read, educated man. And if he'd shot himself, he wouldn't drag himself to a church afterwards and say "sanctuary". Sanctuary means that you're pursued, and when you get into a church you're safe. Your pursuers can't touch you. At one time even the law couldn't get at you.'

She looked questioningly at Miss Marple. The latter nodded. Bunch went on, 'Those people, the Eccleses, were quite different. Ignorant and coarse. And there's another thing. That watch—the dead man's watch. It had the initials W.S. on the back of it. But inside—I opened it—in very small lettering there was "To Walter from his father" and a date. *Walter*. But the Eccleses kept talking of him as William or Bill.'

Miss Marple seemed about to speak but Bunch rushed on. 'Oh, I know you're not always called the name you're baptized by. I mean, I can understand that you might be christened William and called "Porgy" or "Carrots" or something. But your sister wouldn't call you William or Bill if your name was Walter.'

'You mean that she wasn't his sister?'

'I'm quite sure she wasn't his sister. They were horrid—both of them. They came to the vicarage to get his things and to find out if he'd said anything before he died. When I said he hadn't I saw it in their faces—relief. I think myself,' finished Bunch, 'it was Eccles who shot him.'

'Murder?' said Miss Marple.

'Yes,' said Bunch. 'Murder. That's why I came to you, darling.'

Bunch's remark might have seemed incongruous to an ignorant listener, but in certain spheres Miss Marple had a reputation for dealing with murder.

'He said "please" to me before he died,' said Bunch. 'He wanted me to do something for him. The awful thing is I've no idea what.'

Miss Marple considered for a moment or two, and then pounced on the point that had already occurred to Bunch. 'But why was he there at all?' she asked.

'You mean,' said Bunch, 'if you wanted sanctuary you might pop into a church anywhere. There's no need to take a bus that only goes four times a day and come out to a lonely spot like ours for it.'

'He must have come there for a purpose,' Miss Marple thought. 'He must have come to see someone. Chipping Cleghorn's not a big place, Bunch. Surely you must have some idea of who it was he came to see?'

Bunch reviewed the inhabitants of her village in her mind before rather doubtfully shaking her head. 'In a way,' she said, 'it could be anybody.'

'He never mentioned a name?'

'He said Julian, or I thought he said Julian. It might have been Julia, I suppose. As far as I know, there isn't any Julia living in Chipping Cleghorn.'

She screwed up her eyes as she thought back to the scene. The man lying there on the chancel steps, the light coming through the window with its jewels of red and blue light.

'Jewels,' said Miss Marple thoughtfully.

'I'm coming now,' said Bunch, 'to the most important thing of all. The reason why I've really come here today. You see, the Eccleses made a great fuss about having his coat. We took it off when the doctor was seeing him. It was an old, shabby sort of coat—there was no reason they should have wanted it. They pretended it was sentimental, but that was nonsense.

'Anyway, I went up to find it, and as I was just going up the stairs I remembered how he'd made a kind of picking gesture with his hand, as though he was fumbling with the coat. So when I got hold of the coat I looked at it very carefully and I saw that in one place the lining had been sewn up again with a different thread. So I unpicked it and I found a little piece of paper inside. I took it out and I sewed it up again properly with thread that matched. I was careful and I don't really think that the Eccleses would know I've done it. I don't *think* so, but I can't be sure. And I took the coat down to them and made some excuse for the delay.'

'The piece of paper?' asked Miss Marple.

Bunch opened her handbag. 'I didn't show it to Julian,' she said, 'because he would have said that I ought to have given it to the Eccleses. But I thought I'd rather bring it to you instead.'

'A cloakroom ticket,' said Miss Marple, looking at it. 'Paddington Station.'

'He had a return ticket to Paddington in his pocket,' said Bunch.

The eyes of the two women met.

'This calls for action,' said Miss Marple briskly. 'But it would be advisable, I think, to be careful. Would you have noticed at all, Bunch dear, whether you were followed when you came to London today?'

'Followed!' exclaimed Bunch. 'You don't think—'

'Well, I think it's *possible*,' said Miss Marple. 'When anything is possible, I think we ought to take precautions.' She rose with a brisk movement. 'You came up here ostensibly, my dear, to go to the sales. I think the right thing to do, therefore, would be for us to *go* to the sales. But before we set out, we might put one or two little arrangements in hand. I don't suppose,' Miss Marple added obscurely, 'that I shall need the old speckled tweed with the beaver collar just at present.'

It was about an hour and a half later that the two ladies, rather the worse for wear and battered in appearance, and both clasping parcels of hardly-won household linen, sat down at a small and sequestered hostelry called the Apple Bough to restore their forces with steak and kidney pudding followed by apple tart and custard.

'Really a prewar quality face towel,' gasped Miss Marple, slightly out of breath. 'With a J on it, too. So fortunate that Raymond's wife's name is Joan. I shall put them aside until I really need them and then they will do for her if I pass on sooner than I expect.'

'I really did need the glass-cloths,' said Bunch. 'And they were very cheap, though not as cheap as the ones that woman with the ginger hair managed to snatch from me.'

A smart young woman with a lavish application of rouge and lipstick entered the Apple Bough at that moment. After looking around vaguely for a moment or two, she hurried to their table. She laid down an envelope by Miss Marple's elbow.

'There you are, miss,' she said briskly.

'Oh, thank you, Gladys,' said Miss Marple. 'Thank you very much. So kind of you.'

'Always pleased to oblige, I'm sure,' said Gladys.

'Ernie always says to me, "Everything what's good you learned from that Miss Marple of yours that you were in service with," and I'm sure I'm always glad to oblige you, miss.'

'Such a dear girl,' said Miss Marple as Gladys departed again. 'Always so willing and so kind.'

She looked inside the envelope and then passed it on to Bunch. 'Now be very careful, dear,' she said. 'By the way, is there still that nice young inspector at Melchester that I remember?'

'I don't know,' said Bunch. 'I expect so.'

'Well, if not,' said Miss Marple thoughtfully. 'I can always ring up the Chief Constable. I *think* he would remember me.'

'Of course he'd remember you,' said Bunch. 'Everybody would remember *you*. You're quite unique.' She rose.

Arrived at Paddington, Bunch went to the luggage office and produced the cloakroom ticket. A moment or two later a rather shabby old suitcase was passed across to her, and carrying this she made her way to the platform.

The journey home was uneventful. Bunch rose as the train approached Chipping Cleghorn and picked up the old suitcase. She had just left her carriage when a man, sprinting along the platform, suddenly seized the suitcase from her hand and rushed off with it.

'Stop!' Bunch yelled. 'Stop him, stop him. He's taken my suitcase.'

The ticket collector who, at this rural station, was a man of somewhat slow processes, had just begun to say, 'Now, look here, you can't do that—' when a smart blow on the chest pushed him aside, and the man with the suitcase rushed out from the station. He made his way towards a waiting car. Tossing the suitcase in, he was about to climb after it, but before he could move a hand fell on his shoulder, and the voice of Police Constable Abel said, 'Now then, what's all this?'

Bunch arrived, panting, from the station. 'He snatched my suitcase. I just got out of the train with it.'

'Nonsense,' said the man. 'I don't know what this lady means. It's my suitcase. I just got out of the train with it.'

He looked at Bunch with a bovine and impartial stare. Nobody would have guessed that Police Constable Abel and Mrs Harmon spent long half-hours in Police Constable Abel's off-time discussing the respective merits of manure and bone meal for rose bushes.

'You say, madam, that this is your suitcase?' said Police Constable Abel.

'Yes,' said Bunch. 'Definitely.'

'And you, sir?'

'I say this suitcase is mine.'

The man was tall, dark and well dressed, with a drawling voice and a superior manner. A feminine voice from inside the car said, 'Of course it's your suitcase, Edwin. I don't know what this woman means.'

'We'll have to get this clear,' said Police Constable Abel. 'If it's your suitcase, madam, what do you say is inside it?'

'Clothes,' said Bunch. 'A long speckled coat with a beaver collar, two wool jumpers and a pair of shoes.'

'Well, that's clear enough,' said Police Constable Abel. He turned to the other.

'I am a theatrical costumer,' said the dark man importantly. 'This suitcase contains theatrical properties which I brought down here for an amateur performance.'

'Right, sir,' said Police Constable Abel. 'Well, we'll

just look inside, shall we, and see? We can go along to the police station, or if you're in a hurry we'll take the suitcase back to the station and open it there.'

'It'll suit me,' said the dark man. 'My name is Moss, by the way, Edwin Moss.'

The police constable, holding the suitcase, went back into the station. 'Just taking this into the parcels office, George,' he said to the ticket collector.

Police Constable Abel laid the suitcase on the counter of the parcels office and pushed back the clasp. The case was not locked. Bunch and Mr Edwin Moss stood on either side of him, their eyes regarding each other vengefully.

'Ah!' said Police Constable Abel, as he pushed up the lid.

Inside, neatly folded, was a long rather shabby tweed coat with a beaver fur collar. There were also two wool jumpers and a pair of country shoes.

'Exactly as you say, madam,' said Police Constable Abel, turning to Bunch.

Nobody could have said that Mr Edwin Moss underdid things. His dismay and compunction were magnificent.

'I do apologize,' he said. 'I really *do* apologize. Please believe me, dear lady, when I tell you how very, very sorry I am. Unpardonable—quite unpardonable—my behaviour has been.' He looked at his watch. 'I must rush now. Probably my suitcase has gone on the train.' Raising his hat once more, he said meltingly to Bunch, 'Do, *do* forgive me,' and rushed hurriedly out of the parcels office.

'Are you going to let him get away?' asked Bunch in a conspiratorial whisper to Police Constable Abel.

The latter slowly closed a bovine eye in a wink.

'He won't get too far, ma'am,' he said. 'That's to say he won't get far unobserved, if you take my meaning.'

'Oh,' said Bunch, relieved.

'That old lady's been on the phone,' said Police Constable Abel, 'the one as was down here a few years ago. Bright she is, isn't she? But there's been a lot cooking up all today. Shouldn't wonder if the inspector or sergeant was out to see you about it tomorrow morning.'

It was the inspector who came, the Inspector Craddock whom Miss Marple remembered. He greeted Bunch with a smile as an old friend.

'Crime in Chipping Cleghorn again,' he said cheerfully. 'You don't lack for sensation here, do you, Mrs Harmon?'

'I could do with rather less,' said Bunch. 'Have you come to ask me questions or are you going to tell me things for a change?'

'I'll tell you some things first,' said the inspector. 'To begin with, Mr and Mrs Eccles have been having an eye kept on them for some time. There's reason to believe they've been connected with several robberies in this part of the world. For another thing, although Mrs Eccles *has* a brother called Sandbourne who has recently come back from abroad, the man you found dying in the church yesterday was definitely not Sandbourne.'

'I knew that he wasn't,' said Bunch. 'His name was Walter, to begin with, not William.'

The inspector nodded. 'His name was Walter St John, and he escaped forty-eight hours ago from Charrington Prison.'

'Of course,' said Bunch softly to herself, 'he was being hunted down by the law, and he took sanctuary.' Then she asked, 'What had he done?'

'I'll have to go back rather a long way. It's a complicated story. Several years ago there was a certain dancer doing turns at the music halls. I don't expect you'll have ever heard of her, but she specialized in an Arabian Night turn, "Aladdin in the Cave of Jewels" it was called. She wore bits of rhinestone and not much else.

'She wasn't much of a dancer, I believe, but she was—well—attractive. Anyway, a certain Asian royalty fell for her in a big way. Amongst other things he gave her a very magnificent emerald necklace.'

'The historic jewels of a Rajah?' murmured Bunch ecstatically.

Inspector Craddock coughed. 'Well, a rather more modern version, Mrs Harmon. The affair didn't last very long, broke up when our potentate's attention was captured by a certain film star whose demands were not quite so modest.

'Zobeida, to give the dancer her stage name, hung on to the necklace, and in due course it was stolen. It disappeared from her dressing-room at the theatre, and there was a lingering suspicion in the minds of the authorities that she herself might have engineered its disappearance. Such things have been known as a publicity stunt, or indeed from more dishonest motives.

'The necklace was never recovered, but during the course of the investigation the attention of the police was drawn to this man, Walter St John. He was a man of education and breeding who had come down in the world, and who was employed as a working jeweller with a rather obscure firm which was suspected of acting as a fence for jewel robberies.

'There was evidence that this necklace had passed through his hands. It was, however, in connection with the theft of some other jewellery that he was finally

157

brought to trial and convicted and sent to prison. He had not very much longer to serve, so his escape was rather a surprise.'

'But why did he come here?' asked Bunch.

'We'd like to know that very much, Mrs Harmon. Following up his trial, it seems that he went first to London. He didn't visit any of his old associates but he visited an elderly woman, a Mrs Jacobs who had formerly been a theatrical dresser. She won't say a word of what he came for, but according to other lodgers in the house he left carrying a suitcase.'

'I see,' said Bunch. 'He left it in the cloakroom at Paddington and then he came down here.'

'By that time,' said Inspector Craddock, 'Eccles and the man who calls himself Edwin Moss were on his trail. They wanted that suitcase. They saw him get on the bus. They must have driven out in a car ahead of him and been waiting for him when he left the bus.'

'And he was murdered?' said Bunch.

'Yes,' said Craddock. 'He was shot. It was Eccles's revolver, but I rather fancy it was Moss who did the shooting. Now, Mrs Harmon, what we want to know is, where is the suitcase that Walter St John actually deposited at Paddington Station?'

Bunch grinned. 'I expect Aunt Jane's got it by now,' she said. 'Miss Marple, I mean. That was her plan. She sent a former maid of hers with a suitcase packed with her things to the cloakroom at Paddington and we exchanged tickets. I collected her suitcase and brought it down by train. She seemed to expect that an attempt would be made to get it from me.'

It was Inspector Craddock's turn to grin. 'So she said when she rang up. I'm driving up to London to see her. Do you want to come, too, Mrs Harmon?'

'Wel-l,' said Bunch, considering. 'Wel-l, as a matter of fact, it's very fortunate. I had a toothache last night so I really ought to go to London to see the dentist, oughtn't I?'

'Definitely,' said Inspector Craddock ...

Miss Marple looked from Inspector Craddock's face to the eager face of Bunch Harmon. The suitcase lay on the table. 'Of course, I haven't opened it,' the old lady said. 'I wouldn't dream of doing such a thing till somebody official arrived. Besides,' she added, with a demurely mischievous Victorian smile, 'it's locked.'

'Like to make a guess at what's inside, Miss Marple?' asked the inspector.

'I should imagine, you know,' said Miss Marple, 'that it would be Zobeida's theatrical costumes. Would you like a chisel, Inspector?'

The chisel soon did its work. Both women gave a slight gasp as the lid flew up. The sunlight coming through the window lit up what seemed like an inexhaustible treasure of sparkling jewels, red, blue, green, orange.

'Aladdin's Cave,' said Miss Marple. 'The flashing jewels the girl wore to dance.'

'Ah,' said Inspector Craddock. 'Now, what's so precious about it, do you think, that a man was murdered to get hold of it?'

'She was a shrewd girl, I expect,' said Miss Marple thoughtfully. 'She's dead, isn't she, Inspector?'

'Yes, died three years ago.'

'She had this valuable emerald necklace,' said Miss Marple, musingly. 'Had the stones taken out of their setting and fastened here and there on her theatrical costume, where everyone would take them for merely coloured rhinestones. Then she had a replica made of the real necklace, and that, of course, was what was stolen. No wonder it never came on the market. The thief soon discovered the stones were false.'

'Here is an envelope,' said Bunch, pulling aside some of the glittering stones.

Inspector Craddock took it from her and extracted two official-looking papers from it. He read aloud, '"Marriage Certificate between Walter Edmund St John and Mary Moss." That was Zobeida's real name.'

'So they were married,' said Miss Marple. 'I see.'

'What's the other?' asked Bunch.

'A birth certificate of a daughter, Jewel.'

'Jewel?' cried Bunch. 'Why, of course. Jewel! *Jill!* That's it. I see now why he came to Chipping Cleghorn. *That's* what he was trying to say to me. Jewel. The Mundys, you know. Laburnum Cottage. They look after a little girl for someone. They're devoted to her. She's been like their own granddaughter. Yes, I remember now, her name *was* Jewel, only, of course, they call her Jill.

'Mrs Mundy had a stroke about a week ago, and the old man's been very ill with pneumonia. They were both going to go to the infirmary. I've been trying hard to find a good home for Jill somewhere. I didn't want her taken away to an institution.

'I suppose her father heard about it in prison and he managed to break away and get hold of this suitcase from the old dresser he or his wife left it with. I suppose if the jewels really belonged to her mother, they can be used for the child now.'

'I should imagine so, Mrs Harmon. *If* they're here.'

'Oh, they'll be here all right,' said Miss Marple cheerfully . . .

★   ★   ★

'Thank goodness you're back, dear,' said the Reverend Julian Harmon, greeting his wife with affection and a sigh of content. 'Mrs Burt always tries to do her best when you're away, but she really gave me some *very* peculiar fish-cakes for lunch. I didn't want to hurt her feelings so I gave them to Tiglath Pileser, but even *he* wouldn't eat them so I had to throw them out of the window.'

'Tiglath Pileser,' said Bunch, stroking the vicarage cat, who was purring against her knee, 'is *very* particular about what fish he eats. I often tell him he's got a proud stomach!'

'And your tooth, dear? Did you have it seen to?'

'Yes,' said Bunch. 'It didn't hurt much, and I went to see Aunt Jane again, too . . .'

'Dear old thing,' said Julian. 'I hope she's not failing at all.'

'Not in the least,' said Bunch, with a grin.

The following morning Bunch took a fresh supply of chrysanthemums to the church. The sun was once more pouring through the east window, and Bunch stood in the jewelled light on the chancel steps. She said very softly under her breath, 'Your little girl will be all right. *I'll* see that she is. I promise.'

Then she tidied up the church, slipped into a pew and knelt for a few moments to say her prayers before returning to the vicarage to attack the piled-up chores of two neglected days.

The Mystery of Hunter's Lodge

'After all,' murmured Poirot, 'it is possible that I shall not die this time.'

Coming from a convalescent influenza patient, I hailed the remark as showing a beneficial optimism. I myself had been the first sufferer from the disease. Poirot in his turn had gone down. He was now sitting up in bed, propped up with pillows, his head muffled in a woollen shawl, and was slowly sipping a particularly noxious *tisane* which I had prepared according to his directions. His eye rested with pleasure upon a neatly graduated row of medicine bottles which adorned the mantelpiece.

'Yes, yes,' my little friend continued. 'Once more shall I be myself again, the great Hercule Poirot, the terror of evildoers! Figure to yourself, *mon ami*, that I have a little paragraph to myself in *Society Gossip*. But yes! Here it is: "Go it—criminals—all out! Hercule Poirot—and believe me, girls, he's some Hercules!—our own pet society detective can't get a grip on you. 'Cause why? 'Cause he's got *la grippe* himself"!'

I laughed.

'Good for you, Poirot. You are becoming quite a public character. And fortunately you haven't missed anything of particular interest during this time.'

'That is true. The few cases I have had to decline did not fill me with any regret.'

Our landlady stuck her head in at the door.

'There's a gentleman downstairs. Says he must see Monsieur Poirot or you, Captain. Seeing as he was in a great to-do—and with all that quite the gentleman—I brought up 'is card.'

She handed me a bit of pasteboard. 'Mr Roger Havering,' I read.

Poirot motioned with his head towards the bookcase, and I obediently pulled forth *Who's Who*. Poirot took it from me and scanned the pages rapidly.

'Second son of fifth Baron Windsor. Married 1913 Zoe, fourth daughter of William Crabb.'

'H'm!' I said. 'I rather fancy that's the girl who used to act at the Frivolity—only she called herself Zoe Carrisbrook. I remember she married some young man about town just before the War.'

'Would it interest you, Hastings, to go down and hear what our visitor's particular little trouble is? Make him all my excuses.'

Roger Havering was a man of about forty, well set up and of smart appearance. His face, however, was haggard, and he was evidently labouring under great agitation.

'Captain Hastings? You are Monsieur Poirot's partner, I understand. It is imperative that he should come with me to Derbyshire today.'

'I'm afraid that's impossible,' I replied. 'Poirot is ill in bed—influenza.'

His face fell.

'Dear me, that is a great blow to me.'

'The matter on which you want to consult him is serious?'

'My God, yes! My uncle, the best friend I have in the world, was foully murdered last night.'

'Here in London?'

'No, in Derbyshire. I was in town and received a telegram from my wife this morning. Immediately upon its receipt I determined to come round and beg Monsieur Poirot to undertake the case.'

'If you will excuse me a minute,' I said, struck by a sudden idea.

I rushed upstairs, and in a few brief words acquainted Poirot with the situation. He took any further words out of my mouth.

'I see. I see. You want to go yourself, is it not so? Well, why not? You should know my methods by now. All I ask is that you should report to me fully every day, and follow implicitly any instructions I may wire you.'

To this I willingly agreed.

An hour later I was sitting opposite Mr Havering in a first-class carriage on the Midland Railway, speeding rapidly away from London.

'To begin with, Captain Hastings, you must understand that Hunter's Lodge, where we are going, and where the tragedy took place, is only a small shooting-box in the heart of the Derbyshire moors. Our real home is near Newmarket, and we usually rent a flat in town for the season. Hunter's Lodge is looked after by a housekeeper who is quite capable of doing all we need when we run down for an occasional weekend. Of course, during the shooting season, we take down some of our own servants from Newmarket. My uncle, Mr Harrington Pace (as you may know, my mother was a Miss Pace of New York), has, for the last three years, made his home with us. He never got on well with my father, or my elder brother, and I suspect that my being somewhat of a prodigal son myself rather increased than diminished his affection towards me. Of course I am a poor man, and my uncle was a rich one—in other words, he paid the piper! But, though exacting in many ways, he was not really hard to get on with, and we all three lived very harmoniously together. Two days ago, my uncle, rather wearied with some recent gaieties of ours in town, suggested that we should run down to Derbyshire for a day or two. My wife telegraphed to Mrs Middleton, the housekeeper, and we went down that same afternoon. Yesterday evening I was forced to return to town, but my wife and my uncle remained on. This morning I received this telegram.' He handed it over to me:

'Come at once uncle Harrington murdered last night bring good detective if you can but do come—Zoe.'

'Then, as yet you know no details?'

'No, I suppose it will be in the evening papers. Without doubt the police are in charge.'

It was about three o'clock when we arrived at the little station of Elmer's Dale. From there a five-mile drive brought us to a small grey stone building in the midst of the rugged moors.

'A lonely place,' I observed with a shiver.

Havering nodded.

'I shall try and get rid of it. I could never live here again.'

We unlatched the gate and were walking up the narrow path to the oak door when a familiar figure emerged and came to meet us.

'Japp!' I ejaculated.

The Scotland Yard inspector grinned at me in a friendly fashion before addressing my companion.

165

'Mr Havering, I think? I've been sent down from London to take charge of this case, and I'd like a word with you, if I may, sir.'

'My wife—'

'I've seen your good lady, sir—and the housekeeper. I won't keep you a moment, but I am anxious to get back to the village now that I've seen all there is to see here.'

'I know nothing as yet as to what—'

'Ex-actly,' said Japp soothingly. 'But there are just one or two little points I'd like your opinion about all the same. Captain Hastings here, he knows me, and he'll go on up to the house and tell them you're coming. What have you done with the little man, by the way, Captain Hastings?'

'He's ill in bed with influenza.'

'Is he now? I'm sorry to hear that. Rather the case of the cart without the horse, you being here without him, isn't it?'

And on his rather ill-timed jest I went on to the house. I rang the bell, as Japp had closed the door behind him. After some moments it was opened to me by a middle-aged woman in black.

'Mr Havering will be here in a moment,' I explained. 'He has been detained by the inspector. I have come down with him from London to look into the case. Perhaps you can tell me briefly what occurred last night.'

'Come inside, sir.' She closed the door behind me, and we stood in the dimly-lighted hall. 'It was after dinner last night, sir, that the man came. He asked to see Mr Pace, sir, and, seeing that he spoke the same way, I thought it was an American gentleman friend of Mr Pace's and I showed him into the gun-room, and then went to tell Mr Pace. He wouldn't give any name, which, of course, was a bit odd, now I come to think of

166

it. I told Mr Pace, and he seemed puzzled like, but he said to the mistress: "Excuse me, Zoe, while I see what this fellow wants." He went off to the gun-room, and I went back to the kitchen, but after a while I heard loud voices, as if they were quarrelling, and I came out into the hall. At the same time, the mistress she comes out too, and just then there was a shot and then a dreadful silence. We both ran to the gun-room door, but it was locked and we had to go round to the window. It was open, and there inside was Mr Pace, all shot and bleeding.'

'What became of the man?'

'He must have got away through the window, sir, before we got to it.'

'And then?'

'Mrs Havering sent me to fetch the police. Five miles to walk it was. They came back with me, and the constable he stayed all night, and this morning the police gentleman from London arrived.'

'What was this man like who called to see Mr Pace?'

The housekeeper reflected.

'He had a black beard, sir, and was about middle-aged, and had on a light overcoat. Beyond the fact that he spoke like an American I didn't notice much about him.'

'I see. Now I wonder if I can see Mrs Havering?'

'She's upstairs, sir. Shall I tell her?'

'If you please. Tell her that Mr Havering is outside with Inspector Japp, and that the gentleman he has brought back with him from London is anxious to speak to her as soon as possible.'

'Very good, sir.'

I was in a fever of impatience to get all the facts. Japp had two or three hours' start on me, and his anxiety to be gone made me keen to be close at his heels.

167

Mrs Havering did not keep me waiting long. In a few minutes I heard a light step descending the stairs, and looked up to see a very handsome young woman coming towards me. She wore a flame-coloured jumper, that set off the slender boyishness of her figure. On her dark head was a little hat of flame-coloured leather. Even the present tragedy could not dim the vitality of her personality.

I introduced myself, and she nodded in quick comprehension.

'Of course I have often heard of you and your colleague, Monsieur Poirot. You have done some wonderful things together, haven't you? It was very clever of my husband to get you so promptly. Now will you ask me questions? That is the easiest way, isn't it, of getting to know all you want to about this dreadful affair?'

'Thank you, Mrs Havering. Now what time was it that this man arrived?'

'It must have been just before nine o'clock. We had finished dinner, and were sitting over our coffee and cigarettes.'

'Your husband had already left for London?'

'Yes, he went up by the 6.15.'

'Did he go by car to the station, or did he walk?'

'Our own car isn't down here. One came out from the garage in Elmer's Dale to fetch him in time for the train.'

'Was Mr Pace quite his usual self?'

'Absolutely. Most normal in every way.'

'Now, can you describe this visitor at all?'

'I'm afraid not. I didn't see him. Mrs Middleton showed him straight into the gun-room and then came to tell my uncle.'

'What did your uncle say?'

'He seemed rather annoyed, but went off at once. It was about five minutes later that I heard the sound of raised voices. I ran out into the hall and almost collided with Mrs Middleton. Then we heard the shot. The gun-room door was locked on the inside, and we had to go right round the house to the window. Of course that took some time, and the murderer had been able to get well away. My poor uncle'—her voice faltered—'had been shot through the head. I saw at once that he was dead. I sent Mrs Middleton for the police, I was careful to touch nothing in the room but to leave it exactly as I found it.'

I nodded approval.

'Now, as to the weapon?'

'Well, I can make a guess at it, Captain Hastings. A pair of revolvers of my husband's were mounted upon the wall. One of them is missing. I pointed this out to the police, and they took the other one away with them. When they have extracted the bullet, I suppose they will know for certain.'

'May I go to the gun-room?'

'Certainly. The police have finished with it. But the body has been removed.'

She accompanied me to the scene of the crime. At that moment Havering entered the hall, and with a quick apology his wife ran to him. I was left to undertake my investigations alone.

I may as well confess at once that they were rather disappointing. In detective novels clues abound, but here I could find nothing that struck me as out of the ordinary except a large blood-stain on the carpet where I judged the dead man had fallen. I examined everything with painstaking care and took a couple of pictures of the room with my little camera which I had brought with me. I also examined the ground outside the window, but it appeared to have been so heavily trampled underfoot that I judged it was useless to waste time over it. No, I had seen all that Hunter's Lodge had to show me. I must go back to Elmer's Dale and get into touch with Japp. Accordingly I took leave of the Haverings, and was driven off in the car that had brought us from the station.

I found Japp at the Matlock Arms and he took me forthwith to see the body. Harrington Pace was a small, spare, clean-shaven man, typically American in appearance. He had been shot through the back of the head, and the revolver had been discharged at close quarters.

'Turned away for a moment,' remarked Japp, 'and the other fellow snatched up a revolver and shot him. The one Mrs Havering handed over to us was fully loaded and I suppose the other one was also. Curious what darn fool things people do. Fancy keeping two loaded revolvers hanging up on your wall.'

'What do you think of the case?' I asked, as we left the gruesome chamber behind us.

'Well, I'd got my eye on Havering to begin with. Oh, yes!'—noting my exclamation of astonishment. 'Havering has one or two shady incidents in his past. When he was a boy at Oxford there was some funny business about the signature on one of his father's cheques. All hushed up of course. Then, he's pretty heavily in debt now, and they're the kind of debts he wouldn't like to go to his uncle about, whereas you may be sure the uncle's will would be in his favour. Yes, I'd got my eye on him, and that's why I wanted to speak to him before he saw his wife, but their statements dovetail all right, and I've been to the station and there's no doubt whatever that he left by the 6.15. That gets up to London about 10.30. He went straight to his club, he says, and if that's confirmed all right—why, he couldn't have been shooting his uncle here at nine o'clock in a black beard!'

'Ah, yes, I was going to ask you what you thought about that beard?'

Japp winked.

'I think it grew pretty fast—grew in the five miles from Elmer's Dale to Hunter's Lodge. Americans that I've met are mostly clean-shaven. Yes, it's amongst Mr Pace's American associates that we'll have to look for the murderer. I questioned the housekeeper first, and then her mistress, and their stories agree all right, but I'm sorry Mrs Havering didn't get a look at the fellow. She's a smart woman, and she might have noticed something that would set us on the track.'

I sat down and wrote a minute and lengthy account to Poirot. I was able to add various further items of information before I posted the letter.

The bullet had been extracted and was proved to have been fired from a revolver identical with the one held by the police. Furthermore, Mr Havering's movements on the night in question had been checked and verified, and it was proved beyond doubt that he had actually arrived in London by the train in question. And, thirdly, a sensational development had occurred. A city gentleman, living at Ealing, on crossing Haven Green to get to the District Railway Station that morning, had observed a brown-paper parcel stuck between the railings. Opening it, he found that it contained a revolver. He handed the parcel over to the local police station, and before night it was proved to be the one we were in search of, the fellow to that given us by Mrs Havering. One bullet had been fired from it.

All this I added to my report. A wire from Poirot arrived whilst I was at breakfast the following morning:

'Of course black-bearded man was not Havering only you or Japp would have such an idea wire me description of housekeeper and what clothes she wore this morning same of Mrs Havering do not waste time taking photographs of interiors they are underexposed and not in the least artistic.'

It seemed to me that Poirot's style was unnecessarily facetious. I also fancied he was a shade jealous of my position on the spot with full facilities for handling the case. His request for a description of the clothes worn by the two women appeared to me to be simply ridiculous, but I complied as well as I, a mere man, was able to.

At eleven a reply wire came from Poirot:

'Advise Japp arrest housekeeper before it is too late.'

Dumbfounded, I took the wire to Japp. He swore softly under his breath.

'He's the goods, Monsieur Poirot: if he says so, there's something in it. And I hardly noticed the woman. I don't know that I can go so far as arresting her, but I'll have her watched. We'll go up right away, and take another look at her.'

But it was too late, Mrs Middleton, that quiet middle-aged woman, who had appeared so normal and respectable, had vanished into thin air. Her box had been left behind. It contained only ordinary wearing apparel. There was no clue to her identity, or as to her whereabouts.

From Mrs Havering we elicited all the facts we could:

'I engaged her about three weeks ago when Mrs Emery, our former housekeeper, left. She came to me from Mrs Selbourne's Agency in Mount Street—a very well-known place. I get all my servants from there. They sent several women to see me, but this Mrs Middleton seemed much the nicest, and had splendid references. I engaged her on the spot, and notified the Agency of the fact. I can't believe that there was anything wrong with her. She was such a nice quiet woman.'

The thing was certainly a mystery. Whilst it was clear that the woman herself could not have committed the crime, since at the moment the shot was fired Mrs Havering was with her in the hall, nevertheless she must have some connection with the murder, or why should she suddenly take to her heels and bolt?

I wired the latest development to Poirot and suggested returning to London and making inquiries at Selbourne's Agency.

Poirot's reply was prompt:

'Useless to inquire at agency they will never have heard of her find out what vehicle took her up to hunters lodge when she first arrived there.'

Though mystified, I was obedient. The means of transport in Elmer's Dale were limited. The local garage had two battered Ford cars, and there were two station flies. None of these had been requisitioned on the date in question. Questioned, Mrs Havering explained that she had given the woman the money for her fare down to Derbyshire and sufficient to hire a car or fly to take her up to Hunter's Lodge. There was usually one of the Fords at the station on the chance of its being required. Taking into consideration the further fact that nobody at the station had noticed the arrival of a stranger, black-bearded or otherwise, on the fatal evening, everything seemed to point to the conclusion that the murderer had come to the spot in a car, which had been waiting near at hand to aid his escape, and that the same car had brought the mysterious housekeeper to her new post. I may mention that inquiries at the Agency in London bore out Poirot's prognostication. No such woman as 'Mrs Middleton' had ever been on their books. They had received the Hon. Mrs Havering's application for a housekeeper, and had sent her various applicants for the post. When she sent them the engagement fee, she omitted to mention which woman she had selected.

Somewhat crestfallen, I returned to London. I found Poirot established in an armchair by the fire in a garish, silk dressing-gown. He greeted me with much affection.

'*Mon ami* Hastings! But how glad I am to see you. Veritably I have for you a great affection! And you have enjoyed yourself? You have run to and fro with the good Japp? You have interrogated and investigated to your heart's content?'

'Poirot,' I cried, 'the thing's a dark mystery! It will never be solved.'

'It is true that we are not likely to cover ourselves with glory over it.'

'No, indeed. It's a hard nut to crack.'

'Oh, as far as that goes, I am very good at cracking the nuts! A veritable squirrel! It is not that which embarrasses me. I know well enough who killed Mr Harrington Pace.'

'You know? How did you find out?'

'Your illuminating answers to my wires supplied me with the truth. See here, Hastings, let us examine the facts methodically and in order. Mr Harrington Pace is a man with a considerable fortune which at his death will doubtless pass to his nephew. Point No 1. His nephew is known to be desperately hard up. Point No 2. His nephew is also known to be—shall we say a man of rather loose moral fibre? Point No 3.'

'But Roger Havering is proved to have journeyed straight up to London.'

'*Précisément*—and therefore, as Mr Havering left Elmer's Dale at 6.15, and since Mr Pace cannot have been killed before he left, or the doctor would have spotted the time of the crime as being given wrongly when he examined the body, we conclude quite rightly, that Mr Havering did *not* shoot his uncle. But there is a Mrs Havering, Hastings.'

'Impossible! The housekeeper was with her when the shot was fired.'

'Ah, yes, the housekeeper. But she has disappeared.'

'She will be found.'

'I think not. There is something peculiarly elusive about that housekeeper, don't you think so, Hastings? It struck me at once.'

'She played her part, I suppose, and then got out in the nick of time.'

'And what was her part?'

'Well, presumably to admit her confederate, the black-bearded man.'

'Oh, no, that was not her part! Her part was what you have just mentioned, to provide an alibi for Mrs Havering at the moment the shot was fired. And no one will ever find her, *mon ami*, because she does not exist! "There's no such person," as your so great Shakespeare says.'

'It was Dickens,' I murmured, unable to suppress a smile. 'But what do you mean, Poirot?'

'I mean that Zoe Havering was an actress before her

marriage, that you and Japp only saw the housekeeper in a dark hall, a dim middle-aged figure in black with a faint subdued voice, and finally that neither you nor Japp, nor the local police whom the housekeeper fetched, ever saw Mrs Middleton and her mistress at one and the same time. It was child's play for that clever and daring woman. On the pretext of summoning her mistress, she runs upstairs, slips on a bright jumper and a hat with black curls attached which she jams down over the grey transformation. A few deft touches, and the make-up is removed, a slight dusting of rouge, and the brilliant Zoe Havering comes down with her clear ringing voice. Nobody looks particularly at the housekeeper. Why should they? There is nothing to connect her with the crime. She, too, has an alibi.'

'But the revolver that was found at Ealing? Mrs Havering could not have placed it there?'

'No, that was Roger Havering's job—but it was a mistake on their part. It put me on the right track. A man who has committed murder with a revolver which he found on the spot would fling it away at once, he would not carry it up to London with him. No, the motive was clear, the criminals wished to focus the interest of the police on a spot far removed from Derbyshire, they were anxious to get the police away as soon as possible from the vicinity of Hunter's Lodge. Of course the revolver found at Ealing was not the one with which Mr Pace was shot. Roger Havering discharged one shot from it, brought it up to London, went straight to his club to establish his alibi, then went quickly out to Ealing by the District, a matter of about twenty minutes only, placed the parcel where it was found and so back to town. That charming creature, his wife, quietly shoots Mr Pace after dinner—you remember he was shot from behind? Another significant point, that!—reloads the revolver and puts it back in its place, and then starts off with her desperate little comedy.'

'It's incredible,' I muttered, fascinated, 'and yet—'

'And yet it is true. *Bien sur*, my friend, it is true. But to bring that precious pair to justice, that is another matter. Well, Japp must do what he can—I have written him fully—but I very much fear, Hastings, that we shall be obliged to leave them to Fate, or *le bon Dieu*, whichever you prefer.'

'The wicked flourish like a green bay tree,' I reminded him.

'But at a price, Hastings, always at a price, *croyez-moi*!'

Poirot's forebodings were confirmed, Japp, though convinced of the truth of his theory, was unable to get together the necessary evidence to ensure a conviction.

Mr Pace's huge fortune passed into the hands of his murderers. Nevertheless, Nemesis did overtake them, and when I read in the paper that the Hon. Roger and Mrs Havering were amongst those killed in the crashing of the Air Mail to Paris I knew that Justice was satisfied.

The World's End

Mr Satterthwaite had come to Corsica because of the Duchess. It was out of his beat. On the Riviera he was sure of his comforts, and to be comfortable meant a lot to Mr Satterthwaite. But though he liked his comfort, he also liked a Duchess. In his way, a harmless, gentlemanly, old-fashioned way, Mr Satterthwaite was a snob. He liked the best people. And the Duchess of Leith was a very authentic Duchess. There were no Chicago pork butchers in her ancestry. She was the daughter of a Duke as well as the wife of one.

For the rest, she was rather a shabby-looking old lady, a good deal given to black bead trimmings on her clothes. She had quantities of diamonds in old-fashioned settings, and she wore them as her mother before her had worn them: pinned all over her indiscriminately. Someone had suggested once that the Duchess stood in the middle of the room whilst her maid flung brooches at her haphazard. She subscribed generously to charities, and looked well after her tenants and dependents, but was extremely mean over small sums. She cadged lifts from her friends, and did her shopping in bargain basements.

The Duchess was seized with a whim for Corsica. Cannes bored her and she had a bitter argument with the hotel proprietor over the price of her rooms.

'And you shall go with me, Satterthwaite,' she said firmly. 'We needn't be afraid of scandal at our time of life.'

Mr Satterthwaite was delicately flattered. No one had ever mentioned scandal in connection with him before. He was far too insignificant. Scandal—and a Duchess—delicious!

'Picturesque you know,' said the Duchess. 'Brigands—all that sort of thing. And extremely cheap, so I've heard. Manuel was positively impudent this morning. These hotel proprietors need putting in their place. They can't expect to get the best people if they go on like this. I told him so plainly.'

'I believe,' said Mr Satterthwaite, 'that one can fly over quite comfortably. From Antibes.'

'They probably charge you a pretty penny for it,' said the Duchess sharply. 'Find out, will you?'

'Certainly, Duchess.'

Mr Satterthwaite was still in a flutter of gratification despite the fact that his role was clearly to be that of a glorified courier.

When she learned the price of a passage by Avion, the Duchess turned it down promptly.

'They needn't think I'm going to pay a ridiculous sum like that to go in one of their nasty dangerous things.'

So they went by boat, and Mr Satterthwaite endured ten hours of acute discomfort. To begin with, as the boat sailed at seven, he took it for granted that there would be dinner on board. But there was no dinner. The boat was small and the sea was rough. Mr Satterthwaite was decanted at Ajaccio in the early hours of the morning more dead than alive.

The Duchess, on the contrary, was perfectly fresh. She never minded discomfort if she could feel she was saving money. She waxed enthusiastic over the scene on the quay, with the palm trees and the rising sun. The whole population seemed to have turned out to watch the arrival of the boat, and the launching of the gangway was attended with excited cries and directions.

'*On dirait,*' said a stout Frenchman who stood beside them, '*que jamais avant on n'a fait cette manoeuvre là!*'

'That maid of mine has been sick all night,' said the Duchess. 'The girl's a perfect fool.'

Mr Satterthwaite smiled in a pallid fashion.

'A waste of good food, I call it,' continued the Duchess robustly.

'Did she get any food?' asked Mr Satterthwaite enviously.

'I happened to bring some biscuits and a stick of chocolate on board with me,' said the Duchess. 'When I found there was no dinner to be got, I gave the lot to her. The lower classes always make such a fuss about going without their meals.'

With a cry of triumph the launching of the gangway was accomplished. A Musical Comedy chorus of brigands rushed aboard and wrested hand-luggage from the passengers by main force.

'Come on, Satterthwaite,' said the Duchess. 'I want a hot bath and some coffee.'

So did Mr Satterthwaite. He was not wholly successful, however. They were received at the hotel by a bowing manager and were shown to their rooms. The Duchess's had a bathroom attached. Mr Satterthwaite, however, was directed to a bath that appeared to be situated in somebody else's bedroom. To expect the water to be hot at that hour in the morning was, perhaps, unreasonable. Later he drank intensely black coffee, served in a pot without a lid. The shutters and the window of his room had been flung open, and the crisp morning air came in fragrantly. A day of dazzling blue and green.

The waiter waved his hand with a flourish to call attention to the view.

'Ajaccio,' he said solemnly. '*Le plus beau port du monde!*' And he departed abruptly.

Looking out over the deep blue of the bay, with the snowy mountains beyond, Mr Satterthwaite was almost inclined to agree with him. He finished his coffee, and lying down on the bed, fell fast asleep.

At *déjeuner* the Duchess was in great spirits.

'This is just what will be good for you, Satterthwaite,' she said. 'Get you out of all those dusty little old-maidish ways of yours.' She swept a *lorgnette* round the room. 'Upon my word, there's Naomi Carlton Smith.'

She indicated a girl sitting by herself at a table in the window. A round-shouldered girl, who slouched as she sat. Her dress appeared to be made of some kind of brown sacking. She had black hair, untidily bobbed.

'An artist?' asked Mr Satterthwaite.

He was always good at placing people.

'Quite right,' said the Duchess. 'Calls herself one anyway. I knew she was mooching around in some queer quarter of the globe. Poor as a church mouse, proud as Lucifer, and a bee in her bonnet like all the Carlton Smiths. Her mother was my first cousin.'

'She's one of the Knowlton lot then?'

The Duchess nodded.

'Been her own worst enemy,' she volunteered. 'Clever girl too. Mixed herself up with a most undesirable young man. One of that Chelsea crowd. Wrote plays or poems or something unhealthy. Nobody took 'em, of course. Then he stole somebody's jewels and got caught out. I forget what they gave him. Five years, I think. But you must remember? It was last winter.'

'Last winter I was in Egypt,' explained Mr Satterthwaite. 'I had 'flu very badly the end of January, and the doctors insisted on Egypt afterwards. I missed a lot.'

His voice rang with a note of real regret.

'That girl seems to me to be moping,' said the Duchess, raising her *lorgnette* once more. 'I can't allow that.'

On her way out, she stopped by Miss Carlton Smith's table and tapped the girl on the shoulder.

'Well, Naomi, you don't seem to remember me?'

Naomi rose rather unwillingly to her feet.

'Yes, I do, Duchess. I saw you come in. I thought it was quite likely you mightn't recognize me.'

She drawled the words lazily, with a complete indifference of manner.

'When you've finished your lunch, come and talk to me on the terrace,' ordered the Duchess.

'Very well.'

Naomi yawned.

'Shocking manners,' said the Duchess, to Mr Satterthwaite, as she resumed her progress. 'All the Carlton Smiths have.'

They had their coffee outside in the sunshine. They had been there about six minutes when Naomi Carlton Smith lounged out from the hotel and joined them. She let herself fall slackly on to a chair with her legs stretched out ungracefully in front of her.

An odd face, with its jutting chin and deep-set grey eyes. A clever, unhappy face—a face that only just missed being beautiful.

'Well, Naomi,' said the Duchess briskly. 'And what are you doing with yourself?'

'Oh, I dunno. Just marking time.'

182

'Been painting?'

'A bit.'

'Show me your things.'

Naomi grinned. She was not cowed by the autocrat. She was amused. She went into the hotel and came out again with a portfolio.

'You won't like 'em, Duchess,' she said warningly. 'Say what you like. You won't hurt my feelings.'

Mr Satterthwaite moved his chair a little nearer. He was interested. In another minute he was more interested still. The Duchess was frankly unsympathetic.

'I can't even see which way the things ought to be,' she complained. 'Good gracious, child, there was never a sky that colour—or a sea either.'

'That's the way I see 'em,' said Naomi placidly.

'Ugh!' said the Duchess, inspecting another. 'This gives me the creeps.'

'It's meant to,' said Naomi. 'You're paying me a compliment without knowing it.'

It was a queer vorticist study of a prickly pear—just recognizable as such. Grey-green with slodges of violent colour where the fruit glittered like jewels. A swirling mass of evil, fleshy—festering. Mr Satterthwaite shuddered and turned his head aside.

He found Naomi looking at him and nodding her head in comprehension.

'I know,' she said. 'But it *is* beastly.'

The Duchess cleared her throat.

'It seems quite easy to be an artist nowadays,' she observed witheringly. 'There's no attempt to copy things. You just shovel on some paint—I don't know what with, not a brush, I'm sure—'

'Palette knife,' interposed Naomi, smiling broadly once more.

'A good deal at a time,' continued the Duchess. 'In lumps. And there you are! Everyone says: "How clever." Well, I've no patience with that sort of thing. Give me—'

'A nice picture of a dog or a horse, by Edwin Landseer.'

'And why not?' demanded the Duchess. 'What's wrong with Landseer?'

'Nothing,' said Naomi. 'He's all right. And you're all right. The tops of things are always nice and shiny and smooth. I respect you, Duchess, you've got force. You've met life fair and square and you've come out on top. But the people who are underneath see the under side of things. And that's interesting in a way.'

The Duchess stared at her.

'I haven't the faintest idea what you're talking about,' she declared.

Mr Satterthwaite was still examining the sketches. He realized, as the Duchess could not, the perfection of technique behind them. He was startled and delighted. He looked up at the girl.

'Will you sell me one of these, Miss Carlton Smith?' he asked.

'You can have any one you like for five guineas,' said the girl indifferently.

Mr Satterthwaite hesitated a minute or two and then he selected a study of prickly pear and aloe. In the foreground was a vivid blur of yellow mimosa, the scarlet of the aloe flower danced in and out of the picture, and inexorable, mathematically underlying the whole, was the oblong pattern of the prickly pear and the sword motif of the aloe.

He made a little bow to the girl.

'I am very happy to have secured this, and I think I have made a bargain. Some day, Miss Carlton Smith, I shall be able to sell this sketch at a very good profit—if I want to!'

The girl leant forward to see which one he had taken. He saw a new look come into her eyes. For the first time she was really aware of his existence, and there was respect in the quick glance she gave him.

'You have chosen the best,' she said. 'I—I am glad.'

'Well, I suppose you know what you're doing,' said the Duchess. 'And I daresay you're right. I've heard that you are quite a connoisseur. But you can't tell me that all this new stuff is art, because it isn't. Still, we needn't go into that. Now I'm only going to be here a few days and I want to see something of the island. You've got a car, I suppose, Naomi?'

The girl nodded.

'Excellent,' said the Duchess. 'We'll make a trip somewhere tomorrow.'

'It's only a two-seater.'

'Nonsense, there's a dickey, I suppose, that will do for Mr Satterthwaite?'

A shuddering sigh went through Mr Satterthwaite. He had observed the Corsican roads that morning. Naomi was regarding him thoughtfully.

'I'm afraid my car would be no good to you,' she said. 'It's a terribly battered old bus. I bought it second-hand for a mere song. It will just get me up the hills—with coaxing. But I can't take passengers. There's quite a good garage, though, in the town. You can hire a car there.'

'Hire a car?' said the Duchess, scandalized. 'What an idea. Who's that nice-looking man, who drove up in a four-seater just before lunch?'

'I expect you mean Mr Tomlinson. He's a retired Indian judge.'

'He seems quite a decent sort of man. I shall talk to him.'

That evening, on coming down to dinner, Mr Satterthwaite found the Duchess resplendent in black velvet and diamonds, talking earnestly to the owner of the four-seater car. She beckoned authoritatively.

'Come here, Mr Satterthwaite, Mr Tomlinson is telling me the most interesting things, and what do you think?—he is actually going to take us on an expedition tomorrow in his car.'

Mr Satterthwaite regarded her with admiration.

'We must go in to dinner,' said the Duchess. 'Do come and sit at our table, Mr Tomlinson, and then you can go on with what you were telling me.'

'Quite a decent sort of man,' the Duchess pronounced later.

'With quite a decent sort of car,' retorted Mr Satterthwaite.

'Naughty,' said the Duchess, and gave him a resounding blow on the knuckles with the dingy black fan she always carried. Mr Satterthwaite winced with pain.

'Naomi is coming too,' said the Duchess. 'In her car. That girl wants taking out of herself. She's very selfish. Not exactly self-centred, but totally indifferent to everyone and everything. Don't you agree?'

'I don't think that's possible,' said Mr Satterthwaite, slowly. 'I mean, everyone's interest must go *somewhere*. There are, of course, the people who revolve round themselves—but I agree with you, she's not one of that kind. She's totally uninterested in herself. And yet she's got a strong character—there must be *something*. I thought at first it was her art—but it isn't. I've never met anyone so detached from life. That's dangerous.'

'Dangerous? What do you mean?'

'Well, you see—it must mean an obsession of some kind, and obsessions are always dangerous.'

'Satterthwaite,' said the Duchess, 'don't be a fool. And listen to me. About tomorrow—'

Mr Satterthwaite listened. It was very much his role in life.

They started early the following morning, taking their lunch with them. Naomi, who had been six months in the island, was to be the pioneer. Mr Satterthwaite went over to her as she sat waiting to start.

'You are sure that—I can't come with you?' he said wistfully.

She shook her head.

'You'll be much more comfortable in the back of the other car. Nicely padded seats and all that. This is a regular old rattle trap. You'd leap in the air going over the bumps.'

'And then, of course, the hills.'

Naomi laughed.

'Oh, I only said that to rescue you from the dickey. The Duchess could perfectly well afford to have hired a car. She's the meanest woman in England. All the same, the old thing is rather a sport, and I can't help liking her.'

'Then I could come with you after all?' said Mr Satterthwaite eagerly.

She looked at him curiously.

'Why are you so anxious to come with me?'

'Can you ask?' Mr Satterthwaite made his funny old-fashioned bow.

She smiled, but shook her head.

'That isn't the reason,' she said thoughtfully. 'It's odd . . . But you can't come with me—not today.'

'Another day, perhaps,' suggested Mr Satterthwaite politely.

'Oh, another day!' she laughed suddenly, a very queer laugh, Mr Satterthwaite thought. 'Another day! Well, we'll see.'

They started. They drove through the town, and then round the long curve of the bay, winding inland to cross a river and then back to the coast with its hundreds of little sandy coves. And then they began to climb. In and out, round nerve-shattering curves, upwards, ever upwards on the tortuous winding road. The blue bay was far below them, and on the other side of it Ajaccio sparkled in the sun, white, like a fairy city.

In and out, in and out, with a precipice first one side of them, then the other. Mr Satterthwaite felt slightly giddy, he also felt slightly sick. The road was not very wide. And still they climbed.

It was cold now. The wind came to them straight off the snow peaks. Mr Satterthwaite turned up his coat collar and buttoned it tightly under his chin.

It was very cold. Across the water, Ajaccio was still bathed in sunlight, but up here thick grey clouds came drifting across the face of the sun. Mr Satterthwaite ceased to admire the view. He yearned for a steam-heated hotel and a comfortable armchair.

Ahead of them Naomi's little two-seater drove steadily forward. Up, still up. They were on top of the world now. On either side of them were lower hills, hills sloping down to valleys. They looked straight across to the snow peaks. And the wind came tearing over them, sharp, like a knife. Suddenly Naomi's car stopped, and she looked back.

'We've arrived,' she said. 'At the World's End. And I don't think it's an awfully good day for it.'

They all got out. They had arrived in a tiny village,

with half a dozen stone cottages. An imposing name was printed in letters a foot high.

'Coti Chiaveeri.'

Naomi shrugged her shoulders.

'That's its official name, but I prefer to call it the World's End.'

She walked on a few steps, and Mr Satterthwaite joined her. They were beyond the houses now. The road stopped. As Naomi had said, this was the end, the back of beyond, the beginning of nowhere. Behind them the white ribbon of the road, in front of them—nothing. Only far, far below, the sea . . .

Mr Satterthwaite drew a deep breath.

'It's an extraordinary place. One feels that anything might happen here, that one might meet—anyone—'

He stopped, for just in front of them a man was sitting on a boulder, his face turned to the sea. They had not seen him till this moment, and his appearance had the suddenness of a conjuring trick. He might have sprung from the surrounding landscape.

'I wonder—' began Mr Satterthwaite.

But at that minute the stranger turned, and Mr Satterthwaite saw his face.

'Why, Mr Quin! How extraordinary. Miss Carlton Smith, I want to introduce my friend Mr Quin to you. He's the most unusual fellow. You are, you know. You always turn up in the nick of time—'

He stopped, with the feeling that he had said something awkwardly significant, and yet for the life of him he could not think what it was.

Naomi had shaken hands with Mr Quin in her usual abrupt style.

'We're here for a picnic,' she said. 'And it seems to me we shall be pretty well frozen to the bone.'

189

Mr Satterthwaite shivered.

'Perhaps,' he said uncertainly, 'we shall find a sheltered spot?'

'Which this isn't,' agreed Naomi. 'Still, it's worth seeing, isn't it?'

'Yes, indeed.' Mr Satterthwaite turned to Mr Quin. 'Miss Carlton Smith calls this place the World's End. Rather a good name, eh?'

Mr Quin nodded his head slowly several times.

'Yes—a very suggestive name. I suppose one only comes once in one's life to a place like that—a place where one can't go on any longer.'

'What do you mean?' asked Naomi sharply.

He turned to her.

'Well, usually, there's a choice, isn't there? To the right or to the left. Forward or back. Here—there's the road behind you and in front of you—nothing.'

Naomi stared at him. Suddenly she shivered and began to retrace her steps towards the others. The two men fell in beside her. Mr Quin continued to talk, but his tone was now easily conversational.

'Is the small car yours, Miss Carlton Smith?'

'Yes.'

'You drive yourself? One needs, I think, a good deal of nerve to do that round here. The turns are rather appalling. A moment of inattention, a brake that failed to hold, and—over the edge—down—down—down. It would be—very easily done.'

They had now joined the others. Mr Satterthwaite introduced his friend. He felt a tug at his arm. It was Naomi. She drew him apart from the others.

'Who is he?' she demanded fiercely.

Mr Satterthwaite gazed at her in astonishment.

'Well, I hardly know. I mean, I have known him for

some years now—we have run across each other from time to time, but in the sense of knowing actually—'

He stopped. These were futilities that he was uttering, and the girl by his side was not listening. She was standing with her head bent down, her hands clenched by her sides.

'He knows things,' she said. 'He knows things . . . How does he know?'

Mr Satterthwaite had no answer. He could only look at her dumbly, unable to comprehend the storm that shook her.

'I'm afraid,' she muttered.

'Afraid of Mr Quin?'

'I'm afraid of his eyes. He sees things . . .'

Something cold and wet fell on Mr Satterthwaite's cheek. He looked up.

'Why, it's snowing,' he exclaimed, in great surprise.

'A nice day to have chosen for a picnic,' said Naomi.

She had regained control of herself with an effort.

What was to be done? A babel of suggestions broke out. The snow came down thick and fast. Mr Quin made a suggestion and everyone welcomed it. There was a little stone Cassecroute at the end of the row of houses. There was a stampede towards it.

'You have your provisions,' said Mr Quin, 'and they will probably be able to make you some coffee.'

It was a tiny place, rather dark, for the one little window did little towards lighting it, but from one end came a grateful glow of warmth. An old Corsican woman was just throwing a handful of branches on the fire. It blazed up, and by its light the newcomers realized that others were before them.

Three people were sitting at the end of a bare wooden table. There was something unreal about the scene to

Mr Satterthwaite's eye, there was something even more unreal about the people.

The woman who sat at the end of the table looked like a duchess—that is, she looked more like a popular conception of a duchess. She was the ideal stage *grande dame*. Her aristocratic head was held high, her exquisitely dressed hair was of a snowy white. She was dressed in grey—soft draperies that fell about her in artistic folds. One long white hand supported her chin, the other was holding a roll spread with *pâté de foie gras*. On her right was a man with a very white face, very black hair, and horn-rimmed spectacles. He was marvellously and beautifully dressed. At the moment his head was thrown back, and his left arm was thrown out as though he were about to declaim something.

On the left of the white-haired lady was a jolly-looking little man with a bald head. After the first glance, nobody looked at him.

There was just a moment of uncertainty, and then the Duchess (the authentic Duchess) took charge.

'Isn't this storm too dreadful?' she said pleasantly, coming forward, and smiling a purposeful and efficient smile that she had found very useful when serving on Welfare and other committees. 'I suppose you've been caught in it just like we have? But Corsica is a marvellous place. I only arrived this morning.'

The man with the black hair got up, and the Duchess with a gracious smile slipped into his seat.

The white-haired lady spoke.

'We have been here a week,' she said.

Mr Satterthwaite started. Could anyone who had once heard that voice ever forget it? It echoed round the stone room, charged with emotion—with exquisite melancholy. It seemed to him that she had said something wonderful, memorable, full of meaning. She had spoken from her heart.

He spoke in a hurried aside to Mr Tomlinson.

'The man in spectacles is Mr Vyse—the producer, you know.'

The retired Indian judge was looking at Mr Vyse with a good deal of dislike.

'What does he produce?' he asked. 'Children?'

'Oh, dear me, no,' said Mr Satterthwaite, shocked by the mere mention of anything so crude in connection with Mr Vyse. 'Plays.'

'I think,' said Naomi, 'I'll go out again. It's too hot in here.'

Her voice, strong and harsh, made Mr Satterthwaite jump. She made almost blindly, as it seemed, for the door, brushing Mr Tomlinson aside. But in the doorway itself she came face to face with Mr Quin, and he barred her way.

'Go back and sit down,' he said.

His voice was authoritative. To Mr Satterthwaite's surprise the girl hesitated a minute and then obeyed. She sat down at the foot of the table as far from the others as possible.

Mr Satterthwaite bustled forward and button-holed the producer.

'You may not remember me,' he began, 'my name is Satterthwaite.'

'Of course!' A long bony hand shot out and enveloped the other's in a painful grip. 'My dear man. Fancy meeting you here. You know Miss Nunn, of course?'

Mr Satterthwaite jumped. No wonder that voice had been familiar. Thousands, all over England, had thrilled to those wonderful emotion-laden tones. Rosina Nunn! England's greatest emotional actress. Mr Satterthwaite too had lain under her spell. No one like her for interpreting a part—for bringing out the finer shades of meaning. He had thought of her always as an intellectual actress, one who comprehended and got inside the soul of her part.

He might be excused for not recognizing her. Rosina Nunn was volatile in her tastes. For twenty-five years of her life she had been a blonde. After a tour in the States she had returned with the locks of the raven, and she had taken up tragedy in earnest. This 'French Marquise' effect was her latest whim.

'Oh, by the way, Mr Judd—Miss Nunn's husband,' said Vyse, carelessly introducing the man with the bald head.

Rosina Nunn had had several husbands, Mr Satterthwaite knew. Mr Judd was evidently the latest.

Mr Judd was busily unwrapping packages from a hamper at his side. He addressed his wife.

'Some more *pâté*, dearest? That last wasn't as thick as you like it.'

Rosina Nunn surrendered her roll to him, as she murmured simply:

'Henry thinks of the most enchanting meals. I always leave the commissariat to him.'

'Feed the brute,' said Mr Judd, and laughed. He patted his wife on the shoulder.

'Treats her just as though she were a dog,' murmured the melancholy voice of Mr Vyse in Mr Satterthwaite's ear. 'Cuts up her food for her. Odd creatures, women.'

Mr Satterthwaite and Mr Quin between them unpacked lunch. Hard-boiled eggs, cold ham and Gruyère cheese were distributed round the table. The Duchess and Miss Nunn appeared to be deep in murmured

194

confidences. Fragments came along in the actress's deep contralto.

'The bread must be lightly toasted, you understand? Then just a *very* thin layer of marmalade. Rolled up and put in the oven for one minute—not more. Simply delicious.'

'That woman lives for food,' murmured Mr Vyse. 'Simply lives for it. She can't think of anything else. I remember in Riders to the Sea—you know "and it's the fine quiet time I'll be having." I could *not* get the effect I wanted. At last I told her to think of peppermint creams—she's very fond of peppermint creams. I got the effect at once—a sort of far-away look that went to your very soul.'

Mr Satterthwaite was silent. He was remembering.

Mr Tomlinson opposite cleared his throat preparatory to entering into conversation.

'You produce plays, I hear, eh? I'm fond of a good play myself. Jim the Penman, now, that was a play.'

'My God,' said Mr Vyse, and shivered down all the long length of him.

'A tiny clove of garlic,' said Miss Nunn to the Duchess. 'You tell your cook. It's wonderful.'

She sighed happily and turned to her husband.

'Henry,' she said plaintively, 'I've never even *seen* the caviare.'

'You're as near as nothing to sitting on it,' returned Mr Judd cheerfully. 'You put it behind you on the chair.'

Rosina Nunn retrieved it hurriedly, and beamed round the table.

'Henry is too wonderful. I'm so terribly absent-minded. I never know where I've put anything.'

'Like the day you packed your pearls in your sponge bag,' said Henry jocosely. 'And then left it behind at the

195

hotel. My word, I did a bit of wiring and phoning that day.'

'They were insured,' said Miss Nunn dreamily. 'Not like my opal.'

A spasm of exquisite heartrending grief flitted across her face.

Several times, when in the company of Mr Quin, Mr Satterthwaite had had the feeling of taking part in a play. The illusion was with him very strongly now. This was a dream. Everyone had his part. The words 'my opal' were his own cue. He leant forward.

'Your opal, Miss Nunn?'

'Have you got the butter, Henry? Thank you. Yes, my opal. It was stolen, you know. And I never got it back.'

'Do tell us,' said Mr Satterthwaite.

'Well—I was born in October—so it was lucky for me to wear opals, and because of that I wanted a real beauty. I waited a long time for it. They said it was one of the most perfect ones known. Not very large—about the size of a two-shilling piece—but oh! the colour and the fire.'

She sighed. Mr Satterthwaite observed that the Duchess was fidgeting and seemed uncomfortable, but nothing could stop Miss Nunn now. She went on, and the exquisite inflections of her voice made the story sound like some mournful Saga of old.

'It was stolen by a young man called Alec Gerard. He wrote plays.'

'Very good plays,' put in Mr Vyse professionally. 'Why, I once kept one of his plays for six months.'

'Did you produce it?' asked Mr Tomlinson.

'Oh, *no*,' said Mr Vyse, shocked at the idea. 'But do you know, at one time I actually thought of doing so?'

'It had a wonderful part in it for me,' said Miss Nunn. 'Rachel's Children, it was called—though there wasn't anyone called Rachel in the play. He came to talk to me about it—at the theatre. I liked him. He was a nice-looking—and very shy, poor boy. I remember'— a beautiful far-away look stole over her face—'he bought me some peppermint creams. The opal was lying on the dressing-table. He'd been out in Australia, and he knew something about opals. He took it over to the light to look at it. I suppose he must have slipped it into his pocket then. I missed it as soon as he'd gone. There *was* a to-do. You remember?'

She turned to Mr Vyse.

'Oh, I remember,' said Mr Vyse with a groan.

'They found the empty case in his rooms,' continued the actress. 'He'd been terribly hard up, but the very next day he was able to pay large sums into his bank. He pretended to account for it by saying that a friend of his had put some money on a horse for him, but he couldn't produce the friend. He said he must have put the case in his pocket by mistake. I think that was a terribly weak thing to say, don't you? He might have thought of something better than that . . . I had to go and give evidence. There were pictures of me in all the papers. My press agent said it was very good publicity—but I'd much rather have had my opal back.'

She shook her head sadly.

'Have some preserved pineapple?' said Mr Judd.

Miss Nunn brightened up.

'Where is it?'

'I gave it to you just now.'

Miss Nunn looked behind her and in front of her, eyed her grey silk pochette, and then slowly drew up a large purple silk bag that was reposing on the ground beside her. She began to turn the contents out slowly on the table, much to Mr Satterthwaite's interest.

There was a powder puff, a lip-stick, a small jewel case, a skein of wool, another powder puff, two hand-kerchiefs, a box of chocolate creams, an enamelled paper knife, a mirror, a little dark brown wooden box, five letters, a walnut, a small square of mauve crêpe de chine, a piece of ribbon and the end of a *croissant*. Last of all came the preserved pineapple.

'*Eureka*,' murmured Mr Satterthwaite softly.

'I beg your pardon?'

'Nothing,' said Mr Satterthwaite hastily. 'What a charming paper knife.'

'Yes, isn't it? Somebody gave it to me. I can't remember who.'

'That's an Indian box,' remarked Mr Tomlinson. 'Ingenious little things, aren't they?'

'Somebody gave me that too,' said Miss Nunn. 'I've had it a long time. It used always to stand on my dressing-table at the theatre. I don't think it's very pretty, though, do you?'

The box was of plain dark brown wood. It pushed open from the side. On the top of it were two plain flaps of wood that could be turned round and round.

'Not pretty, perhaps,' said Mr Tomlinson with a chuckle. 'But I'll bet you've never seen one like it.'

Mr Satterthwaite leaned forward. He had an excited feeling.

'Why did you say it was ingenious?' he demanded.

'Well, isn't it?'

The judge appealed to Miss Nunn. She looked at him blankly.

'I suppose I mustn't show them the trick of it—eh?' Miss Nunn still looked blank.

'What trick?' asked Mr Judd.

'God bless my soul, don't you know?'

He looked round the inquiring faces.

'Fancy that now. May I take the box a minute? Thank you.'

He pushed it open.

'Now then, can anyone give me something to put in it—not too big. Here's a small piece of Gruyère cheese. That will do capitally. I place it inside, shut the box.'

He fumbled for a minute or two with his hands.

'Now see—'

He opened the box again. It was empty.

'Well, I never,' said Mr Judd. 'How do you do it?'

'It's quite simple. Turn the box upside down, and move the left hand flap half-way round, then shut the right hand flap. Now to bring our piece of cheese back again we must reverse that. The right hand flap halfway round, and the left one closed, still keeping the box upside down. And now—Hey Presto!'

The box slid open. A gasp went round the table. The cheese was there but so was something else. A round thing that blinked forth every colour of the rainbow.

'*My opal!*'

It was a clarion note. Rosina Nunn stood upright, her hands clasped to her breast.

'My opal! How did it get there?'

Henry Judd cleared his throat.

'I—er—I rather think, Rosy, my girl, you must have put it there yourself.'

Someone got up from the table and blundered out into the air. It was Naomi Carlton Smith. Mr Quin followed her.

'But when? Do you mean—?'

Mr Satterthwaite watched her while the truth dawned on her. It took over two minutes before she got it.

'You mean last year—at the theatre.'

'You know,' said Henry apologetically. 'You *do* fiddle with things, Rosy. Look at you with the caviare today.'

Miss Nunn was painfully following out her mental processes.

'I just slipped it in without thinking, and then I suppose I turned the box about and did the thing by accident, but then—but then—' At last it came. 'But then Alec Gerard didn't steal it after all. Oh!'—a full-throated cry, poignant, moving—'How dreadful!'

'Well,' said Mr Vyse, 'that can be put right now.'

'Yes, but he's been in prison a year.' And then she startled them. She turned sharp on the Duchess. 'Who is that girl—that girl who has just gone out?'

'Miss Carlton Smith,' said the Duchess, 'was engaged to Mr Gerard. She—took the thing very hard.'

Mr Satterthwaite stole softly away. The snow had stopped, Naomi was sitting on the stone wall. She had a sketch book in her hand, some coloured crayons were scattered around. Mr Quin was standing beside her.

She held out the sketch book to Mr Satterthwaite. It was a very rough affair—but it had genius. A kaleidoscopic whirl of snowflakes with a figure in the centre.

'Very good,' said Mr Satterthwaite.

Mr Quin looked up at the sky.

'The storm is over,' he said. 'The roads will be slippery, but I do not think there will be any accident—now.'

'There will be no accident,' said Naomi. Her voice was charged with some meaning that Mr Satterthwaite did not understand. She turned and smiled at him—a sudden dazzling smile. 'Mr Satterthwaite can drive back with me if he likes.'

He knew then to what length desperation had driven her.

'Well,' said Mr Quin, 'I must bid you goodbye.'

He moved away.

'Where is he going?' said Mr Satterthwaite, staring after him.

'Back where he came from, I suppose,' said Naomi in an odd voice.

'But—but there isn't anything there,' said Mr Satterthwaite, for Mr Quin was making for that spot on the edge of the cliff where they had first seen him. 'You know you said yourself it was the World's End.'

He handed back the sketch book.

'It's very good,' he said. 'A very good likeness. But why—er—why did you put him in Fancy Dress?'

Her eyes met his for a brief second.

'I see him like that,' said Naomi Carlton Smith.

The Manhood of Edward Robinson

'With a swing of his mighty arms, Bill lifted her right off her feet, crushing her to his breast. With a deep sigh she yielded her lips in such a kiss as he had never dreamed of—'

With a sigh, Mr Edward Robinson put down *When Love is King* and stared out of the window of the underground train. They were running through Stamford Brook. Edward Robinson was thinking about Bill. Bill was the real hundred per cent he-man beloved of lady novelists. Edward envied him his muscles, his rugged good looks and his terrific passions. He picked up the book again and read the description of the proud Marchesa Bianca (she who had yielded her lips). So ravishing was her beauty, the intoxication of her was so great, that strong men went down before her like ninepins, faint and helpless with love.

'Of course,' said Edward to himself, 'it's all bosh, this sort of stuff. All bosh, it is. And yet, I wonder—'

His eyes looked wistful. Was there such a thing as a world of romance and adventure somewhere? Were there women whose beauty intoxicated? Was there such a thing as love that devoured one like a flame?

'This is real life, this is,' said Edward. 'I've got to go on the same just like all the other chaps.'

On the whole, he supposed, he ought to consider

himself a lucky young man. He had an excellent berth—a clerkship in a flourishing concern. He had good health, no one dependent upon him, and he was engaged to Maud.

But the mere thought of Maud brought a shadow over his face. Though he would never have admitted it, he was afraid of Maud. He loved her—yes—he still remembered the thrill with which he had admired the back of her white neck rising out of the cheap four and elevenpenny blouse on the first occasion they had met. He had sat behind her at the cinema, and the friend he was with had known her and had introduced them. No doubt about it, Maud was very superior. She was good looking and clever and very lady-like, and she was always right about everything. The kind of girl, every-one said, who would make such an excellent wife.

Edward wondered whether the Marchesa Bianca would have made an excellent wife. Somehow, he doubted it. He couldn't picture the voluptuous Bianca, with her red lips and her swaying form, tamely sewing on buttons, say, for the virile Bill. No, Bianca was Romance, and this was real life. He and Maud would be very happy together. She had so much common sense . . .

But all the same, he wished that she wasn't quite so— well, sharp in manner. So prone to "jump upon him".

It was, of course, her prudence and her common sense which made her do so. Maud was very sensible. And, as a rule, Edward was very sensible too, but sometimes— He had wanted to get married this Christmas, for instance. Maud had pointed out how much more prudent it would be to wait a while—a year or two, perhaps. His salary was not large. He had wanted to give her an expensive ring—she had been horror stricken, and had forced him to take it back and exchange it for a cheaper one. Her qualities were all excellent qualities, but sometimes Edward wished that she had more faults and less virtues. It was her virtues that drove him to desperate deeds.

For instance—

A blush of guilt overspread his face. He had got to tell her—and tell her soon. His secret guilt was already making him behave strangely. Tomorrow was the first of three days holiday, Christmas Eve, Christmas Day and Boxing Day. She had suggested that he should come round and spend the day with her people, and in a clumsy foolish manner, a manner that could not fail to arouse her suspicions, he had managed to get out of it— had told a long, lying story about a pal of his in the country with whom he had promised to spend the day.

And there was no pal in the country. There was only his guilty secret.

Three months ago, Edward Robinson, in company with a few hundred thousand other young men, had gone in for a competition in one of the weekly papers. Twelve girls' names had to be arranged in order of popularity. Edward had had a brilliant idea. His own preference was sure to be wrong—he had noticed that in several similar competitions. He wrote down the twelve names arranged in his own order of merit, then he wrote them down again this time placing one from the top and one from the bottom of the list alternately.

When the result was announced, Edward had got eight right out of the twelve, and was awarded the first prize of £500. This result, which might easily be ascribed to luck, Edward persisted in regarding as the direct outcome of his 'system.' He was inordinately proud of himself.

The next thing was, what do do with the £500? He knew very well what Maud would say. Invest it. A nice little nest egg for the future. And, of course, Maud would be quite right, he knew that. But to win money as the result of a competition is an entirely different feeling from anything else in the world.

Had the money been left to him as a legacy, Edward would have invested it religiously in Conversion Loan or Savings Certificates as a matter of course. But money that one has achieved by a mere stroke of the pen, by a lucky and unbelievable chance, comes under the same heading as a child's sixpence—'for your very own—to spend as you like'.

And in a certain rich shop which he passed daily on his way to the office, was the unbelievable dream, a small two-seater car, with a long shining nose, and the price clearly displayed on it—£465.

'If I were rich,' Edward had said to it, day after day. 'If I were rich, I'd have you.'

And now he was—if not rich—at least possessed of a lump sum of money sufficient to realize his dream. That car, that shining alluring piece of loveliness, was his if he cared to pay the price.

He had meant to tell Maud about the money. Once he had told her, he would have secured himself against temptation. In face of Maud's horror and disapproval, he would never have the courage to persist in his madness. But, as it chanced, it was Maud herself who clinched the matter. He had taken her to the cinema—and to the best seats in the house. She had pointed out to him, kindly but firmly, the criminal folly of his behaviour— wasting good money—three and sixpence against two and fourpence, when one saw just as well from the latter places.

Edward took her reproaches in sullen silence. Maud felt contentedly that she was making an impression. Edward could not be allowed to continue in these extravagant ways. She loved Edward, but she realized that he was weak—hers the task of being ever at hand to influence him in the way he should go. She observed his worm-like demeanour with satisfaction.

Edward was indeed worm-like. Like worms, he turned. He remained crushed by her words, but it was at that precise minute that he made up his mind to buy the car.

'Damn it,' said Edward to himself. 'For once in my life, I'll do what I like. Maud can go hang!'

And the very next morning he had walked into that palace of plate glass, with its lordly inmates in their glory of gleaming enamel and shimmering metal, and with an insouciance that surprised himself, he bought the car. It was the easiest thing in the world, buying a car!

It had been his for four days now. He had gone about, outwardly calm, but inwardly bathed in ecstasy. And to Maud he had as yet breathed no word. For four days, in his luncheon hour, he had received instruction in the handling of the lovely creature. He was an apt pupil.

Tomorrow, Christmas Eve, he was to take her out into the country. He had lied to Maud, and he would lie again if need be. He was enslaved body and soul by his new possession. It stood to him for Romance, for Adventure, for all the things that he had longed for and had never had. Tomorrow, he and his mistress would take the road together. They would rush through the keen cold air, leaving the throb and fret of London far behind—out into the wide clear spaces . . .

At this moment, Edward, though he did not know it, was very near to being a poet.

Tomorrow—

He looked down at the book in his hand—*When Love is King*. He laughed and stuffed it into his pocket. The car, and the red lips of the Marchesa Bianca, and the amazing prowess of Bill seemed all mixed up together. Tomorrow—

The weather, usually a sorry jade to those who count upon her, was kindly disposed towards Edward. She gave him the day of his dreams, a day of glittering frost, and pale-blue sky, and a primrose-yellow sun.

So, in a mood of high adventure, of dare-devil wickedness, Edward drove out of London. There was trouble at Hyde Park Corner, and a sad *contretemps* at Putney Bridge, there was much protesting of gears, and a frequent jarring of brakes, and much abuse was freely showered upon Edward by the drivers of other vehicles. But for a novice he did not acquit himself so badly, and presently he came out on to one of those fair wide roads that are the joy of the motorist. There was little congestion on this particular road today. Edward drove on and on, drunk with his mastery over this creature of the gleaming sides, speeding through the cold white world with the elation of a god.

It was a delirious day. He stopped for lunch at an old-fashioned inn, and again later for tea. Then reluctantly he turned homewards—back again to London, to Maud, to the inevitable explanation, recriminations . . .

He shook off the thought with a sigh. Let tomorrow look after itself. He still had today. And what could be more fascinating than this? Rushing through the darkness with the headlights searching out the way in front. Why, this was the best of all!

He judged that he had no time to stop anywhere for dinner. This driving through the darkness was a ticklish business. It was going to take longer to get back to London than he had thought. It was just eight o'clock when he passed through Hindhead and came out upon the rim of the Devil's Punch Bowl. There was moon-light, and the snow that had fallen two days ago was still unmelted.

He stopped the car and stood staring. What did it matter if he didn't get back to London until midnight? What did it matter if he never got back? He wasn't going to tear himself away from this at once.

He got out of the car, and approached the edge. There was a path winding down temptingly near him. Edward yielded to the spell. For the next half-hour he wandered deliriously in a snowbound world. Never had he imagined anything quite like this. And it was his, his very own, given to him by his shining mistress who waited for him faithfully on the road above.

He climbed up again, got into the car and drove off, still a little dizzy from that discovery of sheer beauty which comes to the most prosaic men once in a while.

Then, with a sigh, he came to himself, and thrust his hand into the pocket of the car where he had stuffed an additional muffler earlier in the day.

But the muffler was no longer there. The pocket was empty. No, not completely empty—there was some-thing scratchy and hard—like pebbles.

Edward thrust his hand deep down. In another minute he was staring like a man bereft of his senses. The object that he held in his hand, dangling from his fingers, with the moonlight striking a hundred fires from it, was a diamond necklace.

Edward stared and stared. But there was no doubting possible. A diamond necklace worth probably thousands of pounds (for the stones were large ones) had been casually reposing in the side-pocket of the car.

But who had put it there? It had certainly not been there when he started from town. Someone must have come along when he was walking about in the snow, and deliberately thrust it in. But why? Why choose *his* car? Had the owner of the necklace made a mistake? Or was it—could it possibly be *a stolen* necklace?

And then, as all these thoughts went whirling through his brain, Edward suddenly stiffened and went cold all over. *This was not his car.*

It was very like it, yes. It was the same brilliant shade of scarlet—red as the Marchesa Bianca's lips—it had the same long and gleaming nose, but by a thousand small signs, Edward realized that it was not his car. Its shining newness was scarred here and there, it bore signs, faint but unmistakeable, of wear and tear. In that case . . .

Edward, without more ado, made haste to turn the car. Turning was not his strong point. With the car in reverse, he invariably lost his head and twisted the wheel the wrong way. Also, he frequently became entangled between the accelerator and the foot brake with disastrous results. In the end, however, he succeeded, and straight away the car began purring up the hill again.

Edward remembered that there had been another car standing some little distance away. He had not noticed it particularly at the time. He had returned from his walk by a different path from that by which he had gone down into the hollow. This second path had brought him out on the road immediately behind, as he had thought, his own car. It must really have been the other one.

In about ten minutes he was once more at the spot where he had halted. But there was now no car at all by the roadside. Whoever had owned this car must now have gone off in Edward's—he also, perhaps, misled by the resemblance.

Edward took out the diamond necklace from his pocket and let it run through his fingers perplexedly.

What to do next? Run on to the nearest police station? Explain the circumstances, hand over the necklace, and give the number of his own car.

By the by, what was the number of his car? Edward thought and thought, but for the life of him he couldn't remember. He felt a cold sinking sensation. He was going to look the most utter fool at the police station. There was an eight in it, that was all that he could remember. Of course, it didn't really matter—at least . . . He looked uncomfortably at the diamonds. Supposing they should think—oh, but they wouldn't—and yet again they might—that he had stolen the car and the diamonds? Because, after all, when one came to think of it, would anyone in their senses thrust a valuable diamond necklace carelessly into the open pocket of a car?

Edward got out and went round to the back of the motor. Its number was XR10061. Beyond the fact that that was certainly not the number of his car, it conveyed nothing to him. Then he set to work systematically to search all the pockets. In the one where he had found the diamonds he made a discovery—a small scrap of paper with some words pencilled on it. By the light of the headlights, Edward read them easily enough.

'*Meet me, Greane, corner of Salter's Lane, ten o'clock.*'

He remembered the name Greane. He had seen it on a sign-post earlier in the day. In a minute, his mind was made up. He would go to this village, Greane, find Salter's Lane, meet the person who had written the note, and explain the circumstances. That would be much better than looking a fool in the local police station.

He started off almost happily. After all, this was an adventure. This was the sort of thing that didn't happen every day. The diamond necklace made it exciting and mysterious.

He had some little difficulty in finding Greane, and still more difficulty in finding Salter's Lane, but after knocking up two cottages, he succeeded.

Still, it was a few minutes after the appointed hour when he drove cautiously along a narrow road, keeping a sharp look-out on the left-hand side where he had been told Salter's Lane branched off.

He came upon it quite suddenly round a bend, and even as he drew up, a figure came forward out of the darkness.

'At last!' a girl's voice cried. 'What an age you've been, Gerald!'

As she spoke, the girl stepped right into the glare of the headlights, and Edward caught his breath. She was the most glorious creature he had ever seen.

She was quite young, with hair black as night, and wonderful scarlet lips. The heavy cloak that she wore swung open, and Edward saw that she was in full evening dress—a kind of flame-coloured sheath, outlining her perfect body. Round her neck was a row of exquisite pearls.

Suddenly the girl started.

'Why,' she cried; 'it isn't Gerald.'

'No,' said Edward hastily. 'I must explain.' He took the diamond necklace from his pocket and held it out to her. 'My name is Edward—'

He got no further, for the girl clapped her hands and broke in:

'Edward, of course! I am so glad. But that idiot Jimmy told me over the phone that he was sending Gerald

211

along with the car. It's awfully sporting of you to come. I've been dying to meet you. Remember I haven't seen you since I was six years old. I see you've got the necklace all right. Shove it in your pocket again. The village policeman might come along and see it. Brrr, it's cold as ice waiting here! Let me get in.'

As though in a dream Edward opened the door, and she sprang lightly in beside him. Her furs swept his cheek, and an elusive scent, like that of violets after rain, assailed his nostrils.

He had no plan, no definite thought even. In a minute, without conscious volition, he had yielded himself to the adventure. She had called him Edward—what matter if he were the wrong Edward? She would find him out soon enough. In the meantime, let the game go on. He let in the clutch and they glided off.

Presently the girl laughed. Her laugh was just as wonderful as the rest of her.

'It's easy to see you don't know much about cars. I suppose they don't have them out there?'

'I wonder where "out there" is?' thought Edward. Aloud he said, 'Not much.'

'Better let me drive,' said the girl. 'It's tricky work finding your way round these lanes until we get on the main road again.'

He relinquished his place to her gladly. Presently they were humming through the night at a pace and with a recklessness that secretly appalled Edward. She turned her head towards him.

'I like pace. Do you? You know—you're not a bit like Gerald. No one would ever take you to be brothers. You're not a bit like what I imagined, either.'

'I suppose,' said Edward, 'that I'm so completely ordinary. Is that it?'

'Not ordinary—different. I can't make you out. How's poor old Jimmy? Very fed up, I suppose?'

'Oh, Jimmy's all right,' said Edward.

'It's easy enough to say that—but it's rough luck on him having a sprained ankle. Did he tell you the whole story?'

'Not a word. I'm completely in the dark. I wish you'd enlighten me.'

'Oh, the thing worked like a dream. Jimmy went in at the front door, togged up in his girl's clothes. I gave him a minute or two, and then shinned up to the window. Agnes Larella's maid was there laying out Agnes's dress and jewels, and all the rest. Then there was a great yell downstairs, and the squib went off, and everyone shouted fire. The maid dashed out, and I hopped in, helped myself to the necklace, and was out and down in a flash, and out of the place by the back way across the Punch Bowl. I shoved the necklace and the notice where to pick me up in the pocket of the car in passing. Then I joined Louise at the hotel, having shed my snow boots of course. Perfect alibi for me. She'd no idea I'd been out at all.'

'And what about Jimmy?'

'Well, you know more about that than I do.'

'He didn't tell me anything,' said Edward easily.

'Well, in the general rag, he caught his foot in his skirt and managed to sprain it. They had to carry him to the car, and the Larellas' chauffeur drove him home. Just fancy if the chauffeur had happened to put his hand in the pocket!'

Edward laughed with her, but his mind was busy. He understood the position more or less now. The name of Larella was vaguely familiar to him—it was a name that spelt wealth. This girl, and an unknown man called Jimmy, had conspired together to steal the necklace, and

213

had succeeded. Owing to his sprained ankle and the presence of the Larellas' chauffeur Jimmy had not been able to look in the pocket of the car before telephoning to the girl—probably had had no wish to do so. But it was almost certain that the other unknown 'Gerald' would do so at any early opportunity. And in it, he would find Edward's muffler!

'Good going,' said the girl.

A tram flashed past them, they were on the outskirts of London. They flashed in and out of the traffic. Edward's heart stood in his mouth. She was a wonderful driver, this girl, but she took risks!

Quarter of an hour later they drew up before an imposing house in a frigid square.

'We can shed some of our clothing here,' said the girl, 'before we go on to Ritson's.'

'Ritson's?' queried Edward. He mentioned the famous night-club almost reverently.

'Yes, didn't Gerald tell you?'

'He did not,' said Edward grimly. 'What about my clothes?'

She frowned.

'Didn't they tell you *anything*? We'll rig you up some-how. We've got to carry this through.'

A stately butler opened the door and stood aside to let them enter.

'Mr Gerald Champneys rang up, your ladyship. He was very anxious to speak to you, but he wouldn't leave a message.'

'I bet he was anxious to speak to her,' said Edward to himself. 'At any rate, I know my full name now. Edward Champneys. But who is she? Your ladyship, they called her. What does she want to steal a necklace for? Bridge debts?'

In the *feuilletons* which he occasionally read, the beautiful and titled heroine was always driven desperate by bridge debts.

Edward was led away by the stately butler, and delivered over to a smooth-mannered valet. A quarter of an hour later he rejoined his hostess in the hall, exquisitely attired in evening clothes made in Savile Row which fitted him to a nicety.

Heavens! What a night!

They drove in the car to the famous Ritson's. In common with everyone else Edward had read scandalous paragraphs concerning Ritson's. Anyone who was anyone turned up at Ritson's sooner or later. Edward's only fear was that someone who knew the real Edward Champneys might turn up. He consoled himself by the reflection that the real man had evidently been out of England for some years.

Sitting at a little table against the wall, they sipped cocktails. Cocktails! To the simple Edward they represented the quintessence of the fast life. The girl, wrapped in a wonderful embroidered shawl, sipped nonchalantly. Suddenly she dropped the shawl from her shoulders and rose.

'Let's dance.'

Now the one thing that Edward could do to perfection was to dance. When he and Maud took the floor together at the Palais de Danse, lesser lights stood still and watched in admiration.

'I nearly forgot,' said the girl suddenly. 'The necklace?'

She held out her hand. Edward, completely bewildered, drew it from his pocket and gave it to her. To his utter amazement, she coolly clasped it round her neck. Then she smiled up at him intoxicatingly.

'Now,' she said softly, 'we'll dance.'

They danced. And in all Ritson's nothing more perfect could be seen.

Then, as at length they returned to their table, an old gentleman with a would-be rakish air accosted Edward's companion.

'Ah! Lady Noreen, always dancing! Yes, yes. Is Captain Folliot here tonight?'

'Jimmy's taken a toss—racked his ankle.'

'You don't say so? How did that happen?'

'No details as yet.'

She laughed and passed on.

Edward followed, his brain in a whirl. He knew now. Lady Noreen Eliot, the famous Lady Noreen herself, perhaps the most talked of girl in England. Celebrated for her beauty, for her daring—the leader of that set known as the Bright Young People. Her engagement to Captain James Folliot, V.C., of the Household Calvalry, had been recently announced.

But the necklace? He still couldn't understand the necklace. He must risk giving himself away, but know he must.

As they sat down again, he pointed to it.

'Why that, Noreen?' he said. 'Tell me why?'

She smiled dreamily, her eyes far away, the spell of the dance still holding her.

'It's difficult for you to understand, I suppose. One gets so tired of the same thing—always the same thing. Treasure hunts were all very well for a while, but one gets used to everything. "Burglaries" were my idea. Fifty pounds entrance fee, and lots to be drawn. This is the third. Jimmy and I drew Agnes Larella. You know the rules? Burglary to be carried out within three days and the loot to be worn for at least an hour in a public

216

place, or you forfeit your stake and a hundred-pound fine. It's rough luck on Jimmy spraining his ankle, but we'll scoop the pool all right.'

'I see,' said Edward, drawing a deep breath. 'I see.'

Noreen rose suddenly, pulling her shawl round her.

'Drive me somewhere in the car. Down to the docks. Somewhere horrible and exciting. Wait a minute—' She reached up and unclasped the diamonds from her neck. 'You'd better take these again. I don't want to be murdered for them.'

They went out of Ritson's together. The car stood in a small by-street, narrow and dark. As they turned the corner towards it, another car drew up to the curb, and a young man sprang out.

'Thank the Lord, Noreen, I've got hold of you at last,' he cried. 'There's the devil to pay. That ass Jimmy got off with the wrong car. God knows where those diamonds are at this minute. We're in the devil of a mess.'

Lady Noreen stared at him.

'What do you mean? We've got the diamonds—at least Edward has.'

'Edward?'

'Yes.' She made a slight gesture to indicate the figure by her side.

'It's I who am in the devil of a mess,' thought Edward. 'Ten to one this is brother Gerald.'

The young man stared at him.

'What do you mean?' he said slowly. 'Edward's in Scotland.'

'Oh!' cried the girl. She stared at Edward. 'Oh!'

Her colour came and went.

'So you,' she said, in a low voice, 'are the real thing?'

It took Edward just one minute to grasp the situation.

There was awe in the girl's eyes—was it, could it be—admiration? Should he explain? Nothing so tame! He would play up to the end.

He bowed ceremoniously.

'I have to thank you, Lady Noreen,' he said, in the best highwayman manner, 'for a most delightful evening.'

One quick look he cast at the car from which the other had just alighted. A scarlet car with a shining bonnet. His car!

'And I will wish you good-evening.'

One quick spring and he was inside, his foot on the clutch. The car started forward. Gerald stood paralysed, but the girl was quicker. As the car slid past she leapt for it, alighting on the running board.

The car swerved, shot blindly round the corner and pulled up. Noreen, still panting from her spring, laid her hand on Edward's arm.

'You must give it me—oh, you must give it me. I've got to return it to Agnes Larella. Be a sport—we've had a good evening together—we've danced—we've been—pals. Won't you give it to me? To *me*?'

A woman who intoxicated you with her beauty. There were such women then . . .

Also, Edward was only too anxious to get rid of the necklace. It was a heaven-sent opportunity for a *beau geste*.

He took it from his pocket and dropped it into her outstretched hand.

'We've been—pals,' he said.

'Ah!' Her eyes smouldered—lit up.

Then surprisingly she bent her head to him. For a moment he held her, her lips against his . . .

Then she jumped off. The scarlet car sped forward with a great leap.

Romance!
Adventure!

At twelve o'clock on Christmas Day, Edward Robinson
strode into the tiny drawing-room of a house in Clapham
with the customary greeting of 'Merry Christmas'.

Maud, who was rearranging a piece of holly, greeted
him coldly.

'Have a good day in the country with that friend of
yours?' she inquired.

'Look here,' said Edward. 'That was a lie I told you. I
won a competition—£500, and I bought a car with it.
I didn't tell you because I knew you'd kick up a row
about it. That's the first thing. I've bought the car and
there's nothing more to be said about it. The second
thing is this—I'm not going to hang about for years. My
prospects are quite good enough and I mean to marry
you next month. See?'

'Oh!' said Maud faintly.

Was this—could this be—*Edward* speaking in this
masterful fashion?

'Will you?' said Edward. 'Yes or no?'

She gazed at him, fascinated. There was awe and
admiration in her eyes, and the sight of that look was
intoxicating to Edward. Gone was that patient mother-
liness which had roused him to exasperation.

So had the Lady Noreen looked at him last night.
But the Lady Noreen had receded far away, right into
the region of Romance, side by side with the Marchesa Bianca. This was the Real Thing. This was his
woman.

'Yes or no?' he repeated, and drew a step nearer.

'Ye—ye-es,' faltered Maud. 'But, oh, Edward, what
has happened to you? You're quite different today.'

219

'Yes,' said Edward. 'For twenty-four hours I've been a man instead of a worm—and, by God, it pays!'

He caught her in his arms almost as Bill the superman might have done.

'Do you love me, Maud? Tell me, do you love me?'

'Oh, Edward!' breathed Maud. 'I adore you . . .'

Christmas Adventure

The big logs crackled merrily in the wide, open fire-place, and above their crackling rose the babel of six tongues all wagging industriously together. The house-party of young people were enjoying their Christmas.

Old Miss Endicott, known to most of those present as Aunt Emily, smiled indulgently on the clatter.

'Bet you you can't eat six mince-pies, Jean.'

'Yes, I can.'

'No, you can't.'

'You'll get the pig out of the trifle if you do.'

'Yes, *and* three helps of trifle, *and* two helps of plum-pudding.'

'I hope the pudding will be good,' said Miss Endicott apprehensively. 'But they were only made three days ago. Christmas puddings ought to be made a long time before Christmas. Why, I remember when I was a child, I thought the last Collect before Advent—"Stir up, O Lord, we beseech Thee ..."—referred in some way to stirring up the Christmas puddings!'

There was a polite pause while Miss Endicott was speaking. Not because any of the young people were in the least interested in her reminiscences of bygone days, but because they felt that some show of attention was due by good manners to their hostess. As soon as she stopped, the babel burst out again. Miss Endicott sighed, and glanced towards the only member of the party whose years approached her own, as though in search of sympathy—a little man with a curious egg-shaped head and fierce upstanding moustaches. Young people were not what they were, reflected Miss Endicott. In olden days there would have been a mute, respectful circle, listening to the pearls of wisdom dropped by their elders. Instead of which there was all this nonsensical chatter, most of it utterly incomprehensible. All the same, they were dear children! Her eyes softened as she passed them in review—tall, freckled Jean; little Nancy Cardell, with her dark, gipsy beauty; the two younger boys home from school, Johnnie and Eric, and their friend, Charlie Pease; and fair, beautiful Evelyn Haworth ... At thought of the last, her brow contracted a little, and her eyes wandered to where her eldest nephew, Roger, sat morosely silent, taking no part in the fun, with his eyes fixed on the exquisite Northern fairness of the young girl.

'Isn't the snow ripping?' cried Johnnie, approaching the window. 'Real Christmas weather. I say, let's have a snowball fight. There's lots of time before dinner, isn't there, Aunt Emily?'

'Yes, my dear. We have it at two o'clock. That reminds me, I had better see to the table.'

She hurried out of the room.

'I tell you what. We'll make a snowman!' screamed Jean.

'Yes, what fun! I know; we'll do a snow statue of M. Poirot. Do you hear, M. Poirot? The great detective, Hercule Poirot, modelled in snow, by six celebrated artists!'

The little man in the chair bowed his acknowledgements with a twinkling eye.

'Make him very handsome, my children,' he urged. 'I insist on that.'

'Ra-ther!'

The troop disappeared like a whirlwind, colliding in the doorway with a stately butler who was entering with a note on a salver. The butler, his calm re-established, advanced towards Poirot.

Poirot took the note and tore it open. The butler departed. Twice the little man read the note through, then he folded it up and put it in his pocket. Not a muscle of his face had moved, and yet the contents of the note were sufficiently surprising. Scrawled in an illiterate hand were the words: *'Don't eat any plum-pudding.'*

'Very interesting,' murmured M. Poirot to himself. 'And quite unexpected.'

He looked across to the fireplace. Evelyn Haworth had not gone out with the rest. She was sitting staring at the fire, absorbed in thought, nervously twisting a ring on the third finger of her left hand round and round.

'You are lost in a dream, Mademoiselle,' said the little man at last. 'And the dream is not a happy one, eh?'

She started, and looked across at him uncertainly. He nodded reassuringly.

'It is my business to know things. No, you are not happy. Me, too, I am not very happy. Shall we confide in each other? See you, I have the big sorrow because a friend of mine, a friend of many years, has gone away across the sea to the South America. Sometimes, when we were together, this friend made me impatient, his stupidity enraged me; but now that he is gone, I can remember only his good qualities. That is the way of life, is it not? And now, Mademoiselle, what is your trouble? You are not like me, old and alone—you are young and beautiful; and the man you love loves you—oh yes, it is so: I have been watching him for the last half-hour.'

The girl's colour rose.

'You mean Roger Endicott? Oh, but you have made a mistake; it is not Roger I am engaged to.'

'No, you are engaged to Mr Oscar Levering. I know that perfectly. But why are you engaged to him, since you love another man?'

The girl did not seem to resent his words; indeed, there was something in his manner which made that impossible. He spoke with a mixture of kindliness and authority that was irresistible.

'Tell me all about it,' said Poirot gently; and he added the phrase he had used before, the sound of which was oddly comforting to the girl. 'It is my business to know things.'

'I am so miserable, M. Poirot—so very miserable. You see, once we were very well off. I was supposed to be an heiress, and Roger was only a younger son; and—and although I'm sure he cared for me, he never said anything, but went off to Australia.'

'It is droll, the way they arrange the marriages over here,' interpolated M. Poirot. 'No order. No method. Everything left to chance.' Evelyn continued.

'Then suddenly we lost all our money. My mother and I were left almost penniless. We moved into a tiny house, and we could just manage. But my mother became very ill. The only chance for her was to have a serious operation and go abroad to a warm climate. And we hadn't the money, M. Poirot—we hadn't the money! It meant that she must die. Mr Levering had proposed to me once or twice already. He again asked me to marry him, and promised to do everything that could be done for my mother. I said yes—what else could I do? He kept his word. The operation was performed by the greatest specialist of the day, and we went to Egypt for the winter. That was a year ago. My mother is well and strong again; and I—I am to marry Mr Levering after Christmas.'

'I see,' said M. Poirot; 'and in the meantime, M. Roger's elder brother has died, and he has come home—to find his dream shattered. All the same, you are not yet married, Mademoiselle.'

'A Haworth does not break her word, M. Poirot,' said the girl proudly.

Almost as she spoke, the door opened, and a big man with a rubicund face, narrow, crafty eyes, and a bald head stood on the threshold.

'What are you moping in here for, Evelyn? Come out for a stroll.'

'Very well, Oscar.'

She rose listlessly. Poirot rose also and demanded politely:

'Mademoiselle Levering, she is still indisposed?'

'Yes, I'm sorry to say my sister is still in bed. Too bad, to be laid up on Christmas Day.'

'It is indeed,' agreed the detective politely.

A few minutes sufficed for Evelyn to put on her snow-boots and some wraps, and she and her fiancé went out into the snow-covered grounds. It was an ideal Christmas Day, crisp and sunny. The rest of the house-party were busy with the erection of the snowman. Levering and Evelyn paused to watch them.

'Love's young dream, yah!' cried Johnnie, and threw a snowball at them.

'What do you think of it, Evelyn?' cried Jean. 'M. Hercule Poirot, the great detective.'

'Wait till the moustache goes on,' said Eric. 'Nancy's going to clip off a bit of her hair for it. *Vivent les braves Belges!* Pom, pom!'

'Fancy having a real-live detective in the house!'—this from Charlie—'I wish there could be a murder, too.'

'Oh, oh, oh!' cried Jean, dancing about. 'I've got an idea. Let's get up a murder—a spoof one, I mean. And take him in. Oh, do let's—it would be no end of a rag.'

Five voices began to talk at once.

'How should we do it?'

'Awful groans!'

'No, you stupid, out here.'

'Footprints in the snow, of course.'

'Jean in her nightie.'

'You do it with red paint.'

'In your hand—and clap it to your head.'

'I say, I wish we had a revolver.'

'I tell you, Father and Aunt Em won't hear. Their rooms are the other side of the house.'

'No, he won't mind a bit; he's no end of a sport.'

'Yes, but what kind of red paint? Enamel?'

'We could get some in the village.'

'Fat-head, not on Christmas Day.'

'No, watercolour. Crimson lake.'

'Jean can be it.'

'Never mind if you *are* cold. It won't be for long.'

'No, Nancy can be it, Nancy's got those posh pyjamas.'

'Let's see if Graves knows where there's any paint.'

A stampede to the house.

'In a brown study, Endicott?' said Levering, laughing disagreeably.

Roger roused himself abruptly. He had heard little of what had passed.

'I was just wondering,' he said quietly.

'Wondering?'

'Wondering what M. Poirot was doing down here at all.'

Levering seemed taken aback; but at that moment the big gong pealed out, and everybody went in to Christmas dinner. The curtains were drawn in the dining-room, and the lights on, illuminating the long table piled high with crackers and other decorations. It was a real old-fashioned Christmas dinner. At one end of the table was the Squire, red-faced and jovial; his sister faced him at the other. M. Poirot, in honour of the occasion, had donned a red waistcoat, and his plumpness, and the way he carried his head on one side, reminded one irresistibly of a robin redbreast.

The Squire carved rapidly, and everyone fell to on turkey. The carcasses of two turkeys were removed, and there fell a breathless hush. Then Graves, the butler, appeared in state, bearing the plum-pudding aloft— a gigantic pudding wreathed in flames. A hullabaloo broke out.

'Quick. Oh! my piece is going out. Buck up, Graves; unless it's still burning, I shan't get my wish.'

Nobody had leisure to notice a curious expression on the face of M. Poirot as he surveyed the portion of pudding on his plate. Nobody observed the lightning glance he sent round the table. With a faint, puzzled frown he began to eat his pudding. Everybody began to eat pudding. The conversation was more subdued. Suddenly the Squire uttered an exclamation. His face became purple and his hand went to his mouth.

'Confound it, Emily!' he roared. 'Why do you let the cook put glass in the puddings?'

'Glass?' cried Miss Endicott, astonished.

227

The Squire withdrew the offending substance from his mouth.

'Might have broken a tooth,' he grumbled. 'Or swallowed it and had appendicitis.'

In front of each person was a small finger-bowl of water, designed to receive the sixpences and other matters found in the trifle. Mr Endicott dropped the piece of glass into this, rinsed and held it up.

'God bless my soul!' he ejaculated. 'It's a red stone out of one of the cracker brooches.'

'You permit?' Very deftly, M. Poirot took it from his fingers and examined it attentively. As the Squire had said, it was a big red stone, the colour of a ruby. The light gleamed from its facets as he turned it about.

'Gee!' cried Eric. 'Suppose it's real.'

'Silly boy!' said Jean scornfully. 'A ruby that size would be worth thousands and thousands and thousands—wouldn't it, M. Poirot?'

'Extraordinary how well they get up these cracker things,' murmured Miss Endicott. *'But how did it get into the pudding?'*

Undoubtedly that was the question of the hour. Every hypothesis was exhausted. Only M. Poirot said nothing, but carelessly, as though thinking of something else, he dropped the stone into his pocket.

After dinner he paid a visit to the kitchen.

The cook was rather flustered. To be questioned by a member of the house-party, and the foreign gentleman too! But she did her best to answer his questions. The puddings had been made three days ago—'The day you arrived, Sir.' Everyone had come out into the kitchen to have a stir and wish. An old custom—perhaps they didn't have it abroad? After that the puddings were boiled, and then they were put in a row on the top shelf in the larder. Was there anything special to distinguish this pudding from the others? No, she didn't think so. Except that it was in an aluminium pudding-basin, and the others were in china ones. Was it the pudding originally intended for Christmas Day? It was funny that he should ask that. No, indeed! The Christmas pudding was always boiled in a big white china mould with a pattern of holly-leaves. But this very morning (the cook's red face became wrathful) Gladys, the kitchen-maid, sent to fetch it down for the final boiling, had managed to drop and break it. 'And of course, seeing that there might be splinters in it, I wouldn't send it to table, but took the big aluminium one instead.'

M. Poirot thanked her for her information. He went out of the kitchen, smiling a little to himself, as though satisfied with the information he had obtained. And the fingers of his right hand played with something in his pocket.

'M. Poirot! M. Poirot! Do wake up! Something dreadful's happened!'

Thus Johnnie in the early hours of the following morning. M. Poirot sat up in bed. He wore a night-cap. The contrast between the dignity of his countenance and the rakish tilt of the night-cap was certainly droll; but its effect on Johnnie seemed disproportionate. But for his words, one might have fancied that the boy was violently amused about something. Curious sounds came from outside the door, too, suggesting soda-water syphons in difficulty.

'Come down at once, please,' continued Johnnie, his voice shaking slightly. 'Someone's been killed.' He turned away.

'Aha, that is serious!' said M. Poirot.

He arose, and, without unduly hurrying himself, made a partial toilet. Then he followed Johnnie down the stairs. The house-party was clustered round the door into the garden. Their countenances all expressed intense emotion. At sight of him Eric was seized with a violent choking fit.

Jean came forward and laid her hand on M. Poirot's arm.

'Look!' she said, and pointed dramatically through the open door.

'*Mon Dieu!*' ejaculated M. Poirot. 'It is like a scene on the stage.'

His remark was not inapposite. More snow had fallen during the night, the world looked white and ghostly in the faint light of the early dawn. The expanse of white lay unbroken save for what looked like on splash of vivid scarlet.

Nancy Cardell lay motionless on the snow. She was clad in scarlet silk pyjamas, her small feet were bare, her arms were spread wide. Her head was turned aside and hidden by the mass of her clustering black hair. Deadly still she lay, and from her left side rose up the hilt of a dagger, whilst on the snow there was an ever-widening patch of crimson.

Poirot went out into the snow. He did not go to where the girl's body lay, but kept to the path. Two tracks of foot-marks, a man's and a woman's, led to where the tragedy had occurred. The man's footprints went away in the opposite direction alone. Poirot stood on the path, stroking his chin reflectively.

Suddenly Oscar Levering burst out of the house.

'Good God!' he cried. 'What's this?'

His excitement was a contrast to the other's calm.

'It looks,' said M. Poirot thoughtfully, 'like murder.'

Eric had another violent attack of coughing.

'But we must do something,' cried the other. 'What shall we do?'

'There is only one thing to be done,' said M. Poirot. 'Send for the police.'

'Oh!' said everybody at once.

M. Poirot looked inquiringly at them.

'Certainly,' he said. 'It is the only thing to be done. Who will go?'

There was a pause, then Johnnie came forward.

'Rag's over,' he declared. 'I say, M. Poirot, I hope you won't be too mad with us. It's all a joke, you know— got up between us—just to pull your leg. Nancy's only shamming.'

M. Poirot regarded him without visible emotion, save that his eyes twinkled a moment.

'You mock yourselves at me, is that it?' he inquired placidly.

'I say, I'm awfully sorry really. We shouldn't have done it. Beastly bad taste. I apologize, I really do.'

'You need not apologize,' said the other in a peculiar voice.

Johnnie turned.

'I say, Nancy, get up!' he cried. 'Don't lie there all day.'

But the figure on the ground did not move.

'Get up,' cried Johnnie again.

Still Nancy did not move, and suddenly a feeling of nameless dread came over the boy. He turned to Poirot.

'What—what's the matter? Why doesn't she get up?'

'Come with me,' said Poirot curtly.

He strode over the snow. He had waved the others back, and he was careful not to infringe on the other footmarks. The boy followed him, frightened and unbelieving. Poirot knelt down by the girl, then he signed to Johnnie.

'Feel her hand and pulse.'

Wondering, the boy bent down, then started back with a cry. The hand and arm were stiff and cold, and no vestige of a pulse was to be found.

'She's dead!' he gasped. 'But how? Why?'

M. Poirot passed over the first part of the question.

'Why?' he said musingly. 'I wonder.' Then, suddenly leaning across the dead girl's body, he unclasped her other hand, which was tightly clenched over something. Both he and the boy uttered an exclamation. In the palm of Nancy's hand was a red stone that winked and flashed forth fire.

'Aha!' cried M. Poirot. Swift as a flash his hand flew to his pocket, and came away empty.

'The cracker ruby,' said Johnnie wonderingly. Then, as his companion bent to examine the dagger, and the stained snow, he cried out: 'Surely it can't be blood, M. Poirot. It's paint. It's only paint.'

Poirot straightened himself.

'Yes,' he said quietly. 'You are right. It's only paint.'

'Then how—' The boy broke off. Poirot finished the sentence for him.

'How was she killed? That we must find out. Did she eat or drink anything this morning?'

He was retracing his steps to the path where the others waited as he spoke. Johnnie was close behind him.

'She had a cup of tea,' said the boy. 'Mr Levering made it for her. He's got a spirit-lamp in his room.'

Johnnie's voice was loud and clear. Levering heard the words.

'Always take a spirit-lamp about with me,' he declared.

'Most handy thing in the world. My sister's been glad enough of it this visit—not liking to worry the servants all the time you know.'

M. Poirot's eyes fell, almost apologetically as it seemed, to Mr Levering's feet, which were encased in carpet slippers.

'You have changed your boots, I see,' he murmured gently.

Levering stared at him.

'But, M. Poirot,' cried Jean, 'what are we to do?'

'There is only one thing to be done, as I said just now, Mademoiselle. Send for the police.'

'I'll go,' cried Levering. 'It won't take me a minute to put on my boots. You people had better not stay out here in the cold.'

He disappeared into the house.

'He is so thoughtful, that Mr Levering,' murmured Poirot softly. 'Shall we take his advice?'

'What about waking father and—and everybody?'

'No,' said M. Poirot sharply. 'It is quite unnecessary. Until the police come, nothing must be touched out here; so shall we go inside? To the library? I have a little history to recount to you which may distract your minds from this sad tragedy.'

He led the way, and they followed him.

'The story is about a ruby,' said M. Poirot, ensconcing himself in a comfortable arm-chair. 'A very celebrated ruby which belonged to a very celebrated man. I will not tell you his name—but he is one of the great ones of the earth. *Eh bien*, this great man, he arrived in London, incognito. And since, though a great man, he was also a young and a foolish man, he became entangled with a pretty young lady. The pretty young lady, she did not care much for the man, but she did care for his possessions—so much so that she disappeared one day with the historic ruby which had belonged to his house for generations. The poor young man, he was in a quandary. He is shortly to be married to a noble Princess, and he does not want the scandal. Impossible to go to the police, he comes to me, Hercule Poirot, instead. "Recover for me my ruby," he says. *Eh bien*, I know something of this young lady. She has a brother, and between them they have put through many a clever *coup*. I happen to know where they are staying for Christmas. By the kindness of Mr Endicott, whom I chance to have met, I, too, become a guest. But when this pretty young lady hears that I am arriving, she is greatly alarmed. She is intelligent, and she knows that I am after the ruby. She must hide it immediately in a safe place; and figure to yourself where she hides it— in a plum-pudding! Yes, you may well say, oh! She is stirring with the rest, you see, and she pops it into a pudding-bowl of aluminium that is different from the others. By a strange chance, that pudding came to be used on Christmas Day.'

The tragedy forgotten for the moment, they stared at him open-mouthed.

'After that,' continued the little man, 'she took to her bed.' He drew out his watch and looked at it. 'The household is astir. Mr Levering is a long time fetching the police, is he not? I fancy that his sister went with him.'

Evelyn rose with a cry, her eyes fixed on Poirot.

'And I also fancy that they will not return. Oscar Levering has been sailing close to the wind for a long time, and this is the end. He and his sister will pursue their activities abroad for a time under a different name. I alternately tempted and frightened him this morning.

By casting aside all pretence he could gain possession of the ruby whilst we were in the house and he was supposed to be fetching the police. But it meant burning his boats. Still, with a case being built up against him for murder, flight seemed clearly indicated.'

'Did he kill Nancy?' whispered Jean.

Poirot rose.

'Supposing we visit once more the scene of the crime,' he suggested.

He led the way, and they followed him. But a simultaneous gasp broke from their lips as they passed outside the house. No trace of the tragedy remained; the snow was smooth and unbroken.

'Crikey!' said Eric, sinking down on the step. 'It wasn't all a dream, was it?'

'Most extraordinary,' said M. Poirot, 'The Mystery of the Disappearing Body.' His eyes twinkled gently.

Jean came up to him in sudden suspicion.

'M. Poirot, you haven't—you aren't—I say, you haven't been spoofing us all the time, have you? Oh, I do believe you have!'

'It is true, my children. I knew about your little plot, you see, and I arranged a little counterplot of my own. Ah, here is Mlle. Nancy—and none the worse, I hope, after her magnificent acting of the comedy.'

It was indeed Nancy Cardell in the flesh, her eyes shining and her whole person exuberant with health and vigour.

'You have not caught cold? You drank the tisane I sent to your room?' demanded Poirot accusingly.

'I took one sip and that was enough. I'm all right. Did I do it well, M. Poirot? Oh, my arm hurts after that tourniquet!'

'You were splendid, *petite*. But shall we explain to the

others? They are still in the fog, I perceive. See you, *mes enfants*, I went to Mlle. Nancy, told her that I knew all about your little *complot*, and asked her if she would act a part for me. She did it very cleverly. She induced Mr Levering to make her a cup of tea, and also managed that he should be the one chosen to leave footprints on the snow. So when the time came, and he thought that by some fatality she was really dead, I had all the materials to frighten him with. What happened after we went into the house, Mademoiselle?'

'He came down with his sister, snatched the ruby out of my hand, and off they went post-haste.'

'But I say, M. Poirot, what about the ruby?' cried Eric. 'Do you mean to say you've let them have that?'

Poirot's face fell, as he faced a circle of accusing eyes.

'I shall recover it yet,' he said feebly; but he perceived that he had gone down in their estimation.

'Well, I do think!' began Johnnie. 'To let them get away with the ruby—'

But Jean was sharper.

'He's spoofing us again!' she cried. 'You are, aren't you?'

'Feel in my left-hand pocket, Mademoiselle.'

Jean thrust in an eager hand, and drew it out again with a squeal of triumph. She held aloft the great ruby in its crimson splendour.

'You see,' explained Poirot, 'the other was a paste replica I brought with me from London.'

'Isn't he clever?' demanded Jean ecstatically.

'There's one thing you haven't told us,' said Johnnie suddenly. 'How did you know about the rag? Did Nancy tell you?'

Poirot shook his head.

'Then how did you know?'

'It is my business to know things,' said M. Poirot, smiling a little as he watched Evelyn Haworth and Roger Endicott walking down the path together.

'Yes, but do tell us. Oh, do, please! *Dear* M. Poirot, please tell us!'

He was surrounded by a circle of flushed, eager faces.

'You really wish that I should solve for you this mystery?'

'*Yes.*'

'I do not think I can.'

'Why not?'

'*Ma foi*, you will be so disappointed.'

'Oh, do tell us! How *did* you know?'

'Well, you see, I was in the library—'

'Yes?'

'And you were discussing your plans just outside—and the library window was open.'

'Is that all?' said Eric in disgust. 'How simple!'

'Is it not?' said M. Poirot, smiling.

'At all events, we know everything now,' said Jean in a satisfied voice.

'Do we?' muttered M. Poirot to himself, as he went into the house. '*I* do not—I, whose business it is to know things.'

And, for perhaps the twentieth time, he drew from his pocket a rather dirty piece of paper.

'Don't eat any plum-pudding—'

M. Poirot shook his head perplexedly. At the same moment he became aware of a peculiar gasping sound very near his feet. He looked down and perceived a small creature in a print dress. In her left hand was a dust-pan, and in the right a brush.

'And who may you be, *mon enfant*?' inquired M. Poirot.

'Annie 'Icks, please, Sir. Between-maid.'

M. Poirot had an inspiration. He handed her the letter.

'Did you write that, Annie?'

'I didn't mean any 'arm, Sir.'

He smiled at her.

'Of course you didn't. Suppose you tell me all about it?'

'It was them two, Sir—Mr Levering and his sister. None of us can abide 'em; and she wasn't ill a bit—we could all tell that. So I thought something queer was going on, and I'll tell you straight, Sir, I listened at the door, and I heard him say as plain as plain, "This fellow Poirot must be got out of the way as soon as possible." And then he says to 'er, meaning-like, "Where did you put it?" And she answers, "In the pudding." And so I saw they meant to poison you in the Christmas pudding, and I didn't know what to do. Cook wouldn't listen to the likes of me. And then I thought of writing a warning, and I put it in the 'all where Mr Graves would be sure to see it and take it to you.'

Annie paused breathless. Poirot surveyed her gravely for some minutes.

'You read too many novelettes, Annie,' he said at last. 'But you have the good heart, and a certain amount of intelligence. When I return to London I will send you an excellent book upon *le ménage*, also the Lives of the Saints, and a work upon the economic position of woman.'

Leaving Annie gasping anew, he turned and crossed the hall. He had meant to go into the library, but through the open door he saw a dark head and a fair one, very close together, and he paused where he stood. Suddenly a pair of arms slipped round his neck.

'If you *will* stand just under the mistletoe!' said Jean.

'Me too,' said Nancy.

M. Poirot enjoyed it all—he enjoyed it very much indeed.

BIBLIOGRAPHY

Agatha Christie's short stories typically appeared first in magazines and then in her short story books, which tended to be different collections in the UK and the US. This list attempts to catalogue the first publication of each, and gives alternative story titles when used.

Christmas at Abney Hall

Excerpted from *An Autobiography* (1977).

The Chocolate Box

First published in the UK as 'The Clue of the Chocolate Box' in *The Sketch* Number 1582 on 23 May 1924, and in the US in *Blue Book Magazine* Vol. 40, No. 4, in February 1925. Reprinted in *Poirot Investigates* (US edition, 1925) and *Poirot's Early Cases* (UK, 1974).

A Christmas Tragedy

First published in the UK as 'The Hat and the Alibi' in *Storyteller* Vol. 46, No. 273 in January 1930. Reprinted in *The Thirteen Problems* (UK, 1932) aka *The Tuesday Club Murders* (US, 1933).

The Coming of Mr Quin

First published in the UK as 'The Passing of Mr Quinn' in *The Grand Magazine* No. 229 in March 1924 and in the US as 'Mr Quinn Passes By' in *Munsey's Magazine* Vol. 84, No. 2 in March 1925. Reprinted in *The Mysterious Mr Quin* (1930).

The Mystery of The Baghdad Chest

First published in the UK in *Strand Magazine* No. 493 in January 1932, and in the US in *Ladies' Home Journal* Vol. 49, No. 1 also in January 1932. Reprinted in *The Regatta Mystery and Other Stories* (US, 1939) and *While the Light Lasts and Other Stories* (UK, 1997).

The Clergyman's Daughter

First published in the UK as 'The First Wish' in *The Grand Magazine* No. 226 in December 1923. Reprinted in *Partners in Crime* (1929).

The Plymouth Express

First published in the UK as 'The Mystery of the Plymouth Express' in *The Sketch* No. 1575 on 4 April 1923, and in the US as 'The Plymouth Express Affair' in *Blue Book Magazine* Vol. 38, No. 3 in January 1924. Reprinted in *The Under Dog and Other Stories* (US, 1951) and *Poirot's Early Cases* (UK, 1974).

Problem at Pollensa Bay

First published in the UK in *Strand Magazine* No. 539 in November 1935, and in the US as 'Siren Business' in *Liberty* on 5 September 1936. Reprinted in *The Regatta Mystery and Other Stories* (US, 1939) and *Problem at Pollensa Bay and Other Stories* (UK, 1991).

Sanctuary

First published in the UK in *Woman's Journal* in October 1954, and in the US as 'Murder at the Vicarage' in *This Week* in September 1954. Reprinted in *Double Sin and Other Stories* (US, 1961) and *Miss Marple's Final Cases and Two Other Stories* (UK, 1979).

The Mystery of Hunter's Lodge

First published in the UK in *The Sketch* Number 1581 on 16 May 1923, and in the US as 'The Hunter's Lodge Case' in *Blue Book Magazine* Vol. 39, No. 2, in June 1924. Reprinted in *Poirot Investigates* (UK, 1924; US 1925).

The World's End

First published in the UK as 'The World's End' in *Storyteller* magazine No. 238 in February 1927 and in the US in *Flynn's Weekly* Vol. 19, No. 6 on 20 November 1926. Reprinted in *The Mysterious Mr Quin* (1930).

The Manhood of Edward Robinson

First published in the UK as 'The Day of His Dreams' in *The Grand Magazine* No. 238 in December 1924. Reprinted in *The Listerdale Mystery and Other Stories* (UK, 1934) and *The Golden Ball and Other Stories* (US, 1971).

Christmas Adventure

First published in the UK as 'The Adventure of the Christmas Pudding' in *The Sketch* No. 1611 in December 1923. Reprinted in *While the Light Lasts and Other Stories* (UK, 1997). *Midwinter Murder* sees the story's first official publication in the US.